D0477631

ADVANCES IN
EARLY EDUCATION
AND DAY CARE

Volume 1 • 1980

LIST OF CONTRIBUTORS

MARILYN BRADBARD — Auburn University

ROSALIND CHARLESWORTH — Houston, Texas

NORRIS CLASS — Professor Emeritus, University of Southern California, Los Angeles

LELA COSTIN — University of Illinois

RICHARD ENDSLEY — University of Georgia

GRETA FEIN — Merrill-Palmer Institute

EDITH GROTBERG — U.S. Department of Health, Education and Welfare

LILIAN KATZ — University of Illinois, Urbana

BARBARA LANGHAM — Austin, Texas

GWEN MORGAN — Wheelock College

RICHARD ORTON — Texas Department of Human Resources

DOUGLAS POWELL — Merrill-Palmer Institute

MELVIN SHELLY — Bowling Green State University

ADVANCES IN EARLY EDUCATION AND DAY CARE

A Research Annual

Editor: SALLY KILMER
Department of Home Economics
Bowling Green State University

VOLUME 1 • 1980

JAI PRESS INC.
Greenwich, Connecticut

CONTENTS

INTRODUCTION TO THE SERIES

This volume inaugurates a new series developed as a forum for communication and intellectual exchange among those engaged in research and conceptualization relating to the development, education, and care of children. The series is intended to elucidate basic issues through the presentation of original research and critical analyses; and, as such, to provide scholarly references for researchers, teaching faculty, students, and policy makers. It also will furnish opportunities for interface and exchange among scholars in the spectrum of academic disciplines—anthropology, child development, economics, education, medicine, psychology, public policy and administration, sociology, and others—concerned with early childhood research and theory.

For more than 50 years, faculty from various fields have engaged in research in early education and day care, but there has been no common professional outlet for such activities. Depending on the author's professional affiliation, research and reviews have appeared in such journals as *Child Development, American Education Journal, Young Children, Child Welfare, Journal of Home Economics, Pediatrics,* and *Child Care Quar-*

terly. Opportunities for other forms of communication and exchange have been equally as fragmented.

Now, in early 1980, after more than a decade of rapidly increasing numbers of publications, there seems to be a continuing interest in and an increasing quantity of programmatic research and theoretical analyses to sustain an annual volume. The series is broadly conceived. Although specific content will vary from year to year, each volume will include critical reviews which integrate and summarize important conceptual areas as well as reports of original research programs. Some volumes may report a symposium or professional conference; others may focus on a single critical issue, while others will reflect the range of topics in the field.

In sum, the series is envisioned as an annual journal that will present the major advances in theory and research in early education and day care. It is hoped that it will provide a focus, stimulate professional growth, and contribute to the intellectual rigor of the developing field.

Sally Kilmer
Series Editor

INTRODUCTION TO VOLUME I: PROMOTING QUALITY IN PROGRAMS FOR YOUNG CHILDREN

The problem addressed in this first volume of *Advances in Early Education and Day Care* was selected both for its relevance for current public policy and for its abundance of conceptual and research issues. Questions of quality and its maintenance are among the most critical currently before consumers, policy makers, funders, and providers of programs for young children. Present efforts to promote quality are fragmented and sometimes of questionable effectiveness. Yet very little research is available which can be applied to these problems.

The development of this series provided a unique opportunity to facilitate the academic analyses of issues related to the establishment and the maintenance of quality in programs for young children. This volume brings together historical, conceptual, and research perspectives of individuals representing a variety of approaches to program quality. These syntheses of some of the major issues are an initial step in the systematic investigation of variables influencing the quality of programs for young children.

Dissatisfaction with the current techniques for promoting quality centers around three broad but related concerns: *what* should be controlled; *how* it should be implemented; and *who* should be responsible, both for the definition of policy and for its enforcement. Nearly every facet of children's programs is covered in some form in current efforts to promote quality, although the standards and amount of control may vary with sources of funding and geographic location. Responsibility for enforcing or maintaining quality in children's programs is also spread among several different groups: government, providers, and parents. Both the areas of content and mechanisms for enforcement are based on a number of assumptions, reflecting beliefs about characteristics of "good" care and education, and legal and moral obligations for children's well-being.

For the most part we rely on the regulation of what goes into a program or service, such as the specification of training and other qualifications of personnel, group size, ages and other characteristics of users, or amount of physical space, equipment, etc. We have been less inclined to monitor the delivery of the service in process, and only rarely has assessment of the outcomes or results of the service on children been used as a means for quality control.

Formal or legal control (in addition to those covering all businesses), is primarily through requiring a program, home, or staff member to be licensed or certified as meeting specified criteria prior to the provision of any service. Such controls are exercised largely by state governments and some municipalities, although the minimum varies considerably, both among and within jurisdictions (*Survey of State Day Care Licensing Requirements*, 1971; Prescott & Jones, 1972; Lounsbury, Lounsbury, & Brown, 1976). With increased federal funding of the care and education for young children, the federal government has influenced state standards (Early Childhood Project, 1975) and also promulgated its own regulations, the Federal Interagency Day Care Requirements (1969), for program inputs.

Reliance on specification of inputs into a program assumes that the proper use of such elements follows from their presence. Even when standards invoke assessment of the aspects of a program after it is in operation, the inability or reluctance to revoke licensure or to impose other penalties essentially makes the effectiveness of the system dependent upon judgments made prior to the delivery of the service.

A second means of control is the involvement of professionals. Persons with some training related to young children and their families have, at various times, participated in all phases of children's programs from policy development to service delivery to direct assessments of quality.

Professional involvement is presumed to bring both the necessary knowledge and skills and the motivation for providing programs of quality. However, professional participation has varied tremendously and is certainly not even considered essential for service quality by some (O'Neill, 1975).

Probably the most frequent professional participation is working directly with the children. Sometimes training is required as part of licensing standards (*Survey of State Day Care Licensing Requirements, 1971*). In other instances, the employment of professionals, particularly teachers or social workers, is considered a voluntary indicator of a better quality service (AFT Task Force, 1976; Boguslawski, 1966). Even when there are no training requirements or the preparation is below the level of traditional professional training, providers of services are expected to conduct themselves in accord with some professional expectations (cf. Code of Ethics; Project Head Start, n.d.). In addition to meeting standards for preparation and personal conduct, program staff may also be expected to be knowledgeable about indicators of quality and to make accurate judgments of their own program through self-assessment procedures (cf. Mattick & Perkins, 1973; Illinois Department of Children and Family Services Self-Assessment).

Professionals are also involved in assessments of quality apart from direct service delivery, as licensors and as formal evaluators. In either role, critical professional judgments of quality are rendered. Even the selection of variables to assess from the range of possible alternatives conveys information about the relative importance of these factors to both providers and the public. Formal program evaluations, however, are usually summative in nature and rarely establish direct links between inputs or program implementation and outcomes. By their vary nature of being after the delivery of the service, summative evaluations offer no protection for children during the period of enrollment.

Program accreditation such as that of the Child Welfare League of America (1968) is still another form of professional determination of caliber of service. Accreditation certifies the meeting of defined criteria, usually different from minimum licensing standards, but often related to program inputs rather than process.

A third and much more informal form of quality control is that exercised by parents. This mechanism is founded on the belief that parents know what is best for their children (cf. Streuer, 1973). It operates in two different ways, depending on whether or not the parent directly purchases the service. For parents who pay the provider, the American free enterprise system is believed to maintain quality through parents' purchasing the best service available from competing alternatives, thus supporting those of quality while eliminating poorer ones. Control is exerted through their participation in policy making and/or in the actual delivery of the services for parents who do not pay directly for their children's services. Such control is exercised in parent cooperatives and in government-funded programs such as Head Start.

Problems with the current quality control effects include uneven enforcement of standards, lack of evidence of its effectiveness, and limited public support for either the content or the techniques. Dimensions of quality are often poorly defined and difficult to assess. Responsibilities for quality are not commonly agreed upon, and further, the enforcers—parents, staff and other professionals—often lack the background for making informed judgments. What is needed is a coherent *system* in which relations between regulated variables and consequences for children are established, in which responsibility for monitoring is clearly defined and reliably enforced at the points in the delivery of the service which are the most appropriate for assessing the critical variables. While there is beginning to be a body of research defining relations between program dimensions such as staff training, adult-child ratio, and group size (Travers & Roupp, 1978) and quality, there has been little systematic study of an equally critical area, that of the regulation on such variables. This volume addresses some of the issues and assumptions related to the promotion and regulation of quality. It is organized around various mechanisms and the respective roles of governments, of service providers and other professionals, and of parents in attaining and maintaining quality in children's programs. The first section concentrates on the responsibilities of governments and begins with an historical perspective on licensure by Class. Discussions of current issues and alternatives for government involvement follow. First, Grotberg identifies considerations affecting alternative federal roles, and Orton and Langham address issues at the state and local levels, as well. Costin, then, proposes a model for working federal–state relations to resolve some of the current discontinuities. Finally, in this section, Morgan raises questions about governmental regulation of family day care.

The second section focuses on some roles of providers and other professionals. Shelly and Charlesworth review conceptions of evaluation and suggest a perspective for evaluators that would contribute to program quality and Katz discusses the responsibilities and guidelines for personal conduct of those working directly with children.

The final section addresses the roles of parents in promoting quality. Fein's review of the historic roles of parents is followed by two recent research studies of parents in relation to quality control. Bradbard and Endsley investigated the ability of parents to select quality day care, and Powell reports on relations found between parents and staff in programs.

The identification and examination of these issues are first steps in more systematic investigation of variables associated with quality in children's programs. It is hoped that these discussions of assumptions and alternatives will provide a foundation for further research and analyses.

REFERENCES

AFT Task Force on Education Issues. *Putting early childhood and day care services into public schools,* Washington, D.C.: American Federation of Teachers, 1976.

Boguslawski, D. B. *Guide for establishing and operating day care centers for young children.* New York: Child Welfare League of America, 1966.

Child Welfare League of America standards for day care service. New York: Child Welfare League of America, 1968.

Code of Ethics for the Minnesota Association for the Education of Young Children, 1958.

Early Childhood Project. *Day care licensing policies and practices, a state survey* (ECS Report No. 72, EC Report No. 13). Denver: Education Commission of the States, 1975.

Federal Interagency Day Care Requirements 1968. U.S. Department of Health, Education, and Welfare, U.S. Office of Economic Opportunity, U.S. Department of Labor (Publication No. 033-665). Washington, D.C.: U.S. Government Printing Office, 1969.

Lounsbury, J. W., Lounsbury, K. R., & Brown, T. P. The uniformity of application of day care licensing standards. *Child Care Quarterly,* 1976, *5,* 248–261.

Mattick, I., & Perkins, F. J. *Guidelines for observation and assessment: An approach to evaluating the learning environment of a day care center,* Washington, D.C.: Day Care and Child Development Council of America, 1973.

O'Neill, T. P. The vicious and dishonest campaign against the Child and Family Services Bill. *Congressional Record,* December 1, 1975, *121,* n. 175.

Prescott, E., & Jones, E. *The "politics" of day care* (Vol. 1). Washington, D.C.: National Association for the Education of Young Children, 1972.

Project Head Start. *Parent involvement 10A. A workbook of training tips for Head Start Staff.* Washington, D.C.: U.S. Department of Health, Education, and Welfare, n.d.

Self-Assessment. Springfield, Il.: Illinois Department of Children and Family Services Office of Child Development, 1976.

Streuer, E. Current legislative proposals and public policy questions for child care. In P. Roby (Ed.), *Child care who cares.* New York: Basic Books, 1973.

Survey of state day care licensing requirements (Child Care Bulletin No. 4). Washington, D.C.: Day Care and Child Development Council of America, 1971.

Travers, J., & Roupp, R. *National day care study. Preliminary findings and their implications.* Cambridge, Ma.: Abt Associates, 1978.

PART I: ROLES OF GOVERNMENTS

SOME REFLECTIONS ON THE DEVELOPMENT OF CHILD DAY CARE FACILITY LICENSING

Norris E. Class

A PREFATORY NOTE

The content of the following statement on past and present developments in child day care facility licensing is derived from more than a third of a century of professional experience in child care regulatory administration. The experience included administrative operations, university teaching, and consultation to federal and state governments relative to safeguarding of children who experience out-of-home care, either 24-hour foster care or day care. Rather than a formal historical researching of the topic, the content should be regarded as a seriatim of reflections of a person who fortuitously was able to observe the development of child care regulatory administration over a substantial period of time and whose vocational connections permitted the time to analyze his observations. This

Advances in Early Education and Day Care, Volume 1, pages 3–18
Copyright © 1980 by JAI Press Inc.
All rights of reproduction in any form reserved.
ISBN: 0-89232-127-X

statement has, very likely, both the plus and minus of a "participant observer."

Using time as a basis for segmentalization, the major content of the statement trichotomizes into these topics: 1) The development of child day care facility licensing to 1957, the ending of federal funds for day care under the Lanham Act; 2) the achievement in state day care licensing during the period 1957–1977; and 3) current operational challenges in day care facility licensing. The paper concludes with a postscriptive statement to the effect that facility licensing alone is not enough if children are to be truly safeguarded.

DEVELOPMENT OF DAY CARE LICENSING TO 1957

Child day care represents a change in America in the upbringing of children, especially young children under six years of age. It is a major shift from almost complete reliance on the child's biological parents for performing almost all the essential tasks of child rearing to a system of multiple parenting.

Historically, some of the social causation which might account for the emergence of child day care as a social institution in the second half of twentieth-century America includes the following: 1) the decline of the extended family system almost to the point of disappearance; 2) the attenuation of the neighborhood as a mutual aid system due to high population mobility; 3) the decrease in the permanence of marriage and the stability of the home due to increase in divorce; 4) the increased need for community child care support services because of cultural acceptance of the one-parent family; and 5) the need for an ever-increasing amount of day care service due to community acceptance of working mothers, propelled in part by welfare policy and perhaps reinforced by changing concepts of women's roles. What needs to be noted about these dynamic factors is that there is little reason to believe they will be attenuated in the near future. Rather, there will probably be an increase in the need for proper regulatory safeguards.

Any analysis of child day care licensing needs to recognize that it came much later than foster child care licensing. Before the turn of the twentieth century, the licensing and regulation of 24-hour foster care for children had emerged. Institutions, foster homes, and placing agencies were brought under the jurisdiction of newly enacted child care licensing statutes. After the 1909 White House Conference on Child Welfare which focused on the care of dependent children away from their own home and measures to prevent unnecessary removal, child care licensing programs proliferated greatly. By 1920, almost all states had some type of child care licensing, but there was a great variation in the types or categories of foster care regulated. However, it should be emphatically noted that the licensing of child day care was in most instances not specifically named in the statute. Only after 1940, a second World War, and the event of mothers working away from the home in great numbers, would child day care be recognized as a new social institution and in need of serious consideration in policy formulation for both the service program and its regulation. Unfortunately, a wartime and post-wartime era was not the most opportune time for public policy consideration of child day care. First there was the enemy to be dealt with, and then the overwhelming aftermath of social problems. There was little or no public policy discussion of how best to deal with it. The result was the "jamming" of the child day care safeguarding provisions into the existing 24-hour child care licensing statute, regardless of the operational fit.

A high price in the form of administrative confusion and effective operation has been paid for the lack of proper analysis and planning relative to safeguarding children in day care. As ever, simplistic proposals for complex problems tended to result only in increased operational dysfunctionalism and complications. The basic policy issues which were not dealt with properly after the emergence of large child day care operations during and following World War II remained unresolved. The issues were simply covered over for the time being. Perhaps the three most important unresolved issues were: the conceptual nature of day care as a basis for establishing jurisdictional limitation of programs; the differential nature of day care from 24-hour care as a basis for determination of limits of state intervention; and the proper administrative location of day care regulatory responsibilities as a basis for maximizing investment of time, effort, and funds in operations. Each of these issues will be considered briefly.

Conceptual Nature of Day Care[1]

Although the term "child day care" has been in ever-increasing use since World War II, there is still confusion about what it means in respect to community expectations of providers of the service. The sociologist would say there is a lack of cultural institutionalization of the activity. In fact, there may be increasing disagreement over the meaning of the term. Moreover, the difference in usage seems at times to reflect the self-interest of the speaker as much or more than it does the social interest of children. With this lack of agreement, confusion, and uncertainty in respect to what child day care really means, it will be difficult, perhaps impossible, to formulate constitutionally valid licensing statutes and enforceable standards.

Child day care, as the writer sees it, represents the emergence of a new and to some extent ideologically competing social institution for the upbringing of children, especially but not limited to those under six years of age. Generally speaking, prior to World War II a child's legal parents assumed almost complete responsibility for: 1) the daily nurturing of the child including feeding, sheltering, attiring, physically safeguarding, and supervising daily activity; 2) active concern and involvement with the child's physical, psychological, and social development in order to assure optimal self-realization of inherent potentialities; and 3) legally safeguarding the child in respect to rights and entitlements. In addition, when the legal parents, in the event of death or disability, could not carry out the culturally assigned parental responsibilities, these were frequently assumed by near relatives who often were members of the extended family. In this new system of multiple parenting, many persons participate, most of whom are unrelated to and previously unacquainted with the child. Moreover, these persons are often likely to operate behaviorally from a socioeconomic value system quite different from that of the child's parents.

Thus it would seem that child day care must be operationally defined as a community service, under private or public auspice, which provides *supplementary child care* for less than 24 hours a day. The central feature of the service is that someone other than the child's own parents assumes, for a period of the day, parenting responsibility which by legal and cultural decree remains with the parent, but which by circumstance cannot in reality be carried out "at the time" by the parent. A parent, generally speaking, cannot divest his or her care responsibilities arbitrarily by fiat. Granting this, it would seem to follow that a person holding himself or herself to the public as taking on a parenting service (albeit of short duration) inherits for the time being all three of the basic parental responsibilities within defined limits. From the viewpoint of the rights of the child, it is more than mere custodial care. There is an implied developmental and protective service responsibility from the person who assumes responsibility for care in the temporary absence of the parent.

By law, social policy, historical development, and public funding, child care should be viewed as an integrated and indivisible complex of three functions. It serves as an extension of the family in the upbringing of children. Secondly, it aids the process of child development physically, mentally, and socially; and, it is concerned with a child's basic rights and entitlements both as a citizen and as a child. A pragmatic test of having achieved conceptual clarity regarding child day care will be our ability to write a dynamic statutory definition that reflects these three ingredients, rather than one which focuses only on the child's physical custody for a daily time-limited period.

Differential Nature of Day Care Licensing

The functional nature of day care is quite different from 24-hour foster care and therefore the regulatory administrative goals will be different. There is a child protective function in 24-hour foster care which is not present in day care. Twenty-four-hour foster care is truly *substitute* parental care. Both the licensing authority and the placement agency, if present, tend to take on an almost totally protective role. In contrast, the parent or responsible adult using day care not only sees the child before and after care each day, but usually has daily contact with the service. This enables the parent to make certain observations and to confront the operator and staff regarding possible inappropriate care, if such is recognized. *Thus, in contrast to substitute parental care in 24-hour foster care, the adult consumer of day care is likely to regard it as only a supplementary and/or complementary service, that is, as an extension of the parent's own care and responsibility.* Obviously, these functional differences between day care and foster care services raise many questions in respect to structure and operations. One of the most pressing is whether the same rationale for state intervention and safeguards hold for both, or whether there should be a separate statutory policy basis for each program, including legislative directions for enforcement.

Administrative Location of Day Care Licensing

The inclusion of day care safeguarding in statutes providing for existing 24-hour foster care licensing for children usually resulted in an administrative location in state public welfare departments. This factor of administrative location has special significance, especially in relation to standards enforcement. Two things should be noted regarding the public welfare department's involvement with child day care licensing generally, and with enforcement specifically.[2] First, the popular image of "public welfare," rightly or wrongly, is that it is concerned with relief and extremely serious problems of dependency and rehabilitation and is oriented to "social pathology." Child day care, as viewed by the ordinary individual, simply does not fit into this picture of administrative responsibility. Rather, an image of education and (technical) child development service has now been projected onto day care.[3] When persons who are about to start a day care operation learn that they need a license, they are often surprised and distressed when told that the regulatory authority is in a welfare agency. Some providers feel that having to post a license from the welfare department "stigmatizes" the service.

Another possible limitation of having child day care licensing in a welfare department is that the administrative magnitude of public assistance and relief programs tends to deprive day care regulation of top management attention and leadership. It is not that top management personnel are inherently indifferent or insensitive to the needs of day care children. Rather, it is simply that the time and energy demanded by economic public assistance programs require administrative priority. Furthermore, with relief expenditures and costs currently being such emotionally charged issues, it is conceivable that top public welfare administrators may often be reluctant to undertake a vigorous program of licensing standards enforcement if it involves stepping on the toes of members of the community whose support or good will is needed to get the "welfare budget" through the legislature. Thus, an important policy question is immediately at hand: Is it pragmatically possible to revise and internally restructure existing state public welfare departments in order to achieve a totally positive child day care regulatory administration, or, would it be operationally better to relocate such licensing responsibilities?

Of course, raising questions about the feasibility of the present administrative locations of child day care licensing in the state department of public welfare does not in itself provide the answers. Certainly in any decision-making regarding the best administrative location of day care responsibilities, *special attention should be given to the feasibility of having a separate and independent state office of child development.* Such an office should be multifunctional, having among its responsibilities those of implementing community organization programs for child development, possibly also the operation of child development community clinics or parents' consultation service, and the licensing and accreditation of certain categories of child development and child care personnel. Thus, the assignment of day care licensing service to this office would be appropriate, a natural affiliate. Also, an office of child development could play an important role in fiscal regulatory administration such as approving or certifying day care services in relation to the "purchase of service" by public agencies using state or federal funds. After a formative period in which basic organizational aspects unique to child development services were worked through, the integration of this office into a larger administrative structure might then be considered.[4]

ACHIEVEMENT DURING THE 1960s AND 1970s

During the '60s and '70s, day care as a recently evolved social institution for the upbringing of children was affected by two interrelated events, "intellectualization" and "politicalization."[5] Child development theorists endeavored to redefine the functional goals of day care. Proponents of early childhood education saw possibilities of combining it with day care. The intellectualization of day care came at a most propitious moment in terms of American political history. America's historic deep-seated *anti-*

welfare complex, temporarily suppressed during the active phrase of the New Deal, again surfaced in the early '60s: "Work, not welfare" was chanted by both major political party leaders. President Johnson picked up and implemented Kennedy's "Great Society" proposal in which economic security for each and every member of the nation started with concerted community effort to "break the poverty cycle." This antipoverty program was, of course, largely funded by the federal government. Day care was of *double* concern. Day care, per se, was to be the means of getting welfare mothers out of the home and into employment or training for employment. In addition, the content of day care was to be "compensatory" for the constricted home and environmental experiences of poor children. Head Start appealed as a simple solution to a complex problem. It received unusually strong support from the public and many congresspersons long after its efficacy as compensatory education had been questioned by research findings. Later the Federal Interagency Day Care Requirements (FIDCR) could be seen in part as a subsequent development of Head Start and the earlier commitment to breaking the poverty cycle: Care and general supervision of children of working mothers became care and instruction with probably greater emphasis on the latter.

It is important to note that in spite of all of the above federal activity related to children during this period, including the struggle for "quality day care," the question of how best to improve, expand, and operationally refine state child day care facility licensing was addressed only in a limited manner. The federal attitude was often one of indifference, of distrust of state licensure as a safeguarding instrumentality. Interviews with state and local child day care licensing personnel often brought statements to the effect that Head Start personnel frequently seemed to be "antilicensing" and interested only in furthering their own program— "regardless." The FIDCR program developed in part out of feeling that state day care licensing programs were "hopeless" and that the goal of quality care could only be achieved through fiscal operations, rather than through the use of legal authority generated by the legislature. Perhaps the most glaring example of federal indifference to the role of state licensing in safeguarding day care is that until recently, federal funds to the state for child welfare could generally not be used for licensing. At the same time day care programs were expanding as a result of federal policy and funding!

In spite of the above, there were some gains in relation to state child day care facility licensure. Some of these were a result of federal leadership and some developed quite apart from any federal action. Perhaps the most important gains were the improvement of the statutory basis of child care facility licensing, the beginning refinement of the formulation of licensing standards, and the emergence of a professionalism among child care regulatory personnel.

Improvement of Legal Basis

A beginning was made during this period in improving and/or refining the statutory basis of child day care facility licensure. This gain was probably related in part to the federal Office of Child Development's (OCD) Model Act for Child Day Care Licensing put forth in 1973. Although far from perfect, and perpetuating some questionable features of earlier child care licensing laws such as a license duration of one year, the model statute was something which states could immediately work with or against. As such, the Model Act might be regarded as a first step toward achieving a general national uniformity in state licensing laws.

A second contribution in respect to child care facility licensing laws generally, but also applicable to day care specifically, was the 1975 Texas Child Care Licensing Act.[6] In many ways the Texas licensing law was more progressive and innovative than the OCD's Model Act. There were provisions for family day care registration, advisory opinions and declaratory orders, and for a greater array of enforcement measures, including emergency closure, injunction, and civil penalties as well as criminal law penalties. All these should permit flexibility and realistic enforcement operations. The Texas statute coupled with the OCD Model Act constitute basic teaching documents for comparative study.

It should be added that there was increased interest in many parts of the country by licensing staff in the statutory basis of their operations. At staff development meetings the licensing law was examined section by section, often with the assistance of a legal consultant. Some states developed objective tests to assess staff knowledge of the licensing law. Recently, one state legislature (Illinois) enacted an amendment to the child care law requiring licensing personnel to demonstrate knowledge of the statute and standards!

Refinement of Standards

A second gain during this period was that the problem of proper formulation of licensing standards was addressed and a small beginning was made in thinking about the form and substance of licensing requirements. The approach to re-examining day care licensing standards came, perhaps in part, as a result of an OCD community organization operation. Task forces were formed to deal with various areas of standards such as fire safety, health, and program. Members of the respective task forces were experts in the given area of operations. They were selected on a national basis. Funds were available for a limited number of national meetings.

The report of findings of each task group was included in OCD's *Guides for Day Care Licensing* (Department of Health, Education, and Welfare, 1973) which also contained the Model Act referred to above.

As might be expected in such an approach, there was unevenness in achievement and in innovative thinking. Reports were not related to one another. Still, as a whole, the project made a contribution to beginning the refinement of state child day care licensing standards. It is unfortunate that there has been little follow-up of the standards project by the federal government. However, some states, perhaps stimulated in part by the OCD's community organization effort, have re-examined and revised their standards. Even more important, many states have moved to specializing the tasks of standards revision in terms of personnel administration. The presence of specialized personnel and increased recognition of the value of comparative study argues well for formulating "enforceable" standards. In the past, although the intentions of the formulators were most benign, the finished product, namely, the standards, were often not really enforceable. Thus at best, the licensing operation was mainly ritualistic, at worst a mockery. This should change with the presence of technically skilled staff who can begin to be held accountable for the enforceability of the formulated standards.

Professional Development in Child Care Regulatory Administration

Since the early 1960s, there has been an ever-increasing number of staff development operations for child care licensing personnel generally, but especially for day care licensors. The operations were generally paid for with federally derived funds, but other licensing personnel including adult care licensors sometimes attended. The locale of the staff development operations were sometimes within the department and other times at a contracted university. Some universities, such as Tulane and Virginia Commonwealth, have yearly institutes on child day care licensing that are attended by licensing personnel from all parts of the nation. Expenses are frequently paid by the state, and attendance may constitute a formal part of the agency training program. Perhaps as a result of these staff development operations, a beginning effort has been made to define the role of licensing supervisors in relation to responsible teaching and learning of the licensing process. Also there has been an emergence of limited technical literature relating to licensing administration although it is still woefully incomplete. Effort has been made toward a positive disentanglement of the licensing process from other child welfare programs, such as protective care and child placement services. They are, to be sure, closely interrelated but operationally discrete activities. Local child welfare personnel may have to be multi-operational: performing licensing, placement, and protective care functions. However, as a result of training on the functional differences of these respective programs, staff workers now carry out their differential assignments more responsibly.[7]

Out of this increased awareness of the licensing function, there seems to have come a sense of what might be called "regulatory collegiality." The emergence of this regulatory collegiality is attested to by the recent development of the Association for Regulatory Administration (ARA) in 1976. The ARA now has a paid membership of over 400 persons, a full-time secretary and an association journal of good quality, *The ARA Newsletter*. While the membership is generally composed of persons identified with child care regulatory administration, the largest single bloc of members would probably be those with child day care licensing responsibility.

THREE OPERATIONAL CHALLENGES

The achievement—albeit very uneven—that took place during the last 20 years might be said to be "structural" in nature. The licensing law, standards and staff are essential elements for operations, but they themselves are not operations! It is in the area of administrative operations that the least achievement has taken place, especially in relation to communications or interpretation, administrative coordination, and proper and sufficient personnel for enforcement. Yet in my opinion these three administrative activities constitute what are perhaps the most critical administrative determinants for the successful safeguarding of children in day care facilities. Brief comments will be made on each of these administrative challenges.

Communication Aspects of Licensing Administration

The functional difference of child care licensing from most other community service programs for children, such as child placement and protective care, seems not to be fully understood or appreciated. These other children's services are appropriately classified as "social treatment" programs serving particular individuals or small groups. Frequently they are referred to as "helping" services. The functional nature of child care licensing is totally different. Its goal is *not* "individualized helping" or social treatment but a generalized preventive activity. Child care licensing endeavors to reduce risks in day care by requiring compliance with a set of standards in advance of a child's—any child, not a particular one—receiving care there. Child care licensing generally and day care licensing specifically are quite analogous to the public health model of preventive activity in that they endeavor to reduce risks by manipulating the environment.

A critical factor in successful administration of a preventive program is community education. The goals and the means (standards) to achieve these goals must be taught constantly and in many different ways. In fact, one might say that the preventive function of licensing makes it largely a teaching operation rather than a helping or treatment program. Observation and analysis, however, indicate a general lack of administrative attention to the need for systematic interpretation of day care licensing goals and how they are achieved. Yet, without such communication it is difficult to envision how constituency support can be generated so that day care licensing can be stabilized and so be freed of the constant threat of abolishment or of such a degree of operational attenuation that its utility becomes nonexistent.

Administrative Coordination

Child day care facility licensure cannot become isolated. It needs to be administratively related to: 1) other child care licensing, namely, 24-hour care, 2) other types of facility care licensing, such as mental health or corrections which may serve children, 3) regulatory agencies participating in day care licensing, such as health and fire safety, 4) other regulatory programs in the same department, such as adult services licensing, 5) other divisions or bureaus that may utilize the licensed facilities such as placement services, and 6) bureaus that may pay for care in licensed facilities. Then there is also the important administrative coordination of the licensing unit and protective care unit with respect to dealing with problems of child abuse in day care facilities. Yet there seems to be a scarcity of professional literature on these topics and little or no consideration of them at child welfare conferences. Most important of all to note is that there is little or no formal structure, such as an interregulatory agency council, which might at least provide a permanent avenue for dialogue on common administrative coordination problems. It is perhaps the absence of structure to deal with uniform practices in state regulatory programs, or even to resolve "hardship" requirements by a participating regulatory agency that may account for the existence of the antiregulatory attitude that is so seemingly omnipresent. Also, one might speculate that if the matter of coordinative aspects were dealt with, it might constitute the dynamic for achieving better community relations generally, especially with providers' associations and, one hopes, with consumers' groups or organizations. Until day care licensing authorities effect better community relationships with providers and consumers there will really be no valid community participation in licensing administration.

Personnel Aspects of Standards Enforcement[8]

Historically there has been serious lack of enforcement of child care licensing standards including day care. A number of dynamics account for this. One factor was the early philanthropic nature of child care and the attitude that such organizations were "doing the best they can for these poor children." And, of course, there was the added thought that if the philanthropic agency didn't do the job, the burden would fall on taxpayers. The fact that the philanthropic agency was often religiously sponsored added to the operational reluctance to enforce lest there would be charges of entanglement of state and church. Possibly another factor contributing to nonenforcement, but coming later, was the professional philosophy of social workers who frequently staffed child care licensing agencies relative to "the use of authority." Many of these professional social workers seemed to feel that to use legal authority represented failure in effecting "positive treatment relationships." This might be true, but what was not realized was that licensing was not a social treatment program! Thus a pattern of nonenforcement was set and continued long after day care regulation appeared. Time, however, seems to have run out on nonenforcement for a variety of reasons. Perhaps the emergence of proprietary day care is the most important one. Licensed proprietary providers who meet standards are likely to be very critical and vocal if the state licensing authority does not deal with those providers who do not meet standards, or who even operate without applying for a license.

For a sound, vigorous program of positive enforcement many things must happen, including better enforcement provisions in the statute and the development of enforceable standards. However, the most important thing that must take place is the recognition that specialized personnel for enforcement of licensing standards are essential. Very little attention has been given to the need for specialized enforcement personnel. Yet without personnel especially knowledgeable and skilled in enforcement actions, lack of credibility of the child care licensing agency is likely to continue. Thus it is proposed that if a "new deal" in licensing standards enforcement is to take place, consideration must be given to the feasibility of a top management enforcement officer, the redefinition of the line licensing supervisor role to include enforcement activity, and the development of a new line licensing staff position, a regulatory investigation specialist. Brief comment will be made relative to these three points.

There should be a top-level position enforcement officer who would report to the director of the regulatory agency. Preferred qualifications for this position would combine legal training with social work or child development experience and education. Primary responsibilities of the enforcement officer would be to serve as consultant to personnel responsible for directing or supervising line licensing workers who engage in enforcement operations, and to assume responsibility conjointly with line supervisors for directing licensing staff involved in such actions as denial and revocation. Certainly the enforcement officer would assume full responsibility for directing personnel engaged in suppression of illegal operations. In addition to being chairperson of the council on uniform practices, she or he would chair an ad hoc planning committee on enforcement composed of both staff and community persons.

The role of the line supervisor needs to be defined or redefined in respect to enforcement duties and responsibilities. Among other duties, the line licensing supervisor should provide an informal review service when a licensee and a line worker seem to be at an impasse over whether or not a given standard is met. This review service could include going into the field (i.e., facility) to make a separate or a joint inspection. The line licensing supervisor also might play a greater part than at present in the reception and investigation of complaints. Although it is advocated that "regular" licensing workers generally not be involved in suppression of illegal operations, when it is necessary that a line licensing worker make such investigation, the supervisor might join the worker in the visit to the facility. There is much to be said for a joint or team visit in this type of situation. Finally, there should be an expectation that the supervisor play a greater role in "fair hearing" situations, including helping the line worker participate more effectively in the hearing and serving as a link between line worker and legal counsel.

A new type of licensing role is needed in respect to enforcement. It is a staff member who would specialize in the investigation of reported illegal operations and possibly join with the line licensing worker in enforcement activity, as it relates to revocation. A possible job title might be "special licensing investigator." The enforcement officer (referred to above) would be generally responsible for the direction and guidance of these special investigators whether they were in the headquarters office or stationed in a regional office. A special staff development program would be necessary for such workers.

In addition to the above enforcement personnel, it must also be recognized that if successful enforcement operations are to be carried out, there would be a need for the licensing agency to have access to subject-matter specialists in child development. Two important functions of these subject-matter specialists would be to testify as experts at hearings and to provide consultation to licensing staff when revocation is being considered. The basis of employment might vary from full-time or part-time to fee basis, depending on need. Expert testimony in other areas such as fire safety or building standards should preferably be obtained from officials in the particular fields. The presence of a state interregulatory agency council might facilitate this cooperative testifying service which is urgently needed for sound enforcement operations.

A POSTSCRIPT COMMENT: DAY CARE FACILITY
LICENSING ALONE IS NOT ENOUGH

This paper has had as its focus the state of operations of day care facility licensure. Its concern was primarily with administrative analysis. However, in concluding an analysis of how day care facility licensure developed and an identification of some of the important operational challenges, it is important to state two things. The first is that no assumption was made that day care facility licensure was necessarily the best or primary regulatory safeguard for children experiencing family day care. Just as lack of policy planning and sound policy formulation resulted in day care licensing being forced into existing child care licensing statutes, appropriate or not; likewise, little or no thought has been given to whether or not facility licensure is as appropriate for family day care as it is for day care centers. In fact, empirical analysis in many localities seems to indicate that a responsibility to implement a program of formal family day care licensing is impossible. See for example, a federal Office of Child Development publication statement that "Probably 90–95% of the centers are licensed but only about five to ten percent of family care homes are licensed or approved as meeting licensing standards" (Cohen, 1974). Many reasons might explain why, after a reasonable period, family day care licensing has really not caught on. There is the sheer magnitude of numbers. In large states where there is no exemption for a small number of children before a license is required, the total cost can become staggering, and the cost per child safeguarded is questionably high. (Incidentally, it should be noted that exemptions of a given number make for increased enforcement problems because of charges of unfairness and unequal treatment: "Why do I need a license for five but she/he doesn't for four?") In addition to magnitude of number of homes, lack of social visibility and the transitory nature of a great amount of family day care also seem to contribute to nonlicensure. Regardless of the causation, it is apparent licensure will need to give way to regulatory innovation such as registration/self-certification if children in family day care are to be safeguarded.

Secondly, it is important to state that if an optimal degree of safeguarding all day care children in all ways is to take place, it will be necessary to utilize diverse regulatory programs. Besides facility licensure and some innovative program for family day care, consideration also needs to be given to: 1) the credentialing of child care personnel; 2) the certification of facilities to provide a particularized service; 3) fiscal regulatory control of public purchase or funding of private day care services; and 4) the inspection-approval of public day care services since licensing per se is operationally appropriate only for the private sector. Each of these regulatory programs has its positive and negative values with respect to a particular type of day care.

If there is to be a pragmatically valid community safeguarding of day care services, it must have a larger regulatory frame of reference than traditional facility licensure. Both lay and professional leadership need an operational appreciation of the potentialities and limitations of each of the several regulatory programs. The evil of not knowing is that it reduces the making of dynamic choices and thereby constricts freedom of the will. Without greater knowledge of the array of regulatory safeguards there may well be a continuation of the feeling that the choice is a dichotomous one between a facility licensing program or no regulatory safeguard at all. When this is not the case and there is an appreciation of the need for a total system of regulatory safeguards for day care, dialogue will no longer be limited to the need for a model state day care *licensing statute*. Rather, the concern will be with the development of a model state day care *regulatory code*. In such a code there will be separate sections pertaining to licensing, inspection and approval of public facilities, fiscal regulatory administration, certification of technical personnel and specialized facilities, and innovative programs such as family day care registration. In addition, such a code would hopefully be prefaced with an introduction setting forth the rights and entitlements of day care children. When such codes are enacted, and when appropriations and personnel are present to operationalize them, then we might properly state that we have come of age in respect to regulatory administration in the field of child day care.

FOOTNOTES

1. Some of the material in this and the following sections is derived from a paper in preparation by the writer and Richard Orton of the Texas Department of Human Resources, titled, "Towards a Philosophy of Day Care Licensing."

2. Recently there has been a tendency to modify the *name* to Department of Human Resources, but certain assistance programs continue to be functionally present.

3. Historically it should be noted that day care or day nurseries as they emerged and developed in this country were distinctly regarded as a welfare service for working mothers or parents. Day nurseries were listed as social service and were often supported by the "Community Chest." This development was seen as something quite different from nursery school or early childhood education movement whose constituency and support came from the middle class. In a sense, the "paths" of these two developments really did not cross until a very recent date (after World War II) and there is still confusion as to differential functions.

4. Although there has been an advocacy in various parts of the country for state offices of child development only a very few have been established and these generally limited in basic responsibilities. I believe there should be at this time a widespread re-examination of the need for and operational nature of such offices. This re-examination might well be sponsored

by national (private) community organization agencies interested in day care and child development services.

5. Compare with "Intellectualizing Day Care" (Chapter 2) in *The Children's Cause,* by G. Y. Steiner with the assistance of P. H. Milius, Washington, DC: The Brookings Institution, 1976.

6. Child Care Licensing Act (1975) Article 695 c-3. *Vernon's Texas Civil Statutes.*

7. Besides the federal agencies, many national organizations contributed in various ways to this professionalization, including the Child Welfare League of America, American Public Welfare Association, National Day Care and Child Development Council, and National Association for Education of Young Children.

8. The content of this section was largely derived from Class, Gerhart *et al.* "concept paper" on *The Enforcement of Child Day Care Licensing Standards: With Special Reference to Revocation.* (The "concept papers" were scholarly papers commissioned for the FIDCR Appropriateness Report. They were published by the U.S. Department of Health, Education, and Welfare Office of the Assistant Secretary for Planning and Evaluation.)

REFERENCES

Cohen, D. J. *Day care 3. Serving preschool children* (U.S. Department of Health, Education, and Welfare Publication No. OHH 74-1057). Washington, D.C.: U.S. Government Printing Office, 1974.

Guides for Day Care Licensing (U.S. Department of Health, Education, and Welfare Publication No. OCD 73-1053). Washington, D.C.: U.S. Department of Health, Education, and Welfare, 1973.

THE ROLES OF THE FEDERAL GOVERNMENT IN REGULATION AND MAINTENANCE OF QUALITY IN CHILD CARE

Edith H. Grotberg

INTRODUCTION

The issue of federal government involvement, intervention, or intrusion in the quality of early education and day care, to say nothing about roles in regulation and maintenance of quality, is so fraught with emotion that facts or logic are usually lost when addressing the issue. Such strong reactions have their roots in the history of the country, but they have become particularly sharpened as a result of increased government actions in social programs since the early 1960s. To reduce the emotional intensity and to increase the significance of facts and logic, the causes of the emotional reactions are identified and considered first in this review.

Advances in Early Education and Day Care, Volume 1, pages 19–45
ISBN: 0-89232-127-X

Following that discussion is the presentation of some facts about the current federal role in early education and day care, the consumers' indications of what they want, the meaning of standards to children, and what the alternative roles of the federal government are and can be in regulation and maintenance of quality in programs and services for young children.

FEELINGS ABOUT THE FEDERAL ROLE IN REGULATION AND QUALITY MAINTENANCE

Feelings about the federal role in regulation and quality maintenance in early education and day care run high among a number of groups. These include political ideological groups, state officials, business groups, consumer and other advocacy groups. An examination of the concerns these groups express is helpful in understanding some of the problems the federal government faces as it considers alternative roles in assuring quality care for children.

Political Ideologists

Many political ideologists resist any government role in any aspect of the lives of citizens. Their feelings are particularly strong where children are involved, especially preschool children. These same ideologists are not deeply concerned about public schools, compulsory school attendance, and the minimal involvement of citizens in establishing policy regulations and standards for the public schools. They say a great deal, however, about the dangers of government intrusion into the lives of preschool children, suggesting that this would lead to the possibility of state-reared and state-controlled children, which is to be avoided at all costs.

Other political ideologists believe very strongly that government intervention in the lives of children and increasingly in the lives of preschool children is necessary and desirable. They feel that the only way the well-being of young children can be assured is through government initiatives, regulations, and monitoring for quality. It is their opinion that government policy should address the needs of children and that the government should provide the funds and programs to carry out its policy. Early education and day care are seen as responsibilities of the government and not to be left to other groups.

These rather extreme positions of the political ideologists tend to overshadow a more moderate assessment of government involvement in child care.

State Officials

Many state officials, including those in education, human development services, and others in the executive and legislative branches of the states, resent the involvement of the federal government in early education and day care. They do not seriously question state government activity, but any federal regulations or efforts to maintain quality of programs and services are suspect. The federal roles, in their view, should be limited to redistributing funds and helping states accomplish what they want by providing funds and technical assistance. They are not even sure research is a proper area for federal funding or leadership.

State officials cite the Federal Interagency Day Care Requirements (FIDCR) as an example of undesirable activity, and revenue sharing and Title XX of the Social Security Act as examples of a preferred federal role, i.e., providing funds and, at most, asking for a state plan, as for Title XX. The fact that the FIDCR are required in day care under Title XX is frequently seen as an intrusion in an area which should be exclusively state-controlled.

Business Groups

Many business groups ardently oppose any kind of government regulations, and those in the early education and day care business are especially upset by government involvement. They assert that the FIDCR, for example, are too costly to carry out and prevent them from making sufficient profits to stay in business. They, too, are not usually opposed to forms of government subsidies but are vigorously opposed to any accompanying regulations. They argue that an open, competitive market and the choice of consumers will provide sufficient quality control.

Consumer and Advocacy Groups

A number of consumer and advocacy groups, such as women's groups, professional associations, and day care organizations, have firm opinions that day care and, to some extent, early education programs and services, are the rights of parents and children. They hold equally strong views that these programs and services should be supported by public funds. The focus of most of their concern is on the needs of working mothers, and as the population of working mothers with children under the age of six years has increased, so has the advocacy for publicly supported child care. These groups often seem more interested in supporting the rights of working women than in the needs of their children.

The intensity of feelings expressed by all of these groups is caused, then, by strong ideological beliefs about the role of government in providing child care services, establishing standards, and maintaining quality early education and day care programs and services. These beliefs and opinions cannot be ignored, and they will certainly continue to influence the debates and positions taken on the issue of federal involvement in child care. But such feelings often cloud the facts of what is going on, what citizens want, what is at stake for children, and what the federal government is expected to do for the well-being of the citizens.

CURRENT FEDERAL INVOLVEMENT IN EARLY EDUCATION AND DAY CARE

Current federal involvement in early education and day care includes financing, standards and regulations, and research. No sharp lines are drawn among day care, nursery school, cooperative, and Head Start programs. These terms, as well as child care, are used interchangeably except when specific definitions are appropriate.

Financing—The Government as Purchaser

The cost of child care to the consumer depends on the kind of care used, the age of the child, the nature of the caregiver (relative vs. nonrelative, for example), the geographic location, and other factors (Bruce, 1978). A significant amount of care is provided free or for in-kind compensation or other nonmonetary reimbursement. Nevertheless, it is estimated that consumers pay between $6 and $7 billion a year for child care, including intermittent babysitting as well as more formal arrangements. About 33 percent of this amount is spent for in-home care, 40 percent for family day care, and 27 percent for center-based care.

Most day care in this country is paid for by the parents of the children receiving the care or with other private funds. However, the federal government has become increasingly involved in day care and has affected the extensive growth of the day care market. In fiscal 1977, for example, the government obligated about $2.5 billion for federal child care programs. Of that figure, approximately $800 million was planned spending under the Title XX program for the direct purchase of day care, more than twice the amount provided in 1971 under the predecessor of Title XX, Title IV-A.

Differences between care purchased by federal or other government funds and that purchased directly by the parent are in part the consequence of the FIDCR, in part the result of the characteristics of the families and children eligible for public programs, and in part the reflection of policy choices by states. Child care purchased in part or in whole with federal funds (FFP) differed from nonfederally funded day care (non-FFP) in a number of significant ways: who used it, who paid for it, what it offered, and what it cost. Harder to pinpoint was the major cause of that difference: Was it because FFP care had to meet the FIDCR that determined the characteristics of care or was it simply because the government was the purchaser?

Non-FFP care is purchased directly by the parent whose range of choice is limited primarily by income. Of course, even families at the same income level choose to spend widely varying amounts of money for child care. FFP care, in contrast, is purchased by a government entity and provided to qualified recipients. The government-as-purchaser is bound both by law and by bureaucratic considerations. Not only is the government required to purchase care that meets legal requirements (such as the FIDCR), but the agency making the purchase generally determines the modes of care to buy. The variation of mode was shown by the sharp differences among states in their choice of care purchased. Michigan, for example, under its Title XX and Work Incentives (WIN) programs for children in day care full-time, used in-home care 54 percent of the time. California chose center-based care 75 percent of the time. Wisconsin used center care 46 percent of the time and family day care 35 percent (Bruce, 1978).

As is readily apparent, the federal government was and is involved in three kinds of day care: center-based, family day care, and in-home. Each of these has different characteristics in relation to children, staff, staff/child ratio, services, and costs as well as differences from non-FFP day care.

Center-based Care. The majority (60 percent) of Title XX and WIN funding for full-time care was purchased from day care centers. Virtually all centers were state-regulated. Centers operated for profit were much less likely than nonprofit centers to serve FFP children. Thus, most FFP centers were nonprofit. Characteristics of FFP and non-FFP day care centers also revealed some differences.

Black children, children from low-income families, and children from single-parent families were much more apt to be in FFP centers than in non-FFP centers. However, for the nation as a whole, FFP centers were neither overwhelmingly black nor overwhelmingly low-income, although this was true in certain Southern states. In Alabama, for example, 88 percent of FFP enrollment was black compared to 7.5 percent black enrollment in non-FFP centers; likewise, 83 percent of FFP enrollment was low-income while only four percent of non-FFP enrollment was low-income. In nearly one-quarter of these centers, more than 80 percent of children came from single-parent families and more than 90 percent were black. In contrast, nearly half of the non-FFP centers served neither black nor low-income children, although almost all served some children from single-parent families.

While the average caregiver education was approximately the same for all centers, directors of FFP nonprofit centers were much more likely to have 16 or more years of education. FFP centers and nonprofit centers were more likely to have a relatively high percentage of black caregivers. Staff salaries were higher in FFP centers than in non-FFP centers, and higher in nonprofit centers than in profit centers. Staff turnover was somewhat less in FFP and nonprofit centers than in non-FFP and profit centers.

The number of children per staff member for all centers was, on the average, considerably less than the ratios permitted by state licensing law. FFP centers averaged lower child-staff ratios than non-FFP centers and generally had fewer children than allowed by FIDCR. Average child-staff ratios are shown below:

Ratio for all Centers	6.8-1
Ratio for all FFP Centers	5.9-1
Ratio for all Non-FFP Centers	7.6-1
FIDCR Ratio	6.4-1
Average State Licensing Ratio	12.4-1

Although average child-staff ratios for all FFP centers were in compliance with FIDCR, some individual FFP centers did not meet the FIDCR requirement. Below is a breakdown of the percentage of centers meeting state and FIDCR child-staff ratios:

	Percentage Complying with State Requirements	Percentage Complying with FIDCR
All Centers	93.6	50.8
All FFP Centers	95.3	67.6
All Nonprofit Centers	92.3	37.6

FFP centers provided medical, psychological, and social services to children and families with far greater frequency than did non-FFP centers. While all FFP centers were more likely than non-FFP centers to offer a number of social services to parents and health services to children, nonprofit FFP centers stood out in this regard. Sixty-five percent of these centers offered all four of the following family social services: counseling on child's development, counseling on family problems, assistance in obtaining food stamps or financial aid, and assistance in obtaining community services. In contrast, only 17 percent of non-FFP centers did so, and 15 percent offered no family social services.

Costs per child were much higher in FFP centers than in non-FFP centers. Costs for nonprofit FFP centers were markedly higher than for all other types of centers. The average cost of full-time care per child in FFP centers was estimated at $110 per month. Differences in average cost were attributable mainly to differences in classroom staff salaries and to child-staff ratios. Nonprofit FFP centers had an average per child cost of over $200 a month.

The average maximum weekly fee charged by nonprofit centers was $31. (The average cost to the center appeared to be closer to $40 a week, with donations and other factors making up the difference.) The average maximum parent fee in non-FFP profit centers was about $25 a week. According to center directors, relatively few children were paid for with a combination of parent and government fees. Six percent of the average enrollment in nonprofit FFP centers were paid for jointly, and the percentage of split fees was even less in other types of FFP centers. On the other hand, a case study of 300 Title XX day care center recipients in 31 states reported that 63 percent of the respondents said that both they and the social services agency shared in paying for the child care (Bruce, 1978).

In summary, FFP centers were more likely to serve children from black, low-income, or single-parent families, to have better educated directors and more highly paid caregivers, to have lower child-staff ratios, to offer more family and child social services, and were significantly more expensive than non-FFP centers.

Family Day Care. Approximately 2.6 million persons provided child care in their homes for about 5.6 million children for ten or more hours each week. Of these, only about 100–150,000 were regulated through licensing, registration, or approval. Although no national data exist that compare family day care providers who care for FFP children with those who do not, there is information about regulated and unregulated providers. These data can give a general comparison of FFP and non-FFP characteristics, since virtually all unregulated providers care only for children whose fees are fully paid by parents and almost all government subsidized care is provided by regulated caregivers (although only about one-quarter of these caregivers actually care for FFP children).

Regulated homes, as compared to unregulated homes, cared for lower proportions of minority children and for higher proportions of children from one-parent families, and were more likely to care for children to whom they were not related. Further, regulated homes cared for more children on a regular basis, were in operation more hours per week (52 as against 42), and had higher average ratios of children per adult (2.9 to 2.1), and provided almost twice as many child-hours of care per week.

Regarding caregiver characteristics, both types of providers were similar in terms of marital status, age and education. Regulated caregivers in comparison with the unregulated were more experienced in caring for children (56 percent versus 38 percent had four or more years of experience), had higher family incomes, were more likely to be white, and to charge higher hourly fees (67 cents an hour as against 50 cents). The average monthly charge for full-time regulated family day care was $132. The fee for unregulated care was $95. The estimated average FFP reimbursement rate was $91 a month.

In 1976, Title XX Social Service agencies purchased family day care for about 140,000 children, two-thirds of it full-time care.

In-home Care.   There is almost no statistical information available regarding in-home care. It is estimated that 1.5 million households use ten or more hours daily of relative care in the child's home, and 1.2 million households use ten or more hours daily of non-relative in-home care. It is estimated that among households where the mother is employed, three-quarters of those using in-home relative care paid no cash for that service, and 16 percent using in-home nonrelative care did not pay cash.

For paying households in which the mother worked 30 or more hours a week, the average weekly payment for in-home care was $16 for both relative and nonrelative care. These figures are clearly below the minimum wage. (Some in-home care providers may receive in-kind compensation in addition to cash or may provide the service as a personal gesture to friends or family members.) (*Statistical Highlights,* 1976).

No data are available on the characteristics of in-home care providers in general or on those persons providing in-home care to Title XX and WIN children. However, approximately 100,000 Title XX and WIN children received in-home care, with 60 percent of it full-time care.

In summary, most federal financing of day care was to serve children whose parents had low incomes, were in training as part of Federal programs, or qualified for special services for a variety of social, economic, and personal reasons. These facts have influenced the standards and regulations developed by the federal government and account for a good deal of the current debates about what standards are needed and why, and for problems of enforcement and appropriateness.

Development of Standards and Regulations

As a result of its role as a purchaser of day care, the federal government is concerned both with the costs of care and the effects of different arrangements on children and parents. In 1968, the Department of Health, Education, and Welfare, the Department of Labor, and the Office of Economic Opportunity adopted a uniform set of standards intended to control the type and quality of care purchased with federal dollars. These standards, the Federal Interagency Day Care Requirements (FIDCR), apply to all day care centers and family day care homes receiving federal subsidies. Designed to protect children from harm and to promote their development, the 1968 FIDCR cover a variety of center and family day home characteristics.

The 1968 FIDCR were made part of the Code of Federal Regulations in early 1969. Late in 1974 Congress enacted an amendment to the Social Security Act, Title XX, Grants to States for Services, which slightly modified the 1968 version of the FIDCR and made it law, effective October 1, 1975, with potentially severe financial penalties for non-compliance. The modification added staff-child ratio requirements for children under three and made optional the inclusion of an identifiable educational component. Because of controversy at the state and local levels, Congress delayed full implementation of the FIDCR staff-child ratio requirements. Centers were not required to meet the federally prescribed ratios for children aged six weeks to six years. At the same time, states were prohibited from allowing ratios in subsidized centers to fall below actual 1975 levels. The enforcement of the ratio requirements is not yet scheduled to begin (*National Day Care Study,* 1977).

The FIDCR cover a number of program characteristics: staff-child ratio and size of group; suitability and safety of facilities; the provision of social, health, and nutritional services; staff training and parent involvement; as well as aspects of administrative coordination and program evaluation.

To understand the application of the FIDCR to day care centers, it is helpful, when comparing extremely diverse center-based programs, to think of centers as comprising two distinct levels of program operations. A day care center may be seen as having a Core Program, consisting of a standard core and a varying core, and a Supplemental Services Program.

The standard core covers the day-to-day delivery of essential services to the child. It is this component of day care which is found in all centers across the country. It consists of the facility, caregivers, meals, first aid, and the administrative structure that supports direct delivery of care. The standard core program always includes basic care of the child (protecting, "nurturing," feeding, etc.) and usually involves some minimum "educational" activity during part of the day as well. The varying core includes some additional health and transportation services which may be provided by the center or some other agency, depending on local circumstances.

The Supplemental Services Program comprises elements generally considered to benefit the child indirectly, and includes such areas as family social services and staff training. In addition to these program requirements, the FIDCR set external administration/coordination/evaluation requirements.

Barriers to Compliance. The issue of compliance continues not only because of the present status of Congressional involvement but also because of barriers identified by day care service providers in the states

(*Assessment of Barriers,* 1976). There were barriers in the environment which were outside the requirements or the system for enforcement. Examples of this type of barrier were changes in the day care market, lack of agreement over purpose of day care, and federal regulations with no federal administration.

There were also barriers in the system which were related to the capacity of the system for implementation and enforcement. Examples were no federal implementation plan for assistance to states, no clear delegation of responsibility, and lack of procedures for monitoring and enforcement of the standards.

Finally, there were barriers in the requirements related to the specific FIDCR. These included lack of agreement about the purpose of the FIDCR, differing philosophical attitudes toward some of the requirements, support for state day care standards, and lack of clarity and measurability of requirements.

Degree of Compliance.   Non-FFP centers are required to comply only with state day care regulations, while FFP centers must comply with the FIDCR as well as state regulations (Travers *et al.*, 1977). Under current federal guidelines (*Federal Register,* 31 January 1977), state day care agencies are permitted to waive the FIDCR compliance in those FFP centers serving no more than five subsidized children or one fifth of the enrollment, whichever is lower. Some states have chosen not to issue waivers, and others have chosen to issue waivers for only some of their waiver-eligible centers. For purposes of the following discussion on the degree of regulatory compliance, FFP centers have been separated into two categories—those ineligible for FIDCR waivers (FFP/NW) and those who are eligible for waivers (FFP/WE). Of the 8,000 FFP centers, about 1,500 (19 percent) are in the FFP/WE category.

Much of the early debate on the appropriateness of the FIDCR has focused on staff-child ratio requirements. Averaged across all centers, all states, and all ages of children, current state regulations permit a maximum of about twelve children per caregiver, while the maximum permitted by FIDCR is about six children per caregiver. The variability of ratio requirements across states is quite large. The average requirement across all ages of children in Arizona and Hawaii is about 17.5 children per caregiver, but in Connecticut and New York an average of about 6.3 children per caregiver is the legal maximum. Mississippi imposes no ratio requirement at all on non-FFP centers. The major disparities between federal and state ratio requirements occur for children between the ages of two and five years. For children under two years of age and for school-age children, federal and state ratio requirements are relatively similar.

The degree of compliance with state licensing requirements regarding staff-child ratio was very high, regardless of type of center. About 94 percent of all centers had sufficient classroom staff to comply with state requirements. The degree of compliance was slightly higher than average among FFP/NW centers and slightly lower than average among non-FFP centers. Most of the centers which were not in compliance with state requirements were in those states in which the state requirements were very high. For those centers not currently in compliance, a total of only 1,400 additional caregivers would be necessary to achieve compliance. In contrast, those centers which currently comply with state regulations had about 51,000 full-time equivalent caregivers in excess of the minimum numbers required to satisfy state regulations.

The degree of compliance with the FIDCR staff-child ratio requirement varied widely across categories of centers. About 72 percent of FFP/NW centers had sufficient classroom staff to comply with the FIDCR. Among FFP/WE and non-FFP centers only 45 percent and 38 percent, respectively, had sufficient caregivers to satisfy the FIDCR. Within the FFP/NW category, the degree of compliance varied by type of center, 79 percent among nonprofit centers versus only 45 percent among proprietary centers. To bring all noncomplying FFP centers up to FIDCR standards, about 5,500 additional full-time equivalent caregivers would be required. This is an average of about two full-time persons per noncomplying center. Among those FFP centers satisfying FIDCR, however, about 12,500 full-time equivalent caregivers were currently in excess of the minimum numbers required.

There are various other provisions of the FIDCR for which measures of the degree of compliance are available. The FIDCR specify the maximum number of children that can be placed in a single group or classroom. About 60 percent of FFP centers reported groups or classrooms which met the FIDCR limits. Of the remaining 40 percent, many centers appeared to be organized on an open-classroom basis, for which reported group size may have been much larger than effective group size. The latter being a cluster of children under the direct supervision of one or more caregivers at a given time of day. As a result, it appears that more than 60 percent of FFP centers were in compliance with the FIDCR group size provisions. About 68 percent of non-FFP centers report groups or individual classrooms within a center which met the FIDCR limits. Since the frequency of open-classroom arrangements was lower among non-FFP centers, measures of compliance based on effective group sizes would probably show no differences between FFP and non-FFP centers.

The FIDCR require that FFP centers with more than 40 children enrolled allow parents an active voice in center decision-making. If parent involvement is defined as participation in staff selection or review of programs and budgets, it is estimated that 69 percent of FFP/NW and 45 percent of FFP/WE centers comply with this FIDCR provision. This definition of participation is much narrower than that currently recommended by HEW's Administration for Public Services for monitoring purposes. The Administration's definition includes volunteer work by parents and/or opportunity for parents to observe their children in center classrooms as alternative evidence of FIDCR compliance. Virtually all centers complied with this definition of parent participation.

The FIDCR, as well as most state day care regulations, require that children have a medical examination at the time they enroll in day care centers. About 90 percent of all centers complied with this requirement. The degree of compliance was slightly higher for non-FFP centers (92 percent) than for FFP centers (89 percent). In addition, the FIDCR require that children undergo periodic health examinations during the time they are enrolled in centers. About half of FFP centers versus about 20 percent of non-FFP centers provided or facilitated such examinations for the children they enrolled (Travers et al., 1977).

The basic problem with the FIDCR compliance, however, seems to be cost. Low staff-child ratios and high levels of staff training are the major sources of costs and it is to those aspects of the FIDCR that recent research on the appropriateness of the FIDCR has been addressed. The major findings significant for costs related to staff-child ratio and level of staff training were, first, small groups were found to work best. The size of the group in which preschool children spent their day care hours made the most difference. Small numbers of children and small numbers of adults, interacting with each other, comprised the kind of groups associated with better care for children. Second, staff specialization in child-related fields was another important factor. While formal education per se did not make a difference, specialization in a child-related area was linked to quality care.

Third, for preschoolers, minor variations in staff-child ratio had less effect on the quality of care than group size. If the groups were too large, adding caregivers did not help. In groups with small numbers of children and caregivers, minor variations in ratio had little or no impact. Furthermore, costs were not necessarily affected significantly by group size. They were, however, affected by staff-child ratio, by amount of education caregivers had, and by the length of time caregivers had worked in the center.

Finally, centers that received some or all of their income from the federal government were different from centers that relied on parent fees. Centers serving federally subsidized children had higher staff-child ratios, offered a broader range of supplementary services to children and families, and used more staff providing specialized services, such as nurses or nutritionists (Travers et al., 1977).

Congress has been interested in the appropriateness of the FIDCR for several years and required research into this question. In the meantime, because "many states indicated that they would be unable to meet the FIDCR standards without additional financial assistance", Congress also appropriated $200 million additional Title XX monies for fiscal years 1977 and 1978 to upgrade day care staffing to meet the FIDCR (*Childcare and Preschool*, 1978, p. 39).

Research, Development, Demonstration, and Evaluation

The federal government is the major source of funding of research which has implications for child care. Most of the research is conducted at universities, by nonprofit organizations, and in governmental units. The research includes 3,664 projects at an annual cost of $367.1 million. These are distributed in the following areas (Hertz, 1978).

	Percent of Projects	Percent of Funding
Applied research	32.7	26.9
Demonstrations	32.1	45.1
Basic research	20.3	9.2
Support and utilization of research	4.9	5.2
Policy research	4.7	3.5
Evaluation research	4.1	7.8
Social data analysis	1.2	2.3

Advantages of federally supported research include concentration of funds, distribution by equitable criteria, ability to attract researchers across states and to focus on talent rather than location. The federal government is also able to address issues of concern to the entire nation, such as child care, and to provide sufficient funds and continuing attention to issues like the appropriateness of the FIDCR, the characteristics and needs of consumers, and the supply of child care facilities across the country. As a matter of fact, this chapter draws heavily from data and findings generated by studies supported by the Administration for Children, Youth and Families.

The disadvantages of federally supported research include lack of focus on local issues, limited contribution of states to determining needed research, and inadequate dissemination of research findings for utilization at state and local levels.

In summary, the three main areas of federal involvement in early education and day care—financing, standards and regulations, and research—result from a governmental concern for making funds available to providers and consumers of child care on some equitable basis of need, assuring that children are not only protected but stimulated in their development, and supporting the generation of new knowledge about children, early education, and day care in order to improve the quality of child care.

The federal role is currently extensive and complex in early education and day care. It involves cost considerations, program characteristics, and standards of quality. Each of these is subject to debate and differences; each generates strong feelings and the resolutions are not clear. States are expressing their views through continued development of their own standards. Consumers are neither as vocal nor as organized, but their wishes have been identified through surveys and the choices parents make in care for their children. The role of the government in research has not been seriously challenged, except for criticism about the limited dissemination and application of findings.

CONSUMER BEHAVIOR

Most consumers select informal means of child care and express little interest in changing their arrangements. There are, however, identifiable patterns of preference and choice of child care among consumers. These patterns are important when discussing publicly supported services. Further insight into consumer behavior and preference is found in attitudes and opinions expressed about government involvement in child care, financially, programmatically, and in terms of standards and regulations.

Consumer Choice of Day Care Arrangements

The choices consumers make for child care are strongly related to different types of families (Bruce, 1978). For example, while there are far fewer single-parent families than two-parent families, single-parent households were proportionately higher users of day care when occasional babysitting is excluded—52 percent, compared to 36 percent two-parent households.

Most day care users were also employed outside the home. Of the families using ten or more hours of care a week, 50–60 percent of those using in-home care and care by relatives were employed. Of those using nonrelative family day care nearly 90 percent were employed; and nearly 80 percent of those using center care and 60 percent of those using nursery schools were employed.

Most substantial users of day care had incomes near or above the median family income level. The primary reason for this was the high probability that all adults in the family were employed. These above-median-income families tended to use in-home (nonrelative) care and nursery schools more than other income groups. Families with below-poverty income used in-home (relative) or center care more than other forms of care. The near-poor, between the poverty index and the median family income, used higher proportions of relatives (in-home and family day care) than other forms of care.

In general, preschool children received more care by persons other than parents than do children aged 6 through 13. While preschool children constituted only about one-third of the children in this country under the age of 14, they accounted for about 55 percent of the children younger than 14 using ten or more hours of child care per week.

Looking at the overall choices made by consumers of child care, the type of care used breaks down as follows (*Statistical Highlights*, 1976, p. 9):

Type of care	Number of children receiving care (in millions)	Percent of all children receiving care
Own home by relative	9.5	20
Own home by nonrelative	9.7	20
Other home by relative	11.3	24
Other home by nonrelative	7.1	15
Nursery or preschool	1.9	4
Before/after school program	1.6	3
Day care center	1.0	2
Cooperative program	0.5	1
Head Start	0.1	less than 0.5

It is clear from this distribution that 79 percent of all children receiving care were in informal arrangements, with little likelihood of being under day care regulations or standards. When looking at household income, the use of child care increased as income rose. There were two major exceptions: middle-income children used the most care by relatives, and low-income children used the most care in centers and Head Start. In terms of age of children, the greatest use of child care was at two years of age. Beginning at age four, the amount of care steadily decreased. This was essentially true for all types, except for before or after school programs.

Among those consumers who used the principal types of care, the reasons for such use as well as an indication of the most important reason were as follows (*Statistical Highlights*, 1976, p. 17):

	Percent of all users	
	Most important reason	*All reasons*
Work or looking for work	35	42
Going out (social, shopping)	33	67
Socialization	5	23
School preparation	3	14
Child independence	3	22

The most frequent reasons were to go out casually or to work. While child-related reasons were given, they were rarely the most important. It seems that child care is seen more as a need of parents than as a benefit to children.

Most parents were satisfied with their child care arrangements and did not wish to change. When they did express a desire to change, it was generally toward a nursery or preschool type of care. Parents considered a number of factors in making decisions about child care. The most important selection factors were: caregiver reliability or training for center care; "warm and loving" caregivers; a clean and safe place; and a type of care that the child likes. The rankings of the five most frequently given factors (*Statistical Highlights,* 1976, p. 20) are given below.

	Own home	Other home	Center or nursery school
Reliable/dependable caregiver	1	1	NA[1]
Warm and loving caregiver	2	2	2
Child likes this type of care	3	4	4
Discipline given when needed	4	5	
Experienced caregiver	5		
Things are clean and safe		3	3
Planned/supervised group play	NA[1]		
Well trained staff	NA[1]	NA[1]	1

NA indicates that factor was not included in list for this type of care.

Cost was the predominant reason for not using types of care previously considered, especially nursery and preschools or day care centers. Other frequently expressed reasons were availability and transportation, provider reliability, dissatisfaction with provider, and ages of children.

Consumers' Opinions about Government Involvement

The questionnaire used in the National Child Care Consumer Study also included items on attitudes about the general involvement of the government, payment mechanisms, licensing, standards, and staff-child ratios (*Statistical Highlights,* 1976, pp. 22–24). In regard to general government involvement with programs, 16 percent of all respondents agreed that "The government should not be involved in programs to take care of children." Yet, 50 percent of all respondents were either neutral or in agreement with the statement, "I would be willing to have my taxes raised in order to support child care activities."

Regarding method for cash payments, 75 percent of all respondents preferred that "child care funds" be used to make cash payments directly to the provider rather than through working parents. And 82 percent of users preferred sliding fee scales versus either free child care or parents paying for all the costs of the care they used.

In regard to the use of licensed facilities, 85 percent used licensed day care centers, 81 percent used licensed nursery or preschools, and 10 percent used licensed family day care (other home by nonrelative). Of those paying cash to family day care providers, 17 percent of the respondents used licensed providers. As for the general attitude toward licensed providers, one quarter of all respondents agreed that ". . . everyone who takes care of children should be licensed." However, 45 percent of all users answered "yes" to the following question specifically about in-home providers: "Do you think there should be personal qualifications set for nonrelated people who care for children in the children's home? In other words, should sitters be required to pass health exams, educational requirements or meet some other kind of standard if they were providing care in your home?"

In terms of standards, users were highly in favor of regulating centers and nursery schools, though more selective in regard to someone else's home. The following figures indicate the proportion of all users who supported regulating respective aspects of child care facilities:

	Percent of All Users	
	Center or Nursery School	Someone Else's Home
Aspects		
Fire and building safety	94	67
Facility cleanliness and sanitation	94	78
Health conditions of staff and children	89	59
Staff training and qualifications	88	44
Food and nutrition	88	63
Staff-child ratio	86	62
Program content and activities	81	36
Space per child, physical surroundings and equipment	81	47
Counseling and referral services for family and child problems	69	26

In summary, there were several indications that parents with children under 14 favored a government role in day care, though apparently with some reservations. In response to one item in the survey, the general attitude favored government "involvement," but about half would be unwilling to have their taxes increased to support child care activities. Yet, nine out of ten respondents favored a sliding fee scale or universally free day care, which could be interpreted as favoring government involvement.

Regarding standards, users of centers and nursery schools strongly favored regulation of various aspects that are presently included in the federal standards. Support for regulation of certain aspects of care in someone else's home was much lower, though the majority favored safety, cleanliness, ratios, food and nutrition, and health conditions of staff and children. Interestingly enough, compared with users in general, users of care in someone else's home were slightly less favorable to regulations, whereas center and nursery school users were somewhat more favorable to regulation.

Respondents who used some form of care were asked about acceptable numbers of children per adult in someone else's home and in centers or nursery schools. Among all users, only those with children in the respective age groups (0–2, 3–5, 6–9, 10–13) were asked for ratios. Generally, users of these two settings were more accepting of more children per adult than were users in general. Between the two types of care, lenient ratios were more acceptable in centers and nursery schools than in private homes. When compared to federal staffing standards (although the data are not strictly comparable), there was substantial agreement with the ratios for homes but considerably less for day care centers and nursery schools.

Support for licensing was less strong than other indicators of government involvement in day care. Well over one-half of all respondents did not favor licensing for "everyone" who cares for children. This proportion was even greater for users of care in other homes by nonrelatives. This was somewhat confirmed by the relative lack of interest in spending "child care funds" on a "monitoring system to check on caregivers and facilities" (*Statistical Highlights,* 1976, pp. 27–28).

Current Consumer Discussions on Standards

The consumer study provided a good deal of information about the characteristics of consumers, their preferences, and choices of child care. It also provided information on attitudes and opinions about standards and government involvement. The concern of the federal government for encouraging consumer involvement in discussion of policies relating to child care is expressed in a current project. An ongoing contract of the Administration for Children, Youth and Families with the Parent Teachers Association and the College of Human Ecology at Cornell University has distributed packets of issues relating to children, youth and families to PTAs across the country. The PTA Issue Packet No. 1 (Formulating National Policies, 1977) addresses child care for working mothers. The following issues of standards and services are highlighted in the pamphlets for discussion purposes at local PTA chapters.

Standards. Day care offers possibilities to provide several kinds of service—early education, health care, and social services in addition to providing a safe place for children. Obviously, the more services and the higher the standards, the greater the immediate cost. Proponents of high standards maintain that such investments will save money later; opponents maintain that high standards would put private child care providers out of business. Some examples of the issue statements included in the pamphlets to promote discussion are:

— Federal day care standards should only deal with safety and cleanliness of the day care home or center.
— Standards should include, in addition to safety, minimum requirements for the number of children for each adult caretaker.
— In addition to safety and the number of adults, standards should include a minimum level of training and/or knowledge for day care operators.
— In addition to all of the above, a day care center should be required to provide educational experiences for children.

Day Care Services.   A few services that many people believe should be required parts of federally supported day care programs are supervised play and rest, nutritious meals, educational activities, preschool learning, health check-ups, sick-child services when needed, social and psychological service when needed, and emergency night and weekend services. Various PTA chapters are discussing these issues, voting on them to express their position and sending them to the national PTA office for analysis. The resulting information will contribute further to understanding consumer preferences and behavior.

WHAT STANDARDS MEAN TO CHILDREN

No one seriously questions that there should be some standards for child care. The form, scope, and responsibility for maintaining standards are at issue. However, more is involved for the child than standards and services. The development of the child and the role of the parents in contributing to that development are crucial to any discussion of child care. The FIDCR and the Head Start Performance Standards which were derived from the same concepts of child development expect enhanced development and parent involvement to contribute to the development of the child and other members of the family. An examination of parent involvement in Head Start illustrates both the purpose of such involvement and the child and family developmental benefits.

Parent Involvement and Child Development: Head Start
Parent participation has been an integral part of Head Start since its beginning in 1965. Parents have been involved in decision-making about

local program policy and practice through class, center, and program Policy Councils, 50 percent of whose members are required to be Head Start parents. They have also participated in the children's program classrooms as paid staff, volunteers, and observers and in activities for parents which they have helped to develop. In addition, they have worked with their children in their own home or at the center in cooperation with teachers and other staff members. The spectrum of parent participation activities is broad. It encompasses relatively little participation to learning, observing, and helping activities, to active involvement in planning and decision-making at every level of Head Start. Thus, Head Start, while usually thought of as a program for preschool children of the poor, has traditionally involved parents both as contributors and beneficiaries.

Several factors have led to early and continued strong emphasis on parent programs in Head Start. There has been theoretical and research support for involving the family, particularly the mother, in her child's development for the benefit of the child and his/her siblings. Theoretical support for involving the poor in decision-making in order to increase their skills in working through and with community organizations and for parent involvement in decision-making and other aspects of the program to strengthen parents' feelings of competence and ability to initiate worthwhile action, thereby fostering positive attitudes toward themselves and what would be possible for their children, has also contributed to this emphasis. Another factor has been a concern for improving family utilization of community services such as Medicaid and food stamps and improving family ability to secure on their own behalf assistance from public and private sources. Finally, a programmatic need to ensure that Head Start offered relevant high-quality programs responsive to local needs by enlisting the deep concern most Head Start parents have for their children, and the opportunity to improve the family's economic situation and independence through all of these factors and through employment opportunities, career development and training have influenced the emphasis on parent programs.

Additionally, it is believed that parent participation in Head Start is good for the parents themselves, that they learn they are able to control the course of their lives, learn to work within the community structure to reach their own goals and, in the process, develop more positive attitudes toward the community and its institutions such as the schools. Moreover, such participation is also believed to be good for the children. As parents gain self-confidence and inner direction, they might pass on these attitudes to their children.

A review of 67 studies (Mann et al., 1976), including parent involvement in Head Start and Home Start programs, leads to these conclusions: The critical factor appeared to be establishing some kind of change in the parents' behavior that will carry over to the parents' interactions with the child and other members of the family. Thus, parent education projects which emphasized traditional classroom techniques of providing the parent with *information* did not appear to be as effective in producing gains in the child's development as did parent training projects which emphasized the development of new skills to help in child rearing. Modes of parent involvement that attributed a greater sense of importance and responsibility to the parental role appeared to be the most effective, even though the specific nature of the involvement differed. It was found that, within parent training programs, one curriculum did not seem significantly better than another, and professional teachers and social workers were no more effective in training parents than were para-professionals. Parent participation, both in decision-making roles and in learner roles, associated with gains in child development measures, and the extent of participation was more important than the type of participation.

It is difficult to get parent participation in child care programs even when such involvement is required and the positive benefits are so clear. A major challenge to those who care about child and family development, regardless of the income level of the families, is to find ways to bring parents into a closer working relationship with the child care services. The *why* of this is known; the *how* remains a question.

ALTERNATIVE ROLES

There are a number of alternative roles the federal government might play in financing, standards and regulations, and research relating to early education and day care, and these can be presented and discussed. The fact remains, however, that most families do not use child care facilities or make child care arrangements where federal or any government involvement occurs. Suzanne H. Woolsey (1977) summarized the facts and the issues succinctly in this way:

> But whatever the reason, the data seem to show that there is far more interest in informal care in the home or the extended family than anyone would gather from the public debate. Federal policies to help make this sort of care more affordable are listed in the cacophony of contesting arguments over one method of care—formal centers—and one way of funding it—federal support to those centers. What we need is closer concentration on what people need and want to help them cope with their child-care problems (p. 145).

The families presently affected by federal involvement are select groups (e.g., single-parent families with working parent and families with low incomes where parents are in training or are working). Keeping the facts and current practices in mind and recognizing the emotional aspects of federal involvement in early education and day care, let us now examine alternative roles in financing, standards and regulations, and research.

Alternative Roles in Financing
Funds to states with minimal restrictions.   Funds could be available to states with no indication of how the money should be used, as in revenue sharing or as it does with Title XX, require primarily a target population and a published plan. The federal government would primarily redistribute resources among the states in this role. The FIDCR could be removed from Title XX day care services.

The advantages of this role are that states can control their own use of federal money, can apply the money to citizens who are other than the special groups currently served, and can set up their own criteria for who receives the funds. The disadvantages include the tendency of states to give low priority to early education and day care, the difficulty of child advocacy groups within the states to exert sufficient political pressure to assure an adequate share of resources for children, and the limited state legislation on concerns of young children.

Funds to states with maximum restrictions.   The federal government can make funds available to states or local groups, as with Head Start, where the money must be spent for children within some definitive guidelines for the use of that money. This role assures that children benefit from available funds, that they are not left out because of lack of interest in early education and child care, and that the status of legislation or policy in the states does not mitigate against assured services. Another advantage of this role is that the states can address the child care needs of populations other than the ones generally identified by the federal government. However, this role may result in decreased state interest in early education and day care, minimizing the issue as a state issue and eliminating state resources and political commitments to early education and day care.

Alternative Roles in Standards and Regulations
No federal involvement in standards.   The federal government can withdraw from concerns about standards and regulations and leave such standards to state and local authorities or, in light of the informal arrangements parents tend to make, discourage any standards different from the usual public health and safety standards of schools and other public facilities.

This alternative reduces government expenditure on maintaining the standards, permits states to determine their own policies concerning standards, and makes possible the use of state standards which are not linked to public funding and thereby cover a larger population. The problems are that inequities tend to develop among states when no federal guidelines are involved, the greater possibility of pressure groups attempting to minimize standards for business reasons, and the lack of resources in the states to study the needs of child care and the impact of standards and regulations.

Extensive federal involvement in standards. The federal government can insist on requiring any child care program receiving federal funds to comply with federally determined standards irrespective of state standards. The benefits are an assurance of common standards across the country, a model of standards for the states, and a guarantee of equitable distribution of resources related to standards. The drawbacks include conflict with state interests regarding their own standards, application of federal standards limited to select groups and not including the broader consumer population, and focusing a disproportionate amount of money to those child care facilities which receive some federal funds.

A study for Congress on the *Appropriateness of the Federal Interagency Day Care Requirements* (1978) indicates that a decision has already been made to begin the process of revising the FIDCR.

> The Notice of Intent to revise the regulations was published in the Federal Register on April 26, 1978, and a press release was issued the same day to apprise the professional community and the general public of the Department's decision.
>
> The Department expects to publish proposed new regulations in the Federal Register in the winter of 1978–79. That publication will be preceded by national and regional meetings and workshops with the States to obtain comments on preliminary draft regulations. Formal hearings will follow publication of the proposed new FIDCR. The Department will review all comments on the proposed regulations and then publish the final regulations (p. x).

The revision process is participatory and the meetings and workshops will permit a range of participants. A persistent issue that needs to be addressed is the extent to which the federal government will rely upon states to prescribe the content of specific requirements and to enforce the requirements.

> Testimony at the public hearings demonstrated a lack of consensus concerning the proper balance of responsibilities and initiatives by the Federal and State governments.
>
> In general, several models of Federal-State relationships in this area continue to surface in discussions of the FIDCR.
>
> The first model relies heavily upon States to define the specific content of requirements, to upgrade their standards, and to administer and enforce them. The Federal role would consist mainly of prescribing general requirements that States would have to impose (e.g., requiring that the State set an acceptable limit on group size assuring

frequent interactions between caregiver and child); providing financial and other incentives to States to assist them in upgrading their standards and imposing timetables for doing so; furnishing technical assistance to State agencies, providers, and parents; and requiring that the States adopt certain procedures and requirements for information for parents designed to assist public monitoring of day care. Under this model, the Federal Government would regulate not providers but State agencies.

A second model would entail a more directive Federal role. Under this model, the Federal Government would establish minimal Federal requirements for a few critical components (e.g., group size) that appear to be important to the well-being of children in day care. The Federal requirements would act as a safety net to insure that all children in federally financed day care are in programs that minimize risk or harmful situations. States would be actively encouraged to develop requirements that exceeded the Federal regulations and would receive incentives to do so. All federally financed programs would have to meet both State and Federal requirements.

A third model would involve the most extensive Federal role. The Federal Government would draft comprehensive and specific day care requirements, applicable to both the State and to the day care provider. To insure some flexibility to States and providers, the regulations would identify a range of options that States or providers could elect to meet the conditions of the requirements, or provide for waivers from requirements other than those directly related to the safety and well-being of the child (*Appropriateness* . . . (1978), pp. 166–167).

The strengths and weaknesses of these models will be discussed and final new FIDCR made available in 1979.

An important statement in the *Appropriateness* study is that concerning the federal role in child care. The statement is worth quoting because it expresses where the country seems to be in respect to the federal role in child care.

Federal concern for children can be expressed in two ways: the Government's concern for the well-being of all the Nation's children; and the Government's special concern for children when Federal money is being spent for their care. The FIDCR are part of this second concern.

In the first area, the Federal role can be to inform and inspire rather than to coerce. The Government has provided limited guidance and incentives to States, developed model State legislation, suggested standards, and educated the public. For example, HEW developed the Guides for Day Care Licensing, which included model licensing legislation, a model fire safety code, model licensing codes, guidance material for local zoning officials, and incentive funds for States to improve their regulatory systems. This Federal leadership has had an impact on the quality of all day care regardless of whether enrolled children are subsidized by Federal funds.

In the second area, the Government has shown its special concern for children enrolled in federally funded day care by developing the FIDCR. These regulations focus on one particular group of children—those defined by each State (within federally established limits) as eligible for subsidy.

The Federal Government does not have the right to dictate to the States the content of their licensing requirements, which are developed through a political process by each State. The Government does have a legitimate right, however, to go beyond persuasion, inspiration, and incentives and to use negative sanctions to assure itself that its specifications are met when Federal funds are used to purchase day care.[1]

An important task for the future is to relate the Government's two roles. The FIDCR are designed to protect one group of children, but they will effect policy goals for all children. In general, the Federal Government should not drive costs so high with its regulations that private, fee-paying parents cannot afford to purchase quality care for their children in the same community-based programs. If only poor children eligible for subsidy can use the programs, the stigmatizing effect on such segregated care might have a strongly negative effect on the quality of care, and on children, parents, and society (Ibid., pp. 167–168).

The statement says nothing about the research role of the federal government, a role that is, in fact, a part of federal involvement in child care. There can be alternative federal roles in research support, also.

Alternative Roles in Research
Distribute research funds to states. The federal government can distribute the research moneys to the states and permit them to conduct their own research or support local researchers and research organizations. This would enable each state to address the research question it deemed important. It would also permit a greater number of states to conduct research and would encourage the development of local researchers familiar with local child care needs and problems. Disadvantages are that national needs for knowledge would not be met; there is insufficient research talent across states because talent tends to be concentrated in certain geographic areas; and the research would tend to become idiosyncratic to special local situations having no generalizability.

Retain research funds at federal level. The federal government can continue in its present mode of determining at the federal level what research will be funded but with input from the states and from the research community on the significant areas needing study. Often research is generated because of a national problem, such as child care or because of a desire to know the impact of federal programs and standards, such as Head Start.

This alternative has the advantages of concentrating research money in large amounts to address a national problem. Many researchers from all over the country can contribute to the resolution of the problem; national policy can reflect the research findings; and the best talent can be supported. The problems which may result include the probability of not addressing local needs sufficiently, not helping state research capability to increase, not having a state or local voice in determining the research areas needing attention and, most important, not letting states and local levels benefit from the research findings. The dissemination and utilization difficulty continues and is not resolved even though some efforts have been made to improve that situation.

SUMMARY

In summary, the federal government can play a number of alternative roles in relationship to financing, standards and regulations, and research concerning early education and day care. The choices of alternatives emerge from public debate and political considerations. The questions that should guide the selection of an alternative are these:

— How much federal government involvement?
— What kinds of involvement?
— What relationships between federal and state levels?
— What combinations of federal, state and local involvements?
— What benefits do any or all of the above have for children who are in early education or day care programs?

Finally, most parents do not use publicly supported child care facilities. They make informal arrangements. How can these parents benefit from the knowledge and information which has been generated concerning what are good child care facilities and what are good child care programs? The fact that many parents asked for referral centers and help in selecting child care facilities and programs suggests their concern about making good choices (*Statistical Highlights*, 1976). It may be necessary, however, to challenge the current emphasis on child care for the convenience or needs of parents more than on the needs or benefits to children.

FOOTNOTES

1. This right has been upheld in *Stiner vs. Califano*, 438 F. Supp. 796 (1977).

REFERENCES

Appropriateness of the Federal Interagency Day Care Requirements (FIDCR): Report of findings and recommendations. [U.S. Department of Health, Education, and Welfare, Office of the Assistant Secretary of Planning & Evaluation No. 260-923/5035(78)]. Washington, D.C.: U.S. Government Printing Office, 1978.
Assessment of barriers to compliance with the Federal interagency day care requirements in Region V. Arlington, Va.: UNCO, 1976.
Bruce, P. *Early childhood education: Early childhood day care in the United States.* Washington, D.C.: U.S. Department of Health, Education, and Welfare, Administration for Children, Youth, and Families, 1978.
Childcare and preschool: Options for Federal support (Background Paper). Washington, D.C.: Congress of the United States, Congressional Budget Office, 1978.
Formulating national policies on child and family development (HEW-105-77-1053). Con-

tract in progress with U.S. Department of Health, Education, and Welfare, Administration for Children, Youth, and Families, 1977.

Hertz, W. *Toward interagency coordination: FY '77 Federal research and development on early childhood.* Washington, D.C.: George Washington University Social Research Group, 1978.

Mann, A. J., Harrell, A. V., & Hurt, M., Jr. *A review of Head Start research since 1969.* Washington, D.C.: George Washington University Social Research Group, December 1976. (ERIC Document Reproduction Service No. ED 132 805).

National Day Care Study: First annual report, 1974–1975, Volume 1: An Overview of the Study (U.S. Department of Health, Education, and Welfare Publication No. OHDS 77-31094). Cambridge, Ma.: Abt Associates, 1977.

Statistical highlights from the National Child Care Consumer study (DHEW Publication No. OHDS 76-31096). Washington, D.C.: U.S. Department of Health, Education, and Welfare, 1976.

Travers, J., Coelen, C., Ruopp, R., Bache, W., Connell, D., Glantz, N., Goodrich, N., Goodrich, R., Goodson, B., Hewitt, K., & Layzer, J. *National Day Care Study: Second annual report 1975–1976. Phase II results and phase III design.* Cambridge, Ma.: Abt Associates, 1977.

Travers, J., Ruopp, R., Coelen, C., Connell, D., Glantz, N., Goodrich, H., Goodrich, R., Goodson, B., Layzer, J., Smith, A., & Spence, C. *National day care study: Preliminary findings and their implications* (S. Weiser, Ed.). Cambridge, Ma.: Abt Associates, 1978.

Woolsey, Suzanne H. Pied Piper politics and the child care debate. *Daedalus,* 1977, *106,* 127–146.

WHAT IS GOVERNMENT'S ROLE
IN QUALITY DAY CARE?

Richard E. Orton

Barbara Langham

INTRODUCTION

Even the harshest critics of government agree that children's health and safety should be safeguarded by some public regulating body. On the other end of the political spectrum are those who advocate a much heavier role, i.e., regulation of every ingredient of a day care operation in the interest of quality. The current dilemma can be simply stated: What is the proper governmental role in the maintenance of quality care?

This chapter will review this question from the standpoint of what government now does, what some of the problems are, and what government might do to solve some of these problems. This review assumes that government's role is open to examination at any time, and that as society changes so may a government's role. It further assumes that parents have total responsibility for quality care when children are cared for in the

Advances in Early Education and Day Care, Volume 1, pages 47–62
Copyright © 1980 by JAI Press Inc.
All rights of reproduction in any form reserved.
ISBN: 0-89232-127-X

home and that parents are the best judges of what that care should be at home. But when they place a child in a day care center, a preschool, a Head Start program, a family day home, or a before- and after-school program, parents are assigning responsibility for care to someone else. When this happens, they expect government, acting for them, to assume some of that responsibility.

What constitutes quality is an issue in itself. Quality can be viewed as a continuum of care, ranging from minimum safeguards for health and safety at the lowest level to the provision of numerous services, such as health, nutrition, social services, and education, at the highest. Some would argue that "minimum" or "lowest" has no place in a definition of quality, because quality means superiority or excellence. In this discussion, however, "quality" will be defined as a gradation from minimum to the most sophisticated.

All three levels of government (federal, state and local) intervene varyingly along this continuum. The following highlights some of the more significant activities at those levels.

WHAT GOVERNMENTS DO

The Federal Government

The federal government currently performs three principal roles: program funding, staff training, and leadership to the states.

Program Funding.   Although the federal government provided short-lived day care in 1933 for parents employed by the Works Project Administration and in 1942 for mothers employed in war industries, the first sustained federal effort came in the 1960s. The Economic Opportunity Act of 1964 permitted the creation of Head Start and the 1967 amendments to the Social Security Act made federal matching funds for day care available to the states. Child care, in the sense of enhancing child development, has never been an end in itself, but rather a support for something else. Even Head Start, government's most comprehensive child development program, was designed to break the so-called poverty cycle.

Though a relative newcomer, the federal government now has a substantial annual investment in day care. In 1977 the federal government spent approximately $2.5 billion (HEW, 1978, p. xix) for day care. The bulk of these funds support Head Start and day care programs paid for through Title XX of the Social Security Act.

Other federal programs include the Department of Health, Education and Welfare's (HEW) Title IV-A (Work Incentive Program) and Title IV-B (Vocational Rehabilitation), and Education for Handicapped Children programs; the Department of Labor's manpower training programs; the Department of Housing and Urban Development's community development services program; the Community Services Administration's day care for migrants program; and the Interior Department's Indian child welfare programs. One source listed 20 separate funding authorities for fiscal 1975 (Educational Policy Research Center, 1975). In addition, the federal government subsidizes day care for families in the form of tax credits of over $500 million a year and provides loans to profit-making child care centers under the Small Business Act.

With funding goes accountability. The federal government, when it exercises its public responsibility for the expenditure of public funds for day care, generally does so through purchase standards—that is, requiring the day care provider to meet certain standards of service as a condition for funding. The legal basis for this comes from 1967 amendments to the Economic Opportunity Act, directing the Secretary of HEW (and the Director of the Office of Economic Opportunity)[1] "to coordinate programs under their jurisdiction which provide day care" and to establish "a common set of program standards and regulations, and mechanisms for coordination at the state and local levels" (Economic Opportunity, 1967). The Federal Interagency Day Care Requirements (FIDCR), published in 1968, cover nine components—type of facility, environment, educational services, social services, health and nutrition, staff training, parent involvement, administration and coordination, and evaluation. The FIDCR are supposed to apply to nearly all federally assisted day care programs. In reality they are applied primarily to Title XX funded programs. This problem will be discussed later.

Staff Training. Because the interactions of child care staff with children directly impact quality of care, the federal government has taken a significant role in staff training. Under the Social Security Act, institutions of higher learning receive grants to train personnel for child care and child welfare. The training provisions of Title XX provide hundreds of thousands of dollars of training for child care providers. Under the Comprehensive Employment and Training Act, states and local governments may use grants to train people in the field of child care services.

A new kind of training aimed at demonstrated competency in working with children began in the early 1970s under the auspices of the Office of Child Development (OCD), now the Administration for Children, Youth, and Families (ACYF). OCD funded a national consortium to develop a system for measuring competency and awarding a credential, the Child Development Associate (CDA). It also funded 13 pilot projects across the country to develop training programs, with at least 50 percent of training time to be spent in the field actually working with children. By August

1979 the national Child Development Associate Consortium, Inc., had awarded the CDA credential to almost 5,000 child care personnel in the United States. Head Start teaching staff, who continue to receive subsidized training in the form of college child development courses, will eventually be required to earn the CDA or its equivalent. As of this writing, nine states have incorporated CDA as an alternative requirement for day care staff in their state licensing standards.

Leadership to the States.   Before 1968 and the publishing of the FIDCR, there were no federal standards for day care. However, the Children's Bureau did encourage state and local licensing of day care facilities. Contradictory provisions in state and local licensing codes as well as the inadequacies of codes in some states led HEW in 1970 to develop a model day care licensing code for use by the states. Requirements in the resulting "Guides for Day Care Licensing" related to physical facilities and staffing. OCD also has given small grants to states to assist them in revising their licensing standards.

Federal leadership is also evident in research and demonstration projects. The Office of Education makes grants to private and public agencies for research in early childhood education. OEO, and later HEW, has poured millions of dollars into research projects that affect quality child care. A recent project is the multi-million-dollar National Day Care Study. Its main purpose is to determine the costs and effects associated with different levels of staff-to-child ratio, group size, and staff qualifications. The findings of such research have important implications for programs and licensing codes in the states and localities.

In addition, the federal government grants substantial funds for pilot programs for special groups of young children, e.g., handicapped, bilingual, and migrants. For further discussion of the role(s) of federal government, refer to chapter by Grotberg in this volume.

The State Government
States have three principal functions in attaining and maintaining quality care: licensing, staff development and leadership.

Licensing.   Where the federal government's authority for regulating quality in day care has a fiscal basis, state governments derive theirs from their constitutional responsibility for the general welfare of their citizens. "Welfare," as used here, refers to well-being in the broad sense and is not limited to public assistance to the needy. Day care is a service, and states regulate this service just as they do lawyers, doctors, and nursing homes. Every state has chosen to help insure the welfare of children in day care by granting licenses to facilities which comply with state standards (Committee on Finance, U. S. Senate, 1977, p. 150). Unlike federal standards, which are a prerequisite for funding, state standards are a prerequisite for operation. Without a license, a center cannot legally be in business. As for family day homes, all but three states by mid-1975 required that family day homes be licensed, certified or approved (Costin *et al.*, 1977). As a rule, requirements for family day homes are not as stringent nor as comprehensive as those for day care centers.

State standards affect more children in day care than do federal standards, simply because there are more children in nonfederally supported facilities. Many states have undergone licensing reform since 1960, encouraged to some degree by federal efforts. There is a trend toward higher standards, but there continues to be substantial variation in standards from state to state. State standards cover such elements as staff-to-child ratios, physical facilities, child health and safety, and administration. Some also regulate staff qualifications, group size, and the educational component of day care programs.

The licensing standards of most states fall short of the level of quality of the FIDCR. This minimum level of care in some states reflects the basic difference in the purpose of each form of regulation. In a standard for purchase of care, which does not infringe on the facility's right to operate, the balance is in favor of better care for the child. In a standard which regulates an industry, there must be a balance between the facility's right to operate and the child's right to appropriate care.

The responsibility for day care licensing in most states is assigned to the state welfare or social services department. This department relies on licensing staff from either the state or county offices to inspect facilities for compliance and verify whether a center may be granted a license or license renewal.

States also enforce federal standards for federally assisted day care centers. States administer federal day care funds and contract for day care services, and therefore must account for the funds they spend. States have assumed this enforcement role without additional federal funding for monitoring federally assisted programs, except occasionally through the use of Title XX funds.

Leadership in Communities. Many states offer technical assistance to day care providers, usually in conjunction with the licensing role. This technical assistance can have a substantial impact on quality of existing facilities because it can cover staff training, physical facilities, program content, additional services, as well as administration and management. State government agencies can also help communities assess needs of children and plan child care programs, thus affecting the form child care takes—individual centers, day homes, or systems—as well as the funding sources and standards that are used.

Staff Development and Recognition.   The state plays a major role in training day care staff through its colleges and universities. Almost every major university and a substantial number of community and junior colleges offer early childhood degree programs. The number of institutions of higher education offering these programs has greatly expanded since the inauguration of Head Start in 1965 and continues to grow as public and private expenditures for child care increase.

Unlike the regulation of doctors, plumbers, surveyors, accountants, and public school teachers, states do not usually have strict certification procedures for day care staff. As of 1974, twenty-seven states required center supervisors to have formal training or experience in child development; thirty-two states had similar requirements for child care staff (Morgan, 1977). There are two reasons for this. Certification procedures can have two outcomes: higher quality staff and more expensive staff. As yet there is no substantial consumer demand for the former because of the latter consequence. The other reason may be a shortcoming of the child care profession itself: the lack of a career system for early childhood personnel. There is no defined career ladder whereby child care personnel can advance; and few ways to recognize competence, experience, or training. There is a substantial need for more work in this area.[2]

The Local Government

Of the three government levels, local government could potentially have the greatest impact on quality day care because it is the level closest to children and families. In fact, when one considers child care in its broadest sense to include family child rearing, foster care, and institutional care, one quickly realizes that local governments already have tremendous impact on quality care. Cities and counties provide basic services to families, such as water, sanitation, fire and police protection, health services, parks and playgrounds, libraries, as well as special services such as emergency shelters and sometimes day care. Broadly speaking, every city ordinance and every governmental policy, whether it concerns industrial development or transportation, impacts children and families.

In the specific area of day care, local government generally has two principal roles: regulation and, to a lesser extent, funding.

Regulation.   Cities and counties bear the bulk of responsibility for inspecting day care facilities to help assure a safe physical environment.

The local fire marshal's office conducts a safety inspection and the local health department conducts a health and sanitation inspection, usually covering plumbing, food handling, water supply, and sewage system. Local regulations usually increase in stringency as the population increases in density. Larger cities may impose zoning requirements; require building, electrical, and plumbing permits; and demand a local business license, or even a local day care license, beyond the state license. If a facility has pet animals or a swimming pool, it may be subject to still other local ordinances. As a result, many of the key decisions affecting whether a day care facility is granted a license are made by local agencies.

Funding. Some cities and counties provide funding for day care, contributing to the 25 percent local match required by Title XX funding regulations. In 1975 local taxes accounted for nearly a third of the revenue to the children's centers in California (Grubb & Lazerson, 1977). Local governments usually contract with community organizations to operate these federally assisted centers but may operate programs themselves. Day care is usually a low priority for local governments, however, for two reasons: One, local governments historically have relied on the state and private organizations to support services for children and families; and secondly, there are relatively few resources for local governments to work with. Those resources generally go for streets, sewers, parks and recreation, libraries, and the like.

SOME QUESTIONS AND PROBLEMS

At the Federal Level

First, there is a basic question as to whether the federal government should even fund day care. Is funding out-of-home care more cost-effective than paying a mother to stay home with a child? The earnings of a mother with more than one child are frequently at minimum wage scale which turn out to be less than the cost of day care for her children.[3] This is particularly true in federally subsidized centers.

And what about day care subsidized by federal income tax credits? Child care purchased with federal funds must meet standards, but there are no stipulations for the quality of care families use as credits on their income tax. Is this an acceptable inconsistency?

Then there are some major problems with current application of federal quality controls:

— selective application and, in some cases, failure to apply the FIDCR altogether

— the appropriateness of the standards themselves
— high costs for compliance, particularly because of the staff-to-child ratio
— reliance on states for enforcement.

The wording of the law which forms the legal basis for the FIDCR implies that they were to apply to all federally assisted day care programs. In actuality, they are applied almost exclusively to Title XX programs. Local communities which purchase day care with funds authorized by the Community Development Act or by the Comprehensive Employment and Training Act (CETA), have been told they do not have to comply with FIDCR. Other federally assisted day care programs remain exempt from FIDCR. Why is there such limited application? The FIDCR appropriateness report (HEW, 1978) indicates FIDCR may not be sufficient to meet the needs of certain children and that new legislation may be required for FIDCR to apply to all federally assisted day care.

A larger question in the application of FIDCR is this: Can one set of standards be devised which should be applied to all programs across the country? One set of standards assumes that children in federally subsidized care in all 50 states have the same needs. This, of course, is not so. Children's needs vary enormously, and different parents want different things for their children. In view of a diversity of children's needs, is one set of federal standards consistent with a pluralistic society?

Just as day care needs of children and families are varied, so are the objectives of federal programs. For example, Head Start objectives are primarily compensatory. Day care for Department of Labor manpower programs supports these programs. Perhaps several sets of standards should be developed to coincide with specific program objectives. There should be common elements in the various sets of standards, for example minimum health and safety requirements, which can be regulated uniformly.

It has been said that FIDCR are standards for compensatory care (Morgan, 1977). Yet day care is primarily a family supportive service for healthy children who do not need compensatory standards. If the federal standards are compensatory, that would imply that *all* children in centers complying with FIDCR need compensatory care. Even in the case of Title XX children, this is not necessarily the case. Because Title XX authorizes a state to provide care for children whose families make up to 115 percent of the state's median family income, families eligible under Title XX could be considerably better off financially than poverty families eligible under Head Start. The higher income Title XX families could presumably meet more of their children's needs, such as medical and dental care, for example, than poverty families. At issue here, then, is this: Should the federal government require, and therefore pay for, comprehensive services for children of all Title XX families or just those at the lower end of the income scale?

The comprehensive support services and the high staff-to-child ratio have been a chief source of complaints against FIDCR. Extensive services and larger staffs cause federally assisted programs to be more expensive than nonfederally assisted programs. The result has been a type of class system in day care. Centers which meet FIDCR cater almost exclusively to lower-income families. They often cannot serve nonsubsidized children because their families cannot afford the cost of care. The number of services in centers which meet FIDCR is usually higher than in centers which do not; consequently lower income children are receiving higher quality care than children of middle-class families. Should they? And some eligible children in centers not meeting FIDCR are not receiving the higher quality of care they would if they were in centers meeting FIDCR. Is this fair to those eligible children?

Enforcement also poses some puzzling questions. As mentioned earlier, the states, as administrators of Title XX funds, actually enforce the FIDCR, making sure that FIDCR standards are met before issuing a contract for day care services. This has contributed to continuing confusion and resentment among day care providers—distinguishing between FIDCR and state licensing requirements and having to deal with two regulators from the same agency. Why should the states enforce FIDCR? There is not much support for federal day care inspectors, so perhaps there should be additional federal funding to states to monitor FIDCR. State standards affect vastly greater numbers of children than FIDCR. Would federal money be better spend helping states strengthen their own licensing requirements rather than imposing purchase standards for federally assisted care? Likewise, would federal money be better spent training state licensing personnel and day care staff?

How serious is the federal government about the worth of the FIDCR? When states do not enforce FIDCR, Title XX funds can be withheld or day care payments can be denied. In fact, this has never happened. The reasons for this lack of enforcement lie in the harsh penalty for noncompliance and the confusion about what actually constitutes a violation. Already HEW is looking into a system of graduated sanctions, with built-in training, consultation, and assistance. The goal of sanctions should not be to deliver punishment but to give states and providers ample opportunity to learn what constitutes quality care and how to deliver it in the most effective fashion.

At the State Level

Problems at the state level include improving licensing standards, regulation of family day homes, and strengthening qualifications for day care personnel.

In many states the licensing standards represent a minimum level of quality in the sense of protecting the child from harm. From another viewpoint, minimal could be defined in terms of basic elements required for positive growth and development. According to the latter approach, standards might include provisions for physical, cognitive, and social development. Developmental standards would raise costs. Can parents pay for higher quality? Will the people accept that level of intrusion into what essentially are privately supported businesses?

In addition, there are some basic needs that all children share: the need for safety, for caring and affection, for opportunities to succeed, and for a healthy self-image. But some children such as infants and the handicapped have special needs. Are state standards sufficient to cover special needs?

One answer might be that state standards replace federal standards in federally assisted day care centers. This alternative would seem to alleviate some of the administrative and enforcement problems with FIDCR. But, if standards remained at varying levels of quality among the states, the quality of care purchased with federal funds in one state would not be the same level of quality as in another state. Would this be fair to the children served? Licensing standards are lower in some states because child care and human services are not a high priority with officials in these states. Would replacement of federal standards with state standards result in an overall lowering of quality child care? With regard to the standards themselves, many states need to review the specifics of such elements as staff training, parent involvement, protection of cultural diversity, record keeping, and evaluation. Critical to the state's ability to upgrade these specifics is consensus among parents and providers that changes are both worthwhile and practical. Cost is probably the major factor inhibiting states from upgrading standards—costs to the licensing agency in monitoring more stringent standards and to providers in bringing their facilities into compliance. If states raise standards, should costs be offset by diverting some federal funds to pay for more licensing staff or by granting tax credits, loans to profit-making centers, or direct subsidy of staff training to bring centers into compliance with higher standards?

Effective enforcement of state licensing standards requires that the state train personnel to inspect day care facilities uniformly across the state and streamline licensing procedures to prevent delays in either granting or revoking licenses. One study (Consulting Services Corporation, 1971) reported that approximately 15 to 20 major work tasks are required of an applicant in the licensing process and another 35–50 of government officials. If second and third inspections are required, the total number of tasks is even higher. What should comprise an adequate licensing inspection? Do reports used by inspectors give an accurate assessment of the level of quality and compliance with standards? Effective enforcement also requires sufficient legal recourse stated in law so that substandard facilities can be closed. State licensing agencies should have the authority to bring suit against a substandard facility that continues to operate even after its license has been revoked.

What about the regulation of family day homes? In the whole context of government's role in quality child care, it must be said that family day care is an important, often preferred, source of care for families. Because family day homes provide care for a small number of children in a home environment, they lend themselves especially to care for infants and toddlers, and to families who need child care at odd hours, such as nights and weekends. As the states delve further into regulation of family day homes, licensing authorities are discovering that the various methods of regulation (i.e., licensing, certification and registration) produce varying results. Registration, for example, which relies on a statement by the provider and on monitoring by parents that standards have been met, is bringing more family day homes under regulation than licensing.[4] One of the major issues here is the legality of inspecting a private home. It may be that the states' major role in assuring quality in family day care is the training offered to family day home providers.

Because competent staff is a major factor in quality care, should states increase efforts to upgrade the qualifications of day care personnel? If so, what qualifications should day care personnel have? Should the emphasis be on education in the traditional sense, or is it more important that child care personnel be warm, affectionate, and nurturing? How does a paraprofessional credential like the CDA fit in with college degrees in child development and early childhood education? Basic to this issue is the lack of a career ladder for personnel, with room for aides, paraprofessional teachers, master teachers, center directors and so on. For every position, there probably should be requirements for experience and both formal academic training and informal workshop or inservice training, as well as provisions for recognizing competence and achievement. However, if qualifications for personnel are upgraded, how will states determine and verify those qualifications? Will states choose to certify certain day care personnel, similar to the way they certify public school teachers, or public accountants? Or should the early-childhood profession take upon itself the task of certifying the competence of its members, using methods similar to those used by professional groups, such as realtors?

Finally, there is the question of costs. Raising qualifications of staff will undoubtedly raise costs of child care. Are providers prepared to pay higher wages, and are parents as well as governments willing to pay higher fees? Raising the qualifications for personnel might also have the effect of professionalizing child rearing. Would parents look increasingly to such

child care experts and doubt their own competence and values? Or could
higher qualified child care staffs strengthen the parental role by supporting
cultural and religious differences and helping parents regain confidence in
their childrearing abilities?

At the Local Level

A major problem at the local level of government is the concern about
coordination among funding sources as well as the various regulating
bodies. Local governments are not likely to increase their funding toward
quality child care, because they are already strapped for resources in all
areas. Although it is too early to discern the real effects of the tax
"revolt" started by the passage of Proposition 13 in California in 1978, it
is probable that cities, counties, and other forms of local government will
look increasingly to the state and federal government for revenues for
social services, including child care.

With the funding forecast so gloomy, local governments would do well
to make the most of the day care resources they have now. There are
numerous publicly funded agencies already involved in day care, including community action agencies, schools, housing authorities, and manpower programs. Coordination of their resources could have major implications for quality. Public schools, for example, could offer staff training,
equipment, supplies, and unused buildings. Title XX centers work hard to
find comprehensive services from local health and welfare agencies and still
families must go from one part of town to another for medical services,
food stamps, and housing assistance. Head Start programs are required
by 1972 amendments to the Economic Opportunity Act to serve handicapped preschool children from low-income families, but the Education
for All Handicapped Children Act requires that by 1980 schools provide
educational services to all handicapped children as young as age 3. The
local community is where all three levels of government come together,
because that is where services are delivered. How can the various levels
be encouraged to interrelate more effectively?

With regard to licensing, the lack of coordination between state and
local agencies is particularly frustrating. Zoning, fire, safety, health, and
building code requirements are usually not coordinated with state licensing regulations. Inspectors outside the licensing agency frequently do not
have guidelines for applying the regulations to day care facilities. Sometimes applicants do not know what is required of them by the licensing
standards and various local ordinances. Some local requirements conflict
with state requirements. For example, the state requirement for outdoor
play area may be 100 square feet per child, but the city requirement may
be 150. In some areas, such as zoning, local requirements do not cover
day care facilities, so the code for the next most similar type of facility

(i.e., a hospital or restaurant) is used. Such lack of coordination makes for delays in the licensing process, sometimes discouraging an applicant from seeking licensing altogether, as well as inconsistent application of standards.

WHAT GOVERNMENT MIGHT DO

This review now turns to what government might do to begin to answer some of these many questions and problems. Any discussion of government's potential activities implies a goal, a future direction. Where is America going in quality child care? Regrettably, the answer is that no one knows. America has no national policy on child care. Without it, agencies and administrators are indecisive; directives and guidelines are inconsistent; states and localities have no model to follow. Before much progress can be made in assessing the quality of child care and assigning responsibility for it, a national policy should be formulated within the context of a comprehensive policy on children and families. Among those making the call for a national policy on children and families has been the National Research Council's Committee on Child Development (1976).

The Committee's specific recommendations on child care were:

> For those families who, out of necessity or preference, elect some form of substitute care for their children, a range of alternatives should be available. . . . The programs should be available free or at costs that do not require the sacrifice of other essential goods and services.
>
> Mechanisms should be established to ensure that alternative care arrangements meet minimum federal and state standards based on reseach findings of the effects of daytime care and on experience in the administration of programs. These standards include continuity of care, a high ratio of adults to children, cleanliness and nutritional adequacy, health services, safety and a stimulating environment (pp. 4–5).

Certainly care should be available in alternative forms and standards should be based on research findings. What other elements would a national policy contain? One of the most important would be a confirmation of the parents' role in childrearing. As such, quality day care would not undermine or replace parental care but rather support and strengthen it. The real issue then becomes: At what point should government supplement the parental role of assuring quality care for their children, and should government play that role equally for all parents or differentially for some parents? The needs of all children and parents are not the same. Some older children need supervision for two hours after school; some preschool children need the company of playmates a few hours a week; some infants need the care of a warm, nurturing figure on weekdays; some children need an adult at night while parents work the night shift; some children need medical and nutritional services their parents can't afford; and some children need special educational or remedial services because of a handicap or developmental delay. The end result should be that parents have equal opportunities to rear their children the way they want to rear them and that child care facilities will be a source of positive support.

Essential to the formulation of a national policy on child care is concensus of what quality child care is. The federal government should take the lead in bringing about a definition of quality child care because it has the resources to marshal the collection of research findings, to undertake a consensus-building process among parents, professionals, and providers, and to convey that definition to the states and localities. The search for consensus will provoke many questions. How is quality to be measured—purchase standards, licensing standards, perhaps a rating system with standards that increase in quality by degrees? Whose standards will they be: federal, state, local, or some combination? How will standards relate to the goals and objectives of day care programs? To whom and for whom should the standards apply? Who will enforce the standards? How will parents have sufficient opportunity to be informed about quality care and decide what type of care they wish for their children? And most importantly and most difficult: what is the proper balance between what is best for children and what government (the taxpayer) can *afford*.

The American Federation of Teachers, among other organizations, believes that many problems associated with child care could be eliminated by assigning day care to the public schools. Child care for school-age children before and after regular school hours would be particularly convenient for working parents. Here again, though, there are questions. How would such care be supported? What provisions would be made for the children's care: recreation activities, study hall, crafts, snacks? What would be the staff-to-child ratio, and what qualifications would be needed of staff?

Having the public schools provide child care for three- and four-year-olds poses even more serious considerations of quality. Will the environment be the traditional public school classroom with a teacher lecturing, or a room of learning centers with children interacting individually with the teacher and each other? Will the program focus entirely on educational objectives or will there be other objectives, such as social development, health and nutrition, and physical development? Will the teachers be retrained 10th-grade English teachers or specially trained early childhood teachers? Will parents' roles be limited to membership in the Parent-Teacher Association, or will parents sit on a policy council making recommendations on programming and staff hiring? And if public education is extended downward, what will become of Head Start and other day care programs whose objectives are not necessarily educational but compensatory or remedial?

This much is clear. If the federal government provides funding for day care, it should have the means for exercising some control over that care. States have the authority to provide for the well-being of their citizens—in this case, children—and should continue to upgrade licensing standards and procedures. Because all three levels come together at the local level, coordinative mechanisms should be established to ensure consistency and quality in all out-of-home care for children.

Government's role boils down to this: It provides a forum for discussion and resolution of issues. The foregoing clearly points out that the issues are not easy ones. For every possible solution, there are legitimate questions as well as emotional advocates who will raise those questions. In the passage of laws, in the review of regulations, and in the development of policy, government identifies the wishes of the people and lends direction to their preferences. Governments at all levels should join in a partnership, with agreed upon roles for each.

The federal government should take the lead in developing that partnership through a series of forums designed to deal with the issues identified by the affected parties. Child care advocates should also participate. Out of such a national debate should come a basis for accomplishing the first objective—development of a national policy on child care. The forum mechanism can then be used to deal with the other issues in a priority order decided by the participants.

FOOTNOTES

1. OEO Director was dropped from the mandate in 1974.

2. At least one state is attempting to do something about it. In 1975 the Texas Department of Community Affairs provided leadership in the formation of a statewide Committee on Early Childhood Development Careers. The committee was a spin-off of a state-funded pilot CDA training program and the subsequent establishment of CDA training programs in community colleges across the state. The Committee, composed of high school and college educators, day care providers, state agency representatives and leaders of organizations concerned with children, began to develop a career system for early childhood personnel in the areas of 1) preparation and training, 2) career advancement, and 3) career recognition.

An opportunity to apply the Committee's work came in the summer of 1978. The city of Sherman sought assistance from the state in reorganizing the personnel system for the city-operated day care center. With technical assistance and a small grant, the city identified job tasks, assigned tasks to positions, and prepared individualized training for each employee. As a result, city officials believe their new personnel system may serve as a model for other cities, organizations or centers. The success of such a personnel system and the development of a larger career system by the early childhood profession may provide guidance to states, should state legislatures decide that child care workers be examined for their fitness to care for children.

3. Federally subsidized child care which must meet the FIDCR varies in cost in different geographical areas. In Texas, a relatively low-cost state, the annual cost per child is about $1,817.

4. In Texas, for example, only 2,000 family day homes were licensed prior to the passage of a mandatory family home registration law, effective in January 1976. By August 1979, almost 9,900 homes were registered.

REFERENCES

The appropriateness of the Federal Interagency Day Care Requirements [U.S. Department of Health, Education, and Welfare Publication No. 260-923/5035(78)]. Washington, D.C.: U.S. Government Printing Office, 1978.

Child care data and materials. Washington, D.C.: U.S. Senate Committee on Finance, 1977.

Costin, L., Keyserling, M. D., Pierce, W., & Wadlington, W. The challenge of child day care needs and improved federal and state approaches to day care standard setting and enforcement. In *Policy issues in day care: Summaries of 21 papers* (Prepared for the U.S. Department of Health, Education, and Welfare Contract No. 100-77-0017). Washington, D.C.: Center for Systems and Program Development, 1977.

Economic Opportunity Amendments of 1967. P.L. 90-22, sec. 522(d); 42 USC 2032 (d).

Educational Policy Research Center. *Federal Policy for preschool services: Assumptions and evidence.* Menlo Park, Ca.: Stanford Research Institute, 1975.

Grubb, N., & Lazerson, M. Lessons from the California children's centers. *School Review*, 1977, *86*, 1–37.

Morgan, G. Federal day care standards and the law. In *Policy issues in day care: Summaries of 21 papers* (Prepared for the U.S. Department of Health, Education, and Welfare Contract No. 100-77-0017). Washington, D.C.: Center for Systems and Program Development, 1977.

Morgan, G. Federal day care standards in context. In *Policy issues in day care: Summaries of 21 papers* (Prepared for the U.S. Department of Health, Education, and Welfare Contract No. 100-77-0017). Washington, D.C.: Center for Systems and Program Development, 1977.

The National Research Council. *Toward a national policy for children and families.* Washington, D.C.: National Academy of Sciences, 1976.

State and local day care licensing requirements. (Prepared for the U.S. Department of Health, Education, and Welfare Office of Child Development). Washington, D.C.: Consulting Services Corporation, 1971.

FEDERAL–STATE RELATIONS AND CHILDREN'S DAYTIME CARE AND DEVELOPMENT[1]

Lela B. Costin

INTRODUCTION

The increasing incidence of children's daytime care away from their parents has brought augmented efforts to regulate it, chiefly through the application of licensing requirements. This assumption of responsibility by states for the conditions of children's part-time out-of-home care has been relatively recent. In contrast, efforts to inspect, study, and supervise the private organizations and institutions giving full-time foster care to dependent children began in the latter part of the nineteenth century. This difference reflects the greater weight given to continuing parental responsibility in day care compared with foster care and a general reluctance to intervene in arrangements parents make privately for their children's part-time care. Gradually, however, it became apparent that there were also risks involved in the growing use of day care services and that

Advances in Early Education and Day Care, Volume 1, pages 63–76
ISBN: 0-89232-127-X

parents, as private persons, did not have the means, even though they had the competency, to evaluate those services and to enforce adequate standards of operation. States began to acknowledge their responsibility to children whose daytime care was away from their parents. Federal interest in the states' attempts to protect children through the licensing process was slow in coming, however. Today, the federal role in guiding and supporting state agencies' efforts to meet the responsibility for day care regulation is often ambiguous and ineffective.

This paper is concerned with the unclear and often dysfunctional working relations between federal and state governments in their efforts to regulate day care facilities. It identifies the largely unattended but correctable basic problems within the licensing process as currently practiced within the states. It outlines a proposal by which federal and state agencies could address these problems systematically and consistently on a continuing basis and thus achieve common goals for children and families. First, a review of the background to federal-state relations in day care regulation is useful.

FEDERAL INTEREST IN CHILD CARE REGULATION

Even before the 1960s the Children's Bureau of the Department of Health, Education, and Welfare (HEW) had become concerned about the numbers of children being cared for in unregulated and often substandard day care facilities. By 1965 out-of-home day care for children of working mothers was increasing significantly, leading to support for greater governmental activity to make day care more available at a minimum standard of quality at least.

It had become apparent that a surprising array of federal agencies had some involvement with the provision of day care through such legislation as the Elementary and Secondary Education Act of 1965, the Vocational Education Act of 1963, the Education Professions Development Act, the Manpower Training and Development Act, and the Economic Opportunity Act and its Head Start program. In addition, the Women's Bureau of the Department of Labor, under the direction of Mary Dublin Keyserling, was urgently concerned about standards for children's out-of-home daytime care. The Department of Housing and Urban Development had included day care in its Model Cities program; the Department of Agriculture was involved through its surplus food program; and even the Department of Defense had a concern with day care centers on military bases although these facilities continue to be privately funded and subject to neither federal nor state standards (HEW, 1968; Cooper, 1976).

The need for coordination could not be ignored. The result was the appointment of a Federal Panel on Early Childhood with representatives from a variety of departments and agencies, and the development in 1968 of a set of standards—the Federal Interagency Day Care Requirements (FIDCR) applicable to all day care programs receiving federal funds. Five aspects of quality day care were given specific attention: child-staff ratios, parent participation, mental health services, physical health services, and delivery mechanisms and costs.

Following this major step in expression of federal concern for the quantity and quality of day care in the United States, attention turned to a number of other problems, including those connected with state licensing codes. Under the 1962 amendments to the Social Security Act, only day care facilities that met state licensing standards could receive federal aid. Although all states had some kind of child care licensing,

> . . . some states had codes so strict and elaborate that they raised provider costs prohibitively; others had codes so lax that child care specialists considered them wholly inadequate to guarantee even a bare minimum of protection for children. Also, many of the codes constituted jungles of confusing, even contradictory, requirements and red tape that had a tendency to discourage would-be care available nationwide. Finally, if the government was going to increase its support of day care, some measure of the cost implication of state licensing codes was needed (Cooper, 1976, p. 31).

Officials in HEW's Children's Bureau and Office of Child Development (OCD) were concerned about the effect of expanding day care with federal funds while state licensing standards were so varying and poorly enforced. They started work on analyzing existing state laws and preparing model licensing codes that states could be encouraged to adopt (HEW, 1971; *Day Care Licensing Study*, 1971; *Guides for Day Care Licensing*, 1972). The project, carried out from 1970 to 1972, encompassed the points of view and expertise of state and local leaders, federal officials, attorneys, legislators, fire safety marshals, zoning experts and city planners, public health and child development experts, licensing program administrators, day care operators, and parents of children in day care. Representatives from all these groups were brought together to debate, to consult, and finally to agree on drafts of model directions for more effective state licensing practices in behalf of all children in day care. The intent was to "design an effective safety net and at the same time to remove all unnecessary barriers at the state level to swift expansion of day care services" (Cooper, 1976, p. 34).

The model licensing code project encountered serious obstacles before its completion, and results have been disappointing (Cooper, 1976, pp. 36–39). It did, however, act as a catalyst in focusing attention on the urgency of improving child care regulations at the state level and, in the view of some persons, it has been an important force in making inroads against the antiquated licensing statutes and practices in some states (Cohen & Zigler, 1977).

Concern with the provision and quality of day care began to focus on the need for revisions in the FIDCR, and in early 1970 the Federal Panel on Early Childhood was again convened for that purpose. A variety of issues entered into the revision process. For example, (1) imprecisions in language, intended to insure flexibility in application, made the standards difficult to enforce; (2) the standards were primarily concerned with center care of the preschool child to the neglect of attention to those in family day care, school-age children needing out-of-school-hours care, and infants; (3) drafters of the 1968 FIDCR had held that infants should not be in group day care, but working mothers continued to make such arrangements, and (4) there were differences of opinion about child-staff ratios and staff qualifications. Persons primarily concerned with quality day care wanted higher staff requirements. But if requirements for staff were too strict, costs would become excessive and limit the availability of care; (5) the debate over quality versus effective use of limited funds was persistent; (6) and still another issue entered into attempts to revise the 1968 FIDCR, that of defining an appropriate role for parents. Minority and advocacy groups wanted a stronger role in policy making, but by 1972 resistance to this had grown among persons who believed that many in those groups were less interested in child care programs than in using day care policy to gain political influence within their communities.

Progress proved to be difficult to achieve. Changes in personnel at the federal level, overlapping and duplicating assignments, and major disagreements on the issue of quality versus effective use of limited funds and on the best means of enforcement eventually polarized the participants in the revision of FIDCR. In the absence of broad-based support needed for action by Congress on a revised set of standards, the 1972 revisions of FIDCR were stalemated and sent into limbo within the Office of Management and Budget (Cohen and Zigler, 1977; Cooper, 1976).

The Passage of Title XX in 1974 reopened the matter of federal participation in day care standards and enforcement, giving the Secretary of HEW power to revise FIDCR after first submitting to Congress a study of their "appropriateness". Because the significant conflicts were still unresolved, the date for submission of the study was postponed. In the interim, day care facilities were required only to adhere to state licensing standards in order to receive Title XX funds.

Finally, in 1978 the long-awaited HEW report mandated by Congress in 1975 was issued (*Appropriateness*, 1978). It gave strong support to the basic objectives of the FIDCR and offered recommendations for a sound basis for their revision. The future working relations between the federal and state agencies were less clearly addressed with respect to the states' responsibility for licensing not only federally funded facilities but non-funded ones as well.

CURRENT STATUS OF STATE LICENSING CODES

A review of the various states' licensing standards provides convincing evidence that there is genuine concern for children in day care and for the quality of their daytime experiences and opportunity for development. It is upon this countrywide base of concern and readiness to regulate the conditions of children's out-of-home daytime care that any form of federal regulation should build. But considerable variation in licensing standards and practices among the states is also apparent, reflecting the fact that regulation of out-of-home care has been seen as properly a state's responsibility, and to be enforceable the standards must reflect differences from state to state in economic, social and legal conditions. Even within a state there are variations that make it difficult to hold all licensing applicants to one set of mandatory standards. It is hardly surprising that the federal government has found it formidable to apply a single set of standards (the FIDCR) given the diversity among states in licensing standards applicable to all private facilities regardless of source of funding, in community norms and general living conditions, and in organizational structures for child care regulation.

The general thesis of this paper is that the federal government can act effectively as a standard setter in day care only as it takes into account the status of day care regulation in a particular state at a given point in time. Furthermore, the differences in day care regulation between states are not so detrimental as are certain unattended but correctable problems within the licensing process as presently practiced in all states.

BASIC PROBLEMS IN LICENSING PRACTICE

Most licensing personnel are unprepared for their complex duties. Little or no systematic preparation is offered in higher education. With only a few exceptions, schools of social work do not include in their curricula, in any clearly recognizable form, attention to government's regulatory authority or to the process of licensing. Basic concepts relevant to government's role in other welfare services are taught, but even when these also have applicability to the regulation of out-of-home care (for children or aged) they are rarely identified as such. Even if schools of social work more generally gave attention to teaching about licensing as a preventive welfare service, it would not solve the problem entirely, since many licensing personnel come from other areas and backgrounds. Often they are drawn from the field of child development. Although this preparation is particularly useful in helping with the program aspects of the day care operation, such personnel are usually quite uninformed about the investigative, evaluative, and law enforcement aspects of licensing.

Inadequate provision of in-service training and other programs of staff development constitute a major weakness in present-day licensing practice. One large state with a history of strong professional attention to improving the regulation of children's out-of-home care carried out a program evaluation of the state department's activity in day care licensing and regulation. Among the findings was this:

> Licensers were asked what training they had received before being allowed to license facilities on their own. About 20 percent responded that they received none. For the rest, a typical "training procedure" reported was that they were simply given a copy of the standards and told to read it. Some 20 percent reported having been told about licensing procedures in conferences with supervisors. About one-third said they had made joint visits to day care facilities with experienced licensing personnel. Only four licensing workers reported they had some kind of extended training experience. . . . Almost all licensing personnel indicated that they would like to receive more training in one or more particular aspects of their jobs (Illinois Economic and Fiscal Commission, 1974, p. 22).

In most states special workshops for licensing personnel taught by outside experts in day care licensing tend to be planned sporadically or not at all. A licensing staff person may come and leave after considerable experience without having attended such a workshop.

A variety of training settings and structures can be used, but by some combination of mechanisms, basic concepts need to be taught. These include: (a) the basis of governmental regulatory authority, (b) discretionary justice, (c) "floor of protection," (d) prevention vs. protection, (e) the nature of constituted and inherent authority and constructive use of such authority, (f) police power vs. *parens patriae*, (g) licensing as a means of regulating private agencies—but why not public agencies? (h) standard—what it is and the rationale derived from principles of child care and development that underlies each licensing standard, (i) principles and techniques of observation and evaluation, (j) the limits of licensing, (k) the systematic steps in the licensing process, (l) the summary judgment, (m) reasonable compliance.

Systematic training procedures for new licensing personnel might well include the use of a written test on licensing standards and practice that had to be passed before a person was allowed to perform licensing functions (Illinois Economic and Fiscal Commission, 1974, p. 22).

Periodic regional and statewide meetings for day care licensing staff are needed to foster learning about special aspects of the job, such as the application of fire or health standards, or to have opportunity to discuss changes in licensing policy and to provide a means for maintaining a concensus in relation to criteria used in the application of mandatory standards.

A lack of status assigned to the licensing job affects the outcomes negatively. Generally, in state departments of public welfare (or other state organizations with responsibility for child-care regulation) licensing personnel report a lack of status assigned to their work. Many feel that they are held in low esteem by their administrators and by other direct service personnel. The most inexperienced personnel are often assigned to licensing—"anyone can do a licensing study"—or persons are assigned this function without regard for the fact that they aspire to be clinically oriented social workers who can exercise highly individual judgments. Such persons are unlikely to do well in applying licensing standards. A lack of recognition of the amount of specialized knowledge needed to evaluate a day care center, for example, and the evident higher status assigned to direct service in situations of "pathology" or "crisis" contribute to high turnover among licensing staff and loss of personnel who have the potentiality to become excellent regulatory staff. Volunteers and paraprofessionals are often assigned the same duties as are professional licensing staff rather than being assigned selected tasks to assist or supplement the professional staff. As a result, the gains to be realized from the use of volunteers and paraprofessionals are often lost and the self image of the professional licensing staff diminished. The lack of status often is compounded by confusion in the duties of licensing personnel at different levels of agency organization, and a lack of clarity about exact duties and responsibilities. This, in turn, contributes to a conviction on the part of many front-line licensing staff that "we can't deny a license or revoke one even when a situation is clearly below standards because the administration won't back us up."

The lack of a reliable frame of reference for the application of mandatory standards makes for unequal treatment of licensing applicants. Discrepancies and inconsistencies in judgment result from differences in interpretations of the meaning of a particular standard and from differences in applying a given standard even when it is uniformly interpreted. These discrepancies are found in the application of standards across a state, between different licensing personnel, and in the work of the same staff person over time.

Uniform application of standards implies that if two or several licensers inspect a facility at the same time, they would make the same decision as to whether to recommend issuance or denial of license and that there would be agreement as to which standards were in compliance and which were violated. "Tangible" standards relating to physical aspects of the child's growth and development (e.g., health and safety standards, or standards relating to space, etc.) are usually thought to be subject to a considerable degree of agreement. "Intangible" standards that have to do with a desirable psychosocial maturation are expected to present more difficulty in achieving uniformity. One major day care licensing program evaluation found through use of a "paired-observers study" that intangible standards relating to personal characteristics of the day care operators and to the quality of care were subject to fairly high disagreement among licensers. There was also considerable disagreement on such tangible standards as the number of children and staff (Illinois Economic and Fiscal Commission, 1974, pp. 34–39).

The need to administer standards uniformly calls for experimentation with some new procedures and techniques, for example, development of formulas for the licensing decision as might be done by establishing a hierarchy of standards. Violation of any one standard in the highest group—say, fire and safety hazard, child-staff ratio, corporal punishment, serious overenrollment—would indicate a need to deny or revoke license. Violation of two or three standards in the second group—for instance, those relating to outdoor play periods, specific kinds of play equipment or kitchen equipment—would be overlooked before license was denied or revoked. A third group dealing mainly with such matters as record keeping would allow for slightly more violations (Illinois Economic and Fiscal Commission, 1974, pp. 34–39). Obviously great care would be required to arrive at formulas that ensured children protection. In addition, such formulas would have to be developed in consultation with the licensers themselves if they were to be accepted and used uniformly.

In the marginal situations that are so troubling to licensing personnel, a second licenser might be used to inspect and to consult with the first in reaching a decision to recommend issuance or denial of license. In all cases of recommended denial, the day care mother or center operator could be given the right to ask for a visit by a different licenser. Development of better licensing appraisal forms are needed, ones that could be used more effectively for purposes of supervision and monitoring the degree of uniform application of standards.

The maintenance of a concensus among licensing staff as to what each standard means and the measurement of compliance with it can be achieved only through a continuing planned dialogue among licensing staff, part of a program of in-service training/staff development.

"Interest representation" is essential and not always fully utilized in the formulation of mandatory standards. If standards are to be enforceable, it is essential that there be fairness in making rules. This can be achieved only if there is participation in the evolvement of standards by representatives of those who will be required to comply (at both the level of separate state standards and in the federal requirements). Furthermore, if standards, even when complied with, are to help insure quality day care for children, then they must be formulated in realtion to specific desired objectives and an identification of the means known to attain them. Many of the mandatory standards are insufficiently related to factors that affect the child directly, for example, day care practices that enhance or detract from the child's relationship to her/his family. Too often the child-development principle that should provide the rationale for each mandatory standard has been lost sight of through a kind of bureaucratic formalism that adopts rules only because they are traditional or because they are new ones adopted in a neighboring state. The problem is how to move away from a preponderance of lower-level objectives, for example, properly organized boards, record-keeping, etc., in favor of fresh standards directly related to the child's everyday experience in day care. The problem is difficult since, to be enforceable, licensing requirements must be written as clearly and specifically as possible and at a level the public generally is willing to support.

Ineffective enforcement of licensing standards through excessive compromise in instances of noncompliance threatens the welfare of many children in day care and erodes the potential of the licensing process for preventing hazards to children.

Various factors are primary in influencing licensing personnel to overlook noncompliance and fall into a pattern of overbenevolent licensing. The lack of a reliable frame of reference as to what particular standards mean (referred to earlier) leads to indecision and unsupportable judgments. The lack of adequate training for their function leaves many licensing staff persons with an inaccurate understanding of the nature of their authority and the means to use that authority fairly and constructively, e.g., the nature of evidence, the procedures to be followed in denying or revoking a license, and the constructive means of presenting one's authority in a way that can help the licensing applicant toward compliance. The mixture of functions that still goes on in many states—most detrimentally the mixing of responsibility for facility finding, placement into day care, and then licensing that care—forces licensing personnel into overbenevolent practices and unbalanced response to the market factor in day care. Inadequate staff time is allotted for interim supervisory visits, particularly where compliance is known to be marginal. These factors, in turn, inhibit the readiness of supervisors and administrators to provide support and backing to their personnel in the most difficult situations where denial or revocation of license should be carried out.

Participation in the regulatory process on the part of providers (day care personnel) and users (parents of children in day care) is an undeveloped resource for improving children's day care. Day care staff and parents are generally believed to have important roles to play in standard formulation and in monitoring and enforcement. Parents should be a source of valuable opinion as to what they perceive as a minimal standard of day care and which of the existing standards should be modified to more nearly reflect their desires for their children's care.

Yet parents have limited contact with day care licensing personnel and frequently have never seen the published standards. One suggestion has been to give them "Consumer Guides," a summary of standards, and to give them access to the licensing appraisal forms. Periodic surveys of parents could be another valuable means of communication. Not only does this minimal contact make for a "relevancy" gap between parents, operators, and licensers, it also inhibits parents' ability to monitor standard compliance. If they become dissatisfied with their child's care, they may take the only step they can see to take: removing their child from the facility. Even if they are aware of the licensing law, they may not perceive any easy channel of communication to the licensing agency.

Recent research in one large state asked a sample of day care operators, parents, and licensers to rank the relative importance of the different day care participants in monitoring a day care facility. Operators were ranked first, followed by day care staff, parents, licensers, and children (Illinois Economic and Fiscal Commission, 1974, p. 62). Nevertheless, present effectiveness of parent and day care staff in overall monitoring of a community's day care personnel is minimal. Parents often lack time, opportunity, or sufficient basis for sound judgment; day care staff are restrained by their dependent relationship to an employer. (See the chapters by Katz and by Bradbard and Endsley in this volume for further discussion of these issues.)

Despite the rhetoric on the potentiality of parents and providers to contribute to improvement of day care regulation, licensing staff still carry the primary role in ensuring compliance with mandatory standards. If licensing personnel are to more fully involve parents and providers in standard formulation and monitoring of compliance, additional licensing staff and more policy emphasis on community aspects of licensing will be required.

The diversity of agencies concerned with licensing is often a barrier to effective regulation. A common complaint by center operators has been the multiple inspections of their facilities, e.g., not only by licensing staff but also by health, fire, and building code personnel. Interagency committees might be a means of bringing about more joint visits and eliminating some overlapping inspections. Other agencies that are sometimes involved could also endeavor to coordinate their roles, e.g., a state department of education or mental health when day care is purchased for a severely handicapped child for which the public schools have no educational program. Increased communication among the various inspecting agencies could bring about more effective overall monitoring of compliance to safe standards for children. To attain better coordination of the various agencies involved, however, the licensing program will have to be seen in a larger context than usual, that is, in terms of a community's overall day care system rather than in the one-by-one licenser-operator relationship.

AN EFFECTIVE FEDERAL ROLE IN DAY CARE REGULATION

Federal participation in day care regulation, to be effective, must attempt to ameliorate states' regulatory problems as outlined. Until these problems are acknowledged and attacked, federal standards will be relatively ineffective except as a means of channeling money into states for day care at all levels of quality (or nonquality).

If federal funds are to continue to be channeled into day care, then federal participation in setting standards and maintaining the quality of that day care is imperative. Federal involvement is necessary not only for fiscal responsibility but also to meet an obligation to citizens to improve the quality of the nation's day care, and to reduce the discrepancies from state to state in the kind and availability of programs for children's out-of-home daytime experiences.

The question is not whether the federal government should provide leadership in the provision and improvement of children's out-of-home daytime care and development, but the direction that leadership should take and by what means. Given the complexities in effectively implementing a licensing statute, and the attendant problems in licensing practice that impede adequate application and enforcement of the states' mandatory standards, it appears doubtful that simply imposing a revised set of federal standards will achieve the intended goals of assuring developmental day care for children. Differences from state to state are still great in terms of amount of professional personnel for the licensing tasks; resources to permit adequate numbers of staff; degree of sophisticated knowledge about the licensing process; public awareness of the nature of the state's regulatory authority; and the level of care that citizens are prepared to support as essential for all children.

Given these differences, for the federal standards to be enforceable there must be flexibility on the part of the federal government in relation to those differences. This does not mean that the government should waive standards or ignore lack of enforcement in a given state. But the federal government cannot effectively monitor a state's application and enforcement of standards in individual facilities. At present the federal government in effect says, "Here are the standards you must enforce in each facility where federal funds are used," and the state replies, "Yes, that is what we are enforcing." But neither the federal government nor the states have any continuing means to measure the outcomes of such a requirement. The overall result is a deterioration of sound collaboration and confidence between federal and state levels of government and lack of protection to children. This is not to imply that states intend to deceive or default on the matter of standards application and enforcement. They are caught by the basic and complicating problems in licensing that are characteristic generally and by the "state of the art," their own state's particular level of resources and expertise, and a public demand to show eligibility for federal funds.

The federal government must devise a way to interpose its regulations in relation to the status of a particular state at a given point in time. Each state, to be eligible for federal day care funds, could be required to develop a State Day Care Licensing Plan. The plan should contain a factual account and evaluation of the existing status of licensing practice in the state. To do this would require inclusion of the amount of funds allotted to the regulatory function, and a breakdown of the various categories of expenditures; the numbers and qualifications of regulatory staff; the number of licensed facilities of each type and estimates of the number and geographical area of unlicensed facilities; an approximation of the average "case load" among licensing representatives; the kind and frequency of in-service training/staff development for licensing staff over the past two years; an evaluation of the state's licensing statute as compared to the Model Day Care Licensing Statute and an evaluation of the mandatory standards as compared to the Model Code of Standards and to the FIDCR.

The state plan should also include specific objectives within a projected time line for raising the level of its regulatory practice. If these objectives were developed in relation to the basic problems of licensing—revision of statutes, revision of standards, staff qualifications, staff training, funds expended, etc., the outcomes would be measurable at planned intervals.

Each State Day Care Licensing Plan would be individual in the sense that it present the status of day care regulation in a given state at a particular time, its strengths and weaknesses, and showed an agreed upon time line for achievement of a series of measurable objectives that would modify some of the basic problems of licensing administration. Day care standards in a vacuum achieve nothing; mandatory standards, whether federal or state, can only be as good as regulatory administration and practice. Continuing eligibility for federal funds would depend upon progress toward the objectives agreed upon. Encouragement would be given for progress toward objectives that reflected innovative approaches in relation to day care providers and consumers.

Special attention should be given those states with existing standards lower than those set in FIDCR; the objective would be to raise standards and improve enforcement. As states were enabled to strengthen their regulatory programs, gaps between state standards and the FIDCR would be lessened and current difficulties in promulgating two sets of standards—the FIDCR for federally funded programs and less rigorous ones for nonfunded programs would be diminished.

Federal concern about children's out-of-home day care should be couched in terms of the development of public policy affecting the interests of children in all facilities, not only those where federal money is expended. Leadership is needed in (a) developing research in relation to day care, preschool education, and the application of the regulatory authority to such programs; (b) consulting with state agency personnel about alternative ways of meeting goals in licensing practice; (c) developing inservice training/staff development curriculum and (d) meeting some of the increased costs that accompany efforts to bring about more effective child care regulation.

A lesson from history provides some insight into a sound basis for federal-state relations in day care regulation (Department of Labor, 1921). The federal government's first involvement with regulatory aspects of the children's field began in 1916 when Congress passed legislation to protect working children from the disadvantage and exploitation that accompanied premature entrance into employment. Under the farsighted direction of two pace-setting public administrators, Julia Lathrop and Grace Abbott, the child labor division of the Children's Bureau made plans for prompt and effective enforcement of the new legislation for children. The plan was based on the belief that a successful and economical administration of the new measure required federal-state collaboration of a high order. The first consideration in planning federal intervention was the work already being done in the enforcement of existing state child labor laws. Therefore close attention was given to existing administrative standards in the various states. The Children's Bureau was convinced that the full value of a national minimum for the protection of children would never be secured except through "a genuine working relationship between federal and state officials." Needless federal intervention was avoided but when intervention was indicated, it was carried out in ways intended to strengthen respect for both state and federal laws. Insofar as possible federal-state relations were a process of collaboration. The rule was that experience and interest should be pooled. On the basis of existing legislation states were classified roughly into three groups: those with child labor laws with standards higher than those of the federal law; a much larger number with the same requirements; and a smaller number with lower standards. Federal activity was most heavily concentrated in those states in which standards established by law were below those of the federal act or where opposition to a state's standards had prevented their effective enforcement. Research, providing information, suggesting alternative actions to bring about compliance with the law, supporting a state's innovation and individual progress, aiding in public education about essential standards to protect children and promote their well-being, and requiring accountability—these were components of the federal role. A current adaptation of that early model of federal-state collaboration holds promise of improving conditions for all children who require community programs for their daytime care and development.

FOOTNOTE

1. This paper is based on the contributions of the author to a DHEW-contracted Child Welfare League of America "state of the art" paper, "The Challenge of Child Day Care Needs and Improved Federal and State Approaches to Day Care Standard Setting and Enforcement," jointly authored by Mary Dublin Keyserling, Lela B. Costin, William Pierce, and Walter Wadlington.

REFERENCES

Abstracts of state day care licensing requirements. Part 1: Family day care homes and group homes. Part 2: Day care centers (U.S. Department of Health, Education, and Welfare Publication Nos. 72-11 and 72-12). Washington, D.C.: U.S. Government Printing Office, 1971.

Administration of the first Federal child-labor law (Children's Bureau Publication No. 78). Washington, D.C.: U.S. Department of Labor, Children's Bureau, 1921.

The appropriateness of the Federal Interagency Day Care Requirements. Report to the Secretary, U.S. Department of Health, Education, and Welfare [Publication No. 260-923/5035(78)]. Washington, D.C.: U.S. Government Printing Office, 1978.

Cohen, D. J., & Zigler, E. Federal day care standards: rationale and recommendations. *American Journal of Orthopsychiatry, 1977, 47,* 456–465.

Cooper, S. P. *History of Federal interagency day care requirements.* Unpublished manuscript. Washington, D.C.: U.S. Department of Health, Education, and Welfare, 1976.

Day care licensing study: Summary report on Phase 1: State and local day care licensing requirements. Washington, D.C.: U.S. Department of Health, Education, and Welfare, 1971.

Federal Interagency Day Care Requirements 1968. U.S. Department of Health, Education, and Welfare, U.S. Office of Economic Opportunity, U.S. Department of Labor (Publication No. 033-665). Washington, D.C.: U.S. Government Printing Office, 1969.

Guides for day care licensing (U.S. Department of Health, Education, and Welfare Publication No. OCD 73-1053). Washington, D.C.: U.S. Government Printing Office, 1972.

Illinois Economic and Fiscal Commission. *Day care licensing and regulation: A program evaluation.* Springfield Il.: Author, October 1974.

CAN QUALITY FAMILY DAY CARE BE ACHIEVED THROUGH REGULATION?

Gwen Morgan

INTRODUCTION

Every day in the United States 3,500,000 children under 13 go off to meet their friends in day care centers, nursery schools, and family day care homes, where they stay all day long. Another 4,000,000 spend part of their days out of their own home.

The *National Child Care Consumer Study* (Rhodes and Moore, 1976) has shown that for children under six who were cared for more than 30 hours a week, family day care provided for 25.5 percent of the total number, as compared with 29.9 percent in centers and nursery schools. There were about 100,000 licensed or registered family day care homes caring for about 300,000 children. Approximately 18,300 full-day care centers served about 900,000 children. The number of part-day nursery programs was not known.

Advances in Early Education and Day Care, Volume 1, pages 77–102
Copyright © 1980 by JAI Press Inc.
ISBN: 0-89232-127-X

Comparing the number of parents reporting using family day care with the number of children in licensed day care spaces, it is apparent that for preschool children alone there were very many unlicensed homes. When the number of after-school children were included, we found that 16.6 percent of all the children under 14 in families using child care for more than ten hours per week were in family day care. Only 9.4 percent of these children were in centers and nursery schools. At best only one to three out of eight family day care homes were licensed.

As the number of working mothers has dramatically increased over time to become the majority, the number of licensed day care spaces has grown, too, but much more slowly. If 7.5 million young children have working mothers and there are only licensed spaces for one million, it becomes important to know where the other children are. Half of these children of working mothers have relatives who care for them, and approximately another 10 percent have parents who stagger their work hours in order to share care. But for many families it has not been possible to make these arrangements within the family. It has become very difficult to find a person to care for children in their own homes. Centers have grown slowly, inhibited by lack of funds, and are often priced beyond the range of many families. To meet the needs of large numbers of families needing child care, there has been a phenomenal growth of unregulated care in other people's homes.

This is family day care. Large numbers of children are cared for, a few in each place, in a staggering number of licensable units. States have been able to keep pace with the growth of centers, most of which are licensed; but few have been able to license all the day care homes, even though most states have laws requiring it.

The time is past due for state and federal governments to consider family day care and the attitudes that providers and parents have toward its regulation. This chapter will review family day care and will discuss different regulatory and nonregulatory approaches to quality for that care. Alternative options exist for state regulation of family day care, which include improving the licensing system, four different models of registration and deregulation. Decisions among these options must take into account the climate of opinion and past methods of regulation used in the state, as well as criteria of effectiveness.

WHO IS THE FAMILY DAY CARE PROVIDER?

The State of Texas compiled a composite profile of a typical Texas-registered provider of home care.[1] As such, she is not real, since there is no typical provider. However, she has the characteristics most often found among Texas providers of care. Let us call her

Fannie Day Holmes—A Profile

Female, Caucasian, married, age 46
High school graduate
Grew up in rural area
Has been employed as a clerk
Husband is a foreman
Has provided child care continuously for four years
Family income is $10,000 (in 1977)
Lives in a city with population of 500,000
Owns own home—a single-family dwelling worth $20,000; has six
    rooms and one bathroom
Home is in neighborhood of single-family dwellings
Neighborhood is in average condition; home is above average
Has lived in home ten years; in neighborhood fifteen years
Doesn't provide care for children of her own
Cares for four children, two boys and two girls
Children are Caucasian and have both natural parents in the home
Children are young and have been in care only a short time, around
    fifteen months
Provider didn't know children's parents previously; parents referred
    by a friend
No older siblings of children are cared for after school
Children live within two miles of provider's home

Of course, there are many different kinds of caregivers in Texas and elsewhere. Family day care is provided in every social class and by different ethnic groups. Fannie is only a composite average. But, hypothetical as she is, she is more useful than if we were talking about an abstraction. What we need to think about is how much regulation is needed by Fannie? How much does she think she needs? How much protection do parents want when they use her care? Is she likely to provide quality care?

According to the Westat survey, 90 percent of the family day care homes were not licensed in 1970 (Westinghouse Learning Corporation and Westat Research, Inc., 1971). It is possible that this survey did not separate care by friends and relatives, so that the percentage may be too high. But other studies, both national and local, have estimated that at least 80 percent of family day care homes were unlicensed, and most estimated 90 percent (Southeastern Regional Education Board, 1973; Texas Department of Public Welfare, 1973). Twelve states have shifted from traditional licensing to some form of registration, at varying levels of commitment. In those states with a commitment to registration, the percentage of coverage is greater.[2]

The traditional approach to quality control in child care has been to license. There are many reasons why reliance on licensing alone will not achieve quality for family day care. A mix of regulatory and nonregulatory approaches is needed.

ATTITUDES TOWARD FAMILY DAY CARE REGULATION

Regulation, particularly licensing, depends on strong public support. Yet the general public does not assume a need for licensing family day care. Typically, middle-class families consider family day care to be a form of babysitting. (The term "babysitter" does not have the negative connotations among middle-class parents that it has among professionals in the early childhood field. Perhaps its somewhat passive tone has an appeal because it implies that parents themselves are firmly in control of their lives and of their families.) Parents select babysitters with care[3], and one point of consideration is whether they want babysitting in their own home or in the sitter's home. A form of regulation which treats these two forms of child care very differently is neither understood nor supported.

If parents are confident that they can choose, negotiate with, and take responsibility for their children in family day care, then a cumbersome licensing system might only undermine the parental role. If, however, parents feel at the mercy of a much-needed service, not daring to investigate very far, then strong and effective state intervention is needed.

Several years ago a national AFL-CIO conference included a workshop on day care. Most of the group were working-class men. When asked how they felt about regulating family day care, they expressed conviction that it was necessary and important. Several had horror stories to tell from their local communities. Everyone agreed that homes should be licensed. However, when asked whether any of them had been involved in caring for other people's children, two said that their wives had cared for children but had not obtained a license. "We looked into it," said one, "and found it was totally unreasonable. Do you realize they make you get a medical examination for everybody in the house?"

There appeared to be a discrepancy between the abstract endorsement of licensing and the unwillingness to submit to it personally. But these men did not consider their attitudes inconsistent. Somehow the way in which the licensing is carried out failed to reach them in a credible way.

Caring for children is an activity that is down-to-earth, familiar, and natural to many people. However, some of the things which have been traditionally required for licensure are foreign and baffling to someone who wants to care for children. Providers of care feel a certain sense of shock when a firefighter in full regalia invades their kitchen, looking at it as if it were a part of a large and hazardous institution.

Even though providers often consider initial inspection to be sheer bureaucratic insanity as it is presently administered, many are supportive of the concept of an initial licensing inspection. Ongoing supervision is another story. A study years ago in Michigan revealed that neither parents nor providers considered any ongoing supervision as a part of needed regulation; it was only the initial investigation which they saw as licensing.[4]

Most of the unlicensed providers of care have not sought a license, and they do not see themselves as lawbreakers. Nor do parents who use their service regard their use of illegal child care as in any way clandestine.

REASONS WHY FAMILY DAY CARE PROVIDERS DO NOT OBTAIN LICENSES

There are many reasons why day care providers do not obtain a license.[5] Public knowledge of the regulation of family day care is very low, and most people often do not know about the law. Caregivers not only are unaware that there are certain requirements which they should meet, they frequently do not even know that there is a statute.

Licensing may appear too complicated to providers, in contrast to the simple, natural thing they seek to do, to take care of children. The amount and formality of the red tape, forms, certificates, and approvals appear intrusive into what they consider to be their natural right to do what they wish in their own homes. It may also be expensive. Renovations which may be costly are sometimes a required part of the licensing process. Restrictions on the number of children to be served can result in the lowering of needed income.

Providers may also fear and resent the intrusion of inspectors into their homes. Housekeeping and child-rearing practices are part of the self-image of the home-based woman who may be afraid of being measured and possibly criticized on these matters. Licensing inspections may be identified with other kinds of painful inspection and interrogation they have had to undergo in the past, such as qualifying for welfare assistance or dealing with other bureaucratic systems, such as housing authorities. There may be fear or resentment at having to report income from their family day care service to the Internal Revenue Service.

Providers have observed little or no enforcement nor any serious consequences for noncompliance. Parents will use the service whether or not it is licensed and since no increase in income or control of clientele comes with licensing, there seems no compelling reason to be licensed.

REASONS PARENTS DO NOT INSIST ON LICENSING

Parents, too, are not well acquainted with laws regulating child care. Even if they are aware of licensing requirements, parents see no value to their own children from licensing, viewing it as a one-time thing or not wanting to jeopardize desperately needed care. They may feel confident and have a great deal of trust in their own ability to negotiate with the family day care mother without back-up supervision.

If licensing is done by a welfare department, parents may prefer to avoid that agency because of unwillingness to be identified with the recent stigmas that have become associated with the once positive word "welfare."

These points of view of both providers and parents need further systematic investigation. They may be accurate in some geographic areas and not in others; they may be common everywhere; or they may be incorrect assumptions made by biased observers.

A teacher of family day care mothers reports on a misperception of the degree of communication which exists between family day care mothers and parents:

> In one of the classes I gave on household safety, I remarked that, in my experience, this was one of the things that parents worried about most, and therefore it should be very openly discussed between parent and caregiver. I could tell that my opinion wasn't given much weight and, after some questioning, one of the family day care mothers from a family day care system said, "That's just not true. The parents who've come to my house for the most part never bring up the question of safety at all. I think they're either completely ignorant about it or they just don't care." All of the other family day care mothers in the system agreed that this was the case, and that safety wasn't much of a concern with parents. The coordinator of the family day care system sat through the discussion, but finally she said, "This is really amazing. Do you know the parents are always coming to *me* and asking questions about safety in all of your homes. One of your parents, Mrs. P., wanted to know exactly where you keep medicines and your cleaning stuff. One of your parents, Mrs. M., wanted to know if you watched carefully to make sure the children wouldn't fall down the stairs." She gave other examples, to the complete surprise of the family day care mothers. And this family day care system had the highest level of openness and good communication between caregiver and parent that I have ever seen.[6]

More systematic investigation of such parent and caregiver attitudes is of key importance in thinking through the form of regulation needed for family day care.

The familiarity of the parent with the caregiver may be another factor. Family day care from a stranger is different from care given by a friend, though not as different as we might have thought. A key variable is probably whether family day care is offered in a community which can be described as "neighborly" or in a community with a high population turnover and a lack of stability and connectedness among the people who live there.

DO WE KNOW WHAT QUALITY IS?

Those of us who have had a lot of experience with early childhood programs feel that we know quality when we see it. It is evidenced in the way the children respond to us, to each other, and to the caregiver. There are many clues. But, of these, it is baffling to decide which could be regulated. Any of us could make a list of the virtues which a caregiver should have. But by the time we get to "sense of humor" and "stamina" on our list, we may be uncomfortable about what can be regulated.

The most important ingredient in successful child care is *trust* between both parent and caregiver and child and caregiver.[3] While parents may not put this into words, it is a key aspect in their child care decision. Other key ingredients would have to include support for parents in their parenting role[7]—being child-centered is not enough. Good day care also considers parents and their needs and the quality of the relationship between parents and children when they are together; health care—good food, rest, care for physical growth undergirds all the other elements; continuity—children need to be able to count on relationships of trust and love. Constantly shifting child care arrangements are painful.

In addition to these basic ingredients, Pacific Oaks College[8] identified a short and thought-provoking list of the basic things children deserve to find in child care, whether it is provided by center staff, family day caregiver, or by a grandmother.

Softness—this sensory concept includes soft furniture and rugs, laps, furry stuffed toys, messy things, gooey things, mud, water, sand.
Safety and daring—note that safety alone is not enough. Children need to learn to handle potentially dangerous things in a safe way. Overprotectiveness inhibits child development.
Privacy—children have a right to be by themselves some of the time, or alone in an intimate relationship with another person.
Clarity—both the people and the physical environment send clear messages so that the child understands what is expected and what the limits are.
Variety of activities—to include some things to do which are open-ended, unstructured, and some things which have a sense of completion.
Props—some play materials facilitate child-initiated, child-controlled

symbolic play which is not subsumed under "activities." There is
evidence that dramatic play is of great importance both in social development and the development of symbolization.

Variety of people—it is good for children to be with both men and
women, old and young, people who speak different languages, people
of different races and in different work roles such as the mail carrier,
the plumber and the grocer. Different ages of children are also important, offering the opportunity to comfort a younger child or be com-
forted by an older one.

Love—loving relationships can be observed in good day care.

Some of these ingredients, such as softness, could lend themselves to
regulatory approaches, given some ingenuity on the part of the regulators
(Sales, Prescott & Torres, 1977). Others defy regulation.

It is important to understand that licensing is only one of many forms of
regulation aimed at children's services. Further, there are also a number
of other nonregulatory approaches which can be undertaken that are as
important as regulation for achieving quality child care. It is a mistake in
our zeal to try to put all our eggs of quality into the one basket of
licensing. We need to sort out all the different alternatives, both regulatory and nonregulatory, which could lead to quality child care.

If we want to be effective in bringing knowledge to bear on policy, the
appropriate question is not "What should the standards be?" but the
broader, prior question, "What is the most feasible and appropriate mix
of regulatory and nonregulatory actions which is most likely to eliminate
harmful quality and stimulate high-quality child care?"

FORMS OF REGULATION

For family day care one could imagine three possible tiers of quality as
shown in Table 1. Licensing or registration, representing the baseline, is
the lowest tolerable level of quality permitted to exist by the state. This

Table 1. Methods of Regulating Quality

Type of regulation	To whom applied	By whom implemented
Accreditation or Credentialing	All who voluntarily seek it	Peer group, local 4-C or state agency
Fiscal regulation	All using funds from the agency writing the regulation	Funding agency
Licensing	All	State or local licensing agency

minimum can be set as high or low as the citizens of the state wish. However, whether high or low, it is the minimum. Associated with this baseline, but differently administered, are the regulations of the health and safety bureaucracies. These three forms of regulation, licensing, health approval and safety approval, often apply to all child care, whether or not public funds are involved.

Another form of regulation is fiscal regulation. Here the funding agency spells out the quality of care it wishes to purchase. These regulations, therefore, apply only to subsidized child care, not to all care. The Federal Interagency Day Care Requirements are a form of fiscal regulation. The other aspect of fiscal standards is the rate-setting process. Government cannot establish fiscal standards unless it is willing to pay for the cost of meeting the standards.

One way of establishing a potentially higher standard might be a form of voluntary accreditation or credentialing for family day caregivers and babysitters. While not required, this credential or seal of approval might become trusted by the general public over time, giving quality an edge in the marketplace.

High above all these levels of regulatory standards are the goals or ideals of the field, always changing as we learn more about children's programs. Our goals also guide us as nonregulatory approaches to quality are developed.

NONREGULATORY APPROACHES TO QUALITY

There are other methods that may contribute to quality. These can be engaged in by the regulatory agency, or may be more successful if separated from the regulatory agency.

Education of the public is one potential way of contributing to quality. Parents and community expectations of day care should be raised so that the efforts to achieve quality will have public support, and so that parents will make use of regulation as consumer protection.

Providing training for caregivers is another way of improving the quality of care. There are many models of training, including the academic model of pre-service training, the consultative model of ongoing personal development, and the materials model with a place where resources, books, film strips, etc., are available. The second two models are most appropriate for family day care.

The formation of associations by centers or family day care providers offers opportunities to share knowledge. Participation in associations often results in increased status, more information about ways to achieve quality, and better communication with funding sources and the public. Associations, state licensing agencies, state and national organizations and private individuals have also developed newsletters that offer information on quality.

Consultation is another approach to improving quality. True consultation is a relationship voluntarily entered into by both parties and freely ended by either party at any time. That characteristic can never be present in consultation from a regulatory agency. Consultation related to the requirements must be a part of regulation; and it is probable that other kinds of consultation will continue to be made by regulatory staff, since they are in touch with providers of care who may ask for help. The important thing is that the regulator and the regulatee be clear on the difference between requirements and advice. There is no easy solution; the best idea yet may be the suggestion from New York City licensing staff that they always carry a second hat, and actually take off their licensing hat and replace it with a flowery consultant hat to distinguish the difference!

There are now other resources for consultation, about which states can inform caregivers. Vermont pays for outside consultation selected by the caregiver in cases where consultation is related not to the requirements but to the quest for quality. Different states are solving this problem in different ways.

Resource and referral centers have sprung up spontaneously and are expected to continue. A national consumer survey (Rhodes and Moore, 1976) found that parents see a major need for government to provide referral service for parents to inform them about the variety and quality of child care options. Such a consumer-oriented central information center can raise quality through educated parent choice as well as through exchange of information and ideas among caregivers of both center and home care.[9] Examples are the Gathering Place in Tomkins County, New York; Bananas and the Switchboard in California; and the Child Care Resource Center in Cambridge.

One clear way to improve quality is to offer direct services to caregivers. Rather than spend money to regulate whether or not homes are providing "something," it might be more effective to put the money into providing that "thing" to the homes. Support services could include any or all of a long list such as workshops, materials, loan of equipment, toy kits, medical examinations, free TB tests, and the like. Food services are already available when there is an umbrella organization, although there has been much red tape in the implementation. Some states are considering the possibility that with a simple registration system they could apply the savings in potential regulatory costs to raising quality through direct services to homes. The political danger is that legislators might institute the simpler regulatory system without the needed accompanying increase in direct services.

It is evident that there are a number of nonregulatory approaches which could assist the network of family day caregivers to achieve quality. The top two tiers, fiscal regulation of subsidized homes and some voluntary form of credential, are feasible. What is not apparent is what states should do about the bottom line, licensing, which applies to all homes whether or not subsidized. There is no one answer to that question, since states differ greatly in their structure for licensing, their tradition and public support, and their definitions. Many states, however, are rethinking their approach in the face of the fact that they are not achieving coverage of the homes to be licensed with their past methods.

ARGUMENTS AGAINST TRADITIONAL LICENSING AS NOW ADMINISTERED

A number of arguments have been made that the traditional method of licensing day care which is successful for centers may not be so feasible for homes. First, the quantity of family day care units requires large numbers of licensing staff, leading to high costs. This need for staff is further increased by the high turnover of homes offering care. Because of insufficient staff and a lack of public demand for this safeguarding, many homes operate illegally. Failure to license 75–95 percent of family day care homes in states which cannot foresee a time when they will be able to achieve full coverage, is not equal treatment under the law and may arouse public hostility, thus undermining all licensing, including that of centers.

Licensing of some, rather than all, family day care homes also discriminates against the poor. Providing licensure first to families where federal money is used to purchase care imposes two sets of requirements on these homes and has the effect of withholding licensing from homes used only by parents who pay for care out of their own earnings. The poor view this as one more example of unfair state interference in their lives, which is not equally applied to others. This argument was made in Massachusetts by mothers receiving welfare. The state licensing agency argued that they were offering extra protection and priority licensing services, but these women did not find the argument very persuasive.

Routine visits to so many small licensable units also may not be the best use of professional staff time. It diminishes the amount of time available to work with "problem" homes. Licensing agencies staffed for no more than one visit a year cannot provide the guarantee against harmful conditions which the public has learned to associate with the word "license." If an assurance of protection is to be made, staff members must be available to visit each home at least several times a year. Otherwise, parents and community may be led to relax their vigilance, their natural sense of responsibility, and social networks may be undermined by a false sense of security. Without staff, licensure is not a guarantee of protection.

Few parents or providers at present seem to clamor for licensing protection. Instead they appear to view licensing as an unwelcome intrusion where it exists, as in the Michigan study, and to accept responsibility without complaint where it does not, as in Georgia.

Overformal regulation, however well done, may destroy the genuineness of family life shared with children in family day care, creating homelike institutions rather than sharing real homes. It could also undermine the still commonly accepted value that children are the responsibility of their parents. Technical, time-consuming licensing may be not only inappropriate, it may also be counterproductive to the goals of home care.

When a service is defined as something to be licensed by the state, this often brings with it additional regulation imposed by other agencies which derive their authority from other statutes and act independently from the licensing agency. Chief among these other forms of regulation which may be applied to family day care are (a) zoning, deriving its authority from locally passed zoning by-laws under state enabling legislation; (b) safety regulation, deriving its authority from state safety statutes, sometimes with additional local requirements and usually locally enforced; (c) health and sanitation requirements, deriving from public health statutes at the state level, sometimes with additional local requirements and often enforced by several different health officials; and (d) in some places, local licensing in addition to state. The effect of all this regulation and the application of requirements, which were developed for other services more institutional in nature and which are often inappropriate for family day care, is to overwhelm the home with safeguards not required of other family households. This additional regulation may be a major factor that drives family day care underground. Few homes come forward to meet so many demands from such a formidable array of inspectors.

Finally, from a theoretical perspective, family day care licensing does not entirely fit the basic reasons for licensing. There have been two historic developments which have led to the need for licensing. One is our change to a society that is technically specialized, in which the ordinary citizens have neither the expertise nor the access to inspect for quality and safety and, therefore, must rely on the authority of the state for protection. The second is the change to a society in which people have become more mobile, more likely to be strangers to one another, with the result that informal community supervision cannot be fully relied upon. Family day care may not fully fit these rationales. It is not so technical that the citizens cannot understand it and judge its quality, and parents have considerable opportunity to observe their children's care and to make requirements of the day care providers, at least in some geographic areas. There are still communities which exhibit responsibility for the well-being of the children in their midst, such as some small towns and some stable neighborhoods in cities.

ALTERNATIVES TO TRADITIONAL LICENSING

By 1968 Class had begun to suggest that there might be more appropriate ways of regulating family day care, using the word registration but without defining it fully. Different people in different states began talking about and writing about more feasible ways of dealing with family day care (Class, 1968). In Portland, Emlen studied family day care, viewing it as a natural helping network which bureaucratic intervention might destroy.[10]

A number of states began experimenting with different ways of registering family day care homes and several of them gathered systematic information on their experiments. The Michigan Department of Social Services, for example, tried registration in one county, comparing it with licensing in another county.[11] The results were that licensing and enriched licensing achieved greater compliance with the regulations than registration. By definition, a license was not granted until proof of compliance was submitted. Second, the requirements on which licensing achieved greater compliance were those which required collection of papers, such as certificates, medical forms and other written documents. Registration reached many more homes and brought them into the regulatory system. However, because of the increased coverage, costs were greater in the registration county.

The results of registration have also been studied in Texas.[12] In a random sample of 100 registered family day care homes, by and large, a relatively high degree of compliance was found. About 27 percent of the sample were in perfect compliance and the remainder in violation of very few standards. As in Michigan, the particular standards most often violated were those involving the collection of required papers. For example, 43 of the 100 homes did not have an up-to-date immunization record for each child; 41 did not have TB tests for each family member; 25 had not had an annual fire inspection; 21 had not had an annual sanitation inspection. In contrast, only three homes in the sample violated the requirement for the number of children permitted. None violated requirements for caregiver. There was no violation of toy safety requirements nor of the requirements for indoor and outdoor play. One case of abuse/neglect was found, but there were no harsh, cruel or unusual punishments.

OPTIONS FOR STATE REGULATION

Given the arguments against licensing from a practical and a legal point of view, states are assessing their situations and making decisions about future directions in family day care regulation. There are basically six alternatives, ranging from the full implementation of the present licensing codes through four different models for registration (enabling, directing, credentialing, and simple registration with public education), to abandoning both licensing and registration. These alternatives can be conceptualized as a continuum from the most formal regulatory method to the least formal.

Improving the Licensing System

States may continue to try to license family day care homes. This must include realistic planning and commitment of resources to the effort, rather than the present wistful, mythical approach. It is important to begin to be honest about family day care licensing. It is not difficult to specify the number of staff members and the costs for an estimated number of homes to be licensed. This option requires commitment of that staff.

There are additional actions that states can take which will alleviate some of the present problems with licensing. First, states could amend their licensing statutes to provide for the licensing of "family day care systems." Homes which are part of a satellite system administered by a central administrative core, often with a group day care center as a training center and visible focal point, do not need to be licensed independently. If the administration and fiscal accountability is centralized, it might be questionable whether the individual homes have the autonomy to be licensed separately. Instead, the system could be licensed as a single entity with its administration held accountable for seeing that member homes meet basic requirements.

Homes, as parts of a licensed system, would be approved by the system on the basis of state standards. The system itself would also have to meet additional standards which the state would place on systems, covering the number and qualifications of support staff and services to the homes. If a system or one of its homes does not meet requirements, its license could be revoked and penalties applied. It is likely that in such a case the home would be dropped from membership by the system and the state would then require the home to be licensed separately.

The Commonwealth of Massachusetts has developed standards for the operation of family day care systems and plans to issue licenses to systems. However, the responsible agency, the Office for Children, found it extraordinarily difficult to reach agreement on standards. Qualifications for director of such a system, number of staff required for support, and number of visits were issues not easily resolved.

The second action that states might take to improve the licensing of family day care is to examine other statutes to determine whether the number and kinds of codes applied and inspections made by different agencies are appropriate for the size and informal characteristics of homes. Each government agency operates under its own authority derived from its statutory mandate. While there may be logic in requiring a variety of inspections for centers and group homes, regulation of family day care by agencies other than the licensing authority should not go beyond the type of requirements made of homes in which families live with their own children. Currently, other regulators include zoning, health, and safety officials.

Zoning has become in recent years a major obstacle to family day care, as well as to other community-based services. In some states it is possible to define day care as a "customary home use" in the state's enabling zoning statute, allowing family day care as a matter of right in all zones in which people live. At the local level, citizens can see that local zoning by-laws are worded in this way. It is important that the zoning by-law should be defined in such a way that the children's use of the home is not restricted in any way. Often, a customary home use can be limited to just one room or just one part of the house. This kind of thinking, however, is inappropriate for family day care, which involves a sharing of the entire home. Children use the bathroom, the kitchen, the bedrooms and other parts of the house.

The battery of regulators, including the licensing inspector, the fire, building and sanitation inspectors, add up to an overwhelming degree of regulation for the small informal service which family day care is. It is like aiming twenty-one cannons at an ant. This kind of regulation assumes that family day care is a little institution "like a home." If we want to preserve it as a real home, then no requirements for health and safety should be placed upon family day care homes that are not part of those for all residences in which families live. Wherever possible, it is desirable to remove family day care from the jurisdiction of these other disaster-oriented regulatory systems and write all requirements into one code, with one inspector from the licensing agency.

A third action which states can take to increase their coverage in licensing family day care homes is to develop definitions and an appropriate set of requirements for group homes. A group home is usually defined as a residential setting for the care of between seven and twelve children. A group home is not the informal sharing of a home; it is more like a small, informal center. To accommodate as many as twelve children, more than one person is needed, and it is reasonable to require minor structural renovations to assure safety of the group beyond what might be required of a residential dwelling. Health and safety requirements should be suitably tailored to the needs of a very small service, and a set of requirements appropriate to group homes is needed, not only for licensing but also for any other agencies which regulate group homes.

Attention to regulation of group homes is also relevant to improving the coverage of licensure of family day care. Knowledge that the care of more than six children involves meeting all the formal requirements for a center, including a formidable array of expensive modifications to the house or apartment, may encourage illegal family day care. Requirements for group homes which are reasonable and appropriate to the type of service might bring to light some underground family day care as well as the group homes.

These four steps—licensing systems; seeking uniform treatment in zoning codes; consolidating health, safety and licensing inspection; and developing appropriate codes and licensing for group homes could improve the regulation of family day care in many states. However, states must analyze the number of homes to be licensed and the resources available to do the inspections, in order to determine whether they would be able to do the number of prelicensing and supervisory inspections to make the guarantee which the public expects from a license. If not, some other form of regulation should be considered.

FOUR MODELS OF REGULATION

Registration as Enabling Regulation.   This method has elements in common with the next three, since they are all models of registration. The basic components in all four models are a central registry office with minimum records and competent staff. There would be no mandate of fire and health clearances beyond those applied to residential occupancies.

A registry office could be established at the county or area level, which maintains three records: (a) a registration book with the name and registration number of each applicant-registrant; (b) a master-file registration control card, with the immediately accessible information whether the home is pending, active or closed, plus face sheet and decision-type data, such as a checklist for required documents; and (c) statistics giving the total numbers of day care homes, by geographic area and including capacities, number of children, and families.

Staff maintaining the registry would be well-trained and qualified clerical people, supervised by a professional staff member with knowledge of child growth and development, social work, and regulatory concepts. Experimentation is needed to determine the best agency in which to locate the registrars, the feasible geographic area to be covered by each registrar, and the number of registrars who can be supervised by one professional staff person.

Potential providers would go to a central place to register day care home and to report the number of children they are caring for. This procedure gives the method "officiality."

The same information on procedures would be used with both providers and parents. This would include instructions about where and how to register; and information to be posted on the registration card. The file card, the procedural form, and any educational materials would be developed by the agency staff and the public, using the committee method.

These are the common elements which all the registration options share. This enabling model of registration is closest to traditional licensing. In fact, this type of regulation is a form of license. Chapter 551, Section 8, of the Administrative Procedures Act (5 U.S.C. c. 551) provides that a "license includes the whole or any part of any agency permit, certificate, approval, *registration,* charter, membership, statutory exemption or other form of permission" (emphasis added). If a family day care operator must register in order to operate lawfully, if the burden of initiating contact with the administrative process is on the individual who desires to engage in the specific conduct which has been otherwise prohibited by law, and if the state has the power to inspect, to enforce standards set by a regulatory agency, and to prohibit continued operation when those standards are not met, then all the conditions defining licensure are present.

The term "enabling" is based on Freund's (1928) distinction between the future-oriented, time-consuming licensing type of regulatory administration which he called "enabling," and a simpler form of regulation which tells what must be done in the present called "directing." For this reason if a state changes to "enabling" registration under a statute mandating licensure, no statutory change is needed. Such registration is in fact a license, or permission to operate.

There are, however, some major differences between enabling registration and the procedures which have become traditional in licensing centers. The major difference is in the prelicensing inspection. Under enabling registration, the caregiver certifies that the home meets the requirements of the state. One of these requirements is that a copy be given to every parent using the service. On the copy of the requirements which parents receive, complaint procedures are spelled out and parents are enlisted as partners of the state in assuring compliance with requirements.

The state does not routinely inspect each home but, rather spot checks a percentage on a rotating basis. If 10 percent are spot checked, then a home would be inspected only every five to ten years. However, the turnover rate is greater than ten years, so that some homes might never be inspected. The state would also inspect or request from a provider, upon complaints by parents or members of the community, or if there is any questionable response to the self-certification process. References might also be required and these might raise questions leading to a visit. The family day caregiver in each case would be informed about the reason for the inspection.

Upon receiving a potential provider's statement that the home meets the requirements, states would issue a "certificate of registration," a process which, even with the collection of references, normally takes only two or three weeks. This certificate is in fact a license to operate. It is called by another name and is usually less official-looking than traditional licenses, in order to avoid misleading the public into believing that the traditional inspections have been done and the traditional guarantees of quality have been made by the state.

Unless the state is very clear in its intention and educates the community to the differences between this form of registration and licensing in the traditional sense, this model could lead to some confusion, since it has many elements in common with traditional licensing. Confusion would be especially great in a state which had in the past been making a major effort to license family day care traditionally.

With this model, the state's responsibility is less than in traditional licensure. The state does not certify that the day care home meets requirements as it does when it licenses; it certifies that the family day care provider has stated that he or she believes that the home meets requirements and it makes sure that parents are informed about those requirements and of the parents' role in negotiating with the provider on the basis of the requirements. The state makes no routine supervisory home visits. It does maintain records for information on the volume of family day care for planning and possible research. It does make lists of day care homes available, putting day care providers and parents in touch with each other. Having identified the homes, if this model is successful, the state could provide information and services to them.

If the state has additional resources, another level could be added to improve the regulatory model. This would include an office interview for all applicants at the place of registration by a professional, the maintenance of a mini-record with more detail than the simple card, as well as greater use of the media for informing and providing education on child care to the day care mother and to parents.

Still another level of commitment of resources could add group instruction, training and meetings of day care providers and parents, a newsletter and some home visits for individual teaching or consultation. The model does not include visits for supervision, but at every level of design the model includes the idea that staff would be available to visit homes upon a complaint or request for help.

For this, as in all the options, if incentives are offered to providers to make themselves known, the model has greater likelihood of achieving its goals.

Massachusetts has developed a registration model of the "enabling" type for regulating its independent homes, without changing its statute which calls for a license.[13] Massachusetts is also planning to license its family day care systems, which did require statutory definition.

Registration as Directing Regulation. This model is very similar, for all practical purposes, to the preceding one, but its legal basis is quite different. The assumption underlying this model is that licensing is not the appropriate regulatory method for family day care because of the service's lack of social visibility, its informal and transitory nature, the large number of units that are costly to inspect, and the generalist, nontechnical nature of the service. Rather than trying to bend licensing to make it fit a service for which it is inappropriate, an alternative statutory approach is taken.

Instead of the licensing language, "No person shall provide family day care unless . . . ," the statute would read like an order. Wording such as the following would be suitable: Persons providing care of a child or children in family day care (definition elsewhere) shall register their names and addresses (and any other information the state wishes to require) with the department (defined elsewhere), and shall meet such requirements as the department shall determine.

Under this kind of statutory language, the state may enforce requirements but without the heavy preparatory and future-oriented emphasis of enabling language, requiring proof that the requirements will be met before allowing the service to take place.

The major features of this model are similar to the previous model: registration of the fact of providing family day care and the number of children in care, and perhaps their ages; a signed statement of awareness of the nature of state requirements and the provider's belief that the service meets the standards or an agreement to achieve conformity; willingness to submit to inspection; willingness to supply users with a document which includes the state requirements and the manner of filing a complaint. Registration would be mandatory in the statute, but there would be no vested interest in holding a license since no license would be involved. The latter feature is the major difference with the previous model.

Credentialing Model of Registration. This model of registration is closer to a credential than to a license. Instead of establishing standards for the operation of the family day care program, the state would establish competencies for the caregiver. Training would be offered, either for tuition or at the state's expense, and successful completion of the training would be a condition for registration. It is possible that some form of competency assessment could be used as an alternative to the training. No requirements are promulgated or enforced and no supervision is done in this model.

States would have to decide which agency appropriately should provide the training. To avoid conflict, it might be preferable if the training agency were different from the one maintaining the registry. In that case, of course, the two agencies would have to work closely together.

This model relies on a required training program as a way of linking up the family day care providers with one another and with community sources of help. If training can develop competencies and deepen sensitivities to children, then this model has the potential of seeing that providers operate in a relationship with a state agency or agencies which can provide continuing information and support. As in all the options, many services could be provided if the state has the resources and the commitment to provide them.

This model has not been implemented by any states at the present.

Simple Registration with Education of the Community. A state choosing this option would require all family day care providers to register with the state. This required registration would provide a record of all providers with certain needed statistics. No supervision would be done of the homes, and no requirements would be promulgated or enforced. The emphasis would be on playing a helpful role in identifying the providers by name and address in order to send them educational materials. Standards could be included among the educational materials, but they would not be requirements. Proponents of this model believe there is considerable advantage simply in knowing where all the family day care homes are, and they are hopeful that the state can achieve full coverage by this method. This appears to be the model which Texas has begun to develop.

The model relies on nonregulatory services and education of the public for upgrading the quality of the existing family day care network. The purpose of the registration is to identify providers so that the state can provide services to them, as well as to gather data which might be useful in planning.

This model is the least costly in state resources. Those proposing it usually try to use available funds in other ways, rather than trying to save money overall. The argument is that if less were spent on regulatory staff, resources could be offered to the home. Such services as minor renovations, loan equipment, educational kits, help with association newsletters, resource and referral centers, voluntary ongoing training, and health services could be provided with the funds not being spent on inspections.

Deregulation of Family Day Care

The only remaining option for the states, if they do not have resources for licensing and do not choose to implement any one of the models of registration, is to abandon the effort entirely and place major emphasis on other ways of achieving improvement in quality. This suggestion may appear dramatic and drastic but, upon analysis, it is not far from what some states are now doing in practice. Some states which have statutory authority to license family day care are dealing almost entirely with homes which are publicly funded. Even if they did not license, these departments would still be obligated to monitor quality to be sure that federal funding requirements are met. State funding requirements could be adopted. With no licensing authority at all, these states could continue to regulate the same homes through fiscal administration, without promising a preventive service to all children which they are not delivering. Putting staff energy into the task of enforcing fiscal requirements for public funds, without confusing it with licensing, would be more realistic and more logical for such states.

A number of other states do license private homes without confusing licensing with purchase of care or child placement. But some of these states have defined family day care in such a way that most out-of-home care of small numbers of children is exempt from licensing. Some states, such as Tennessee and Missouri, define family day care as the care of four or more children outside their home. Since family day care typically cares for two or three children, such a definition essentially exempts such care from licensure.

The underlying assumption of this option is that parents do not need or want state intervention in family day care, beyond the enforcement of improved legislation for child protection from abusive or neglectful care. A further assumption is that funds which might have gone into routine inspections can go into services to the providers and parents and into education of the public as to the need for quality in the care of children.

DECIDING AMONG THE OPTIONS

As policy makers evaluate the above alternatives for the future of regulation of family day care, they will need to consider factors such as the climate of opinion which will influence whether a constructive change can be accomplished; the past history of regulation in the state; and criteria of effectiveness, such as coverage and effect on family role.

The Climate of Opinion

A part of any strategy for change is assessing environmental constraints and possible favorable opportunities in public opinion. Some of these factors are identified below.

There has been a shift in the use of family day care. Many middle-class families now use this kind of care which formerly included mostly poor people. The licensing representative may find that state intervention meets with hostility rather than gratitude. In fact, some parents brought suit against the State of California[14] because, among other things, they felt the state was inhibiting parental choice of child care by refusing to license certain homes.

There has also been a shift of public concern from merely protecting children in day care to include concern for children who need day care and do not have it. Instead of just being protectors of children, licensors may also be seen negatively as bureaucrats impeding the growth of a needed service.

There is much more understanding today of parental differences in values and the need to support the cultural values of a particular family. Licensors who impose their own values through regulation may be met with great hostility.

Because of the above factors, legislators are apt to curb the authority of regulators. In many states during the past two years, legislation has been filed which would substantially weaken the licensing authority, and some of this legislation has passed. In some cases, the triggering incident was an arbitrary action by a licensor against a family day care home, an action which aroused hostility among caregivers and parents.

There is vast confusion over the Federal Interagency Day Care requirements (FIDCR) which have been controversial at the federal level. Some of that controversy has spilled over into licensing and the general public is not clear on the distinction between FIDCR and state licensing. Operators fearful of federal regulation have moved against state licensing.

The temper of the times is antibureaucracy, anti-big government, and antiregulation. There is a growing revolt against excessive paper work and a presidential commission against red tape.

Decision-makers want hard data to justify standards, but there is a lack of such a knowledge base. Social science research technology has not been able to measure dramatic differences except in the most gross situations. Research data exist but often do not convince policy makers.

There is great interest in due process, creating lengthy delays in any attempted negative action in regulation. Children's rights receive little emphasis when they clash with property rights of operators, with a license under the law being viewed as property. Since the lawyers are deeply interested in due process and rights at this time, they also tend to insist on lengthy and wordy standards that spell out these rights. Registration, to succeed, needs a simple set of requirements, few in number and written in jargon-free English which both parents and providers can understand and find compelling. Legal trends may inhibit or totally defeat that goal.

It is not clear that the right to inspect homes will survive a court test. Even in centers there is some question about whether regulators have the right to enter and inspect without a search warrant, a case now before the Supreme Court.[15] In homes, the issue is even more sensitive. A person's home has for centuries been considered inviolable, and family day care takes place in a real home where people live.

Frequent use of political influence on the part of the regulated causes passivity and apathy in regulatory agencies. Many licensing agencies have become defeatist, no longer struggling to assert children's rights over adult rights.

There is a small and growing self-help movement among parents and an insistence on strengthening family roles and responsibilities (Howell, 1976). Consumerism as a movement is also growing. As families show increasing active interest in the quality of the products they use, this interest could lead to a more active parental role in selecting quality child care and monitoring it. These two factors may be constraints against traditional licensing, but they could offer exciting opportunities for new approaches to regulation. If the regulatory policy makers could plan to link their fortunes with the rising tides of self-help and consumerism, licensing or registration could become a dynamic program for securing child and family rights, with parents playing a key role. Without that development, the rest of the constraints in the current climate of opinion may well overwhelm the effort to license.

Past History of Regulation in the State

For states which have not been making a major effort to license, a shift to one of the registration models is likely to be a positive experience. One licensor describes the change as follows:

> We would get calls from caregivers who wanted to do the right thing, to get a license because it was required. They always expected that it would be a simple thing and that they could begin to care for children at once. We had to tell them that two months was the soonest we could get them the license if we were lucky. It didn't make sense to them that they couldn't care for children during that time; usually there was some child who really needed care next Monday morning. We could look the other way, but it was hard to believe in what we were doing. Now, with the shift to

registration, all of a sudden there are no pending licenses. We're not just pushing
paper around; we're involved in things we think are important—public education,
teaching caregivers what the standards mean, investigating complaints.[16]

For the states which have a substantial number of licensed homes, the
problems are different. Licensed homes may oppose any change.
Licensed centers also oppose anything that looks like easing up on homes.
It would take a careful campaign to win support for registration.

Reasons for Considering Change
If it would be difficult to change the regulatory model, then why do it?
The major reason for change is that licensing may never reach all the
homes, or even half the homes. Some state licensing offices are apparently unaware of how many studies have identified vast numbers of
unregulated homes. We do not have the option of pretending they don't
exist. If we are going to license, we have to license all the homes. That
means identifying a state or local staff large enough to do the job, or
changing the procedure.

Another reason is that registration may be superior to licensing. It
creates a different balance between the state and the parent. The state
does not guarantee anything close to absolute protection to parents because it recognizes that this would be a false guarantee without frequent
inspections. It also recognizes that it would be inappropriate to take over
the responsibility from parents, who should feel in charge of selecting and
evaluating their child care arrangement. By enlisting parents as partners,
the state can reach all family day care homes. The parents must be part of
the educated public that can exert sufficient effort to achieve success.

Arthur Emlen (1973) in Portland firmly believes that licensing *reduces*
the quality of family day care. He feels that bureaucratizing family day
care turns it into a little institution and destroys its quality of neighborly
helping. Many feel this somewhat overstates the case, but this perspective
is shared by many middle-class parents who use family day care and who
resent heavy-handed interference by the government.

SUMMARY

Six options have been identified as alternatives for the regulation of family
day care. They are: improvement of licensing; enabling registration; directing registration; credential registration; simple registration; and deregulation. Some of the questions policy makers should be asking about
these alternatives and investigating through field testing and study include
the following:

— How much protection is needed by the state? What is the nature of family day care in the different geographic areas of the state? To what degree is it offered by neighbors in places where people know each other and share family concerns and values? To what degree is it offered by strangers who are unsupported by a community?
— Is the regulatory method chosen adequate to assure nurture of the child's physical and psychological growth?
— Do homes regulated by this method provide a level of care comparable to that provided through other regulatory methods?
— How important is it to collect paper documentation in order to assure quality?
— Does the regulatory method support the appropriate family role?
— Is the regulation acceptable to parents?
— Does the public support the degree of protection it guarantees? Do legislators understand it?
— Can it reach all the homes equitably?
— If the regulatory method relies heavily on other regulators, will these other actions be taken by the other agencies; will they be taken in a timely way; and will they be appropriate to a real home?
— What is the maximum number of homes which a licensing worker can carry and provide the supervision guaranteed by the method chosen? Given the projected number of homes, is the level of staffing adequate? If not, can additional staff be identified or added?

We know that parents of young children today have less community and extended family support than ever before and that the vast number of children in family day care need the concern of society. A combination of regulatory and nonregulatory action is needed to assure that children receive the care they need. It is time to face up to the policy choices we need in order to make our concern a reality.

FOOTNOTES

1. Texas Welfare Department. *Overview of Registered Family Homes Research and Evaluation Project*. Unpublished report, 1977.
2. Texas Welfare Department. *Proceedings of a conference on family day care registration October 31–November 2, 1977.*
3. Unpublished data from Project Connections. American Institute for Research, Cambridge, Ma.
4. *Licensing power*. Proceedings of the Annual Conference of State Licensing Personnel, U.S. Department of Health, Education, and Welfare, Zion, Il., February 1971.
5. Based on informal discussions with family day care providers at family day care

conference sponsored by Day Care and Child Development Council of America, Washington, D.C., 1977.

6. Personal communication, 1976.

7. *Report to the Congress on the appropriateness of Federal Interagency Day Care Requirements* (Chapter 2). Washington, D.C.: U.S. Department of Health, Education, and Welfare, Office of Assistant Secretary for Planning & Evaluation, 1978.

8. Prescott, E., & Davis, T. G. *Concept paper on the effects of the physical environment on day care.* Prepared for U.S. Department of Health, Education, and Welfare, Assistant Secretary for Planning & Evaluation, 1977.

9. Cranston, A. *Congressional Record*, August 24, 1978.

10. Emlen, A. *Neighborhood family day care as a child-rearing environment.* Paper presented at the annual meeting of the National Association for the Education of Young Children. Boston, November 1970.

11. Michigan Department of Social Services, *Demonstration Project for the Registration of Family Day Care Homes (Interim Report).* February 12, 1976.

12. Texas Welfare Department. Randomly sampled registered family homes. *Standard by standard evaluation.* Unpublished report, 1977.

13. McCauley, L. *Registration of family day care homes in Massachusetts.* Massachusetts Office for Children Family Day Care Licensing Unit. Boston, 1975.

14. Petition 465428-7. Filed June 5, 1975, in Superior Court, California, in and for the County of Alameda.

15. Camera vs. Municipal Court. 387 U.S. 523. 1967. Massachusetts licensing staff discussion at New England Institute on Day Care Licensing, unpublished, Tufts University, Medford, Massachusetts, 1976.

16. Personal interview, 1977.

REFERENCES

Belben, J. E., and Tagg, C. A. *Family day care systems: Results of a survey of systems in Massachusetts.* Boston: Massachusetts Office for Children, 1978.

Class, N. *Licensing of child care facilities by state welfare departments* (Children's Bureau Publication No. 462). Washington, D.C.: U.S. Department of Health, Education, and Welfare, 1968.

Emlen, A. Slogans, slots, and slanders—the myth of day care need. *American Journal of Orthopsychiatry, 1973, 43,* 23–36.

Freund, E. *Administrative powers over persons and property.* Chicago: The University of Chicago Press, 1928.

Howell, M. *Helping ourselves, families and the human network.* Boston: Beacon Press, 1976.

Problems of licensing family day care homes (Southeastern Day Care Bulletin No. 4). Atlanta, Ga.: Southeastern Regional Education Board, 1973.

Rhodes, T. W., & Moore, J. C. *National child care consumer study.* (Vol. 1, 2, 3). (Prepared under Contract HEW-105-74-1007 for U.S. Department of Health, Education, and Welfare, Office of Child Development.) Arlington, Va.: UNCO, 1976.

Sales, J., Prescott, E., & Torres, Y. *The right ingredients.* Pasadena, Ca.: Pacific Oaks College, 1977. (Filmstrip and cassette tape)

Survey of unlicensed day care in Texas. Austin, Tx.: Texas Department of Public Welfare, April 23, 1973.

U.S. Bureau of the Census. Daytime care of children. In *Current Population Reports* (Series P20, No. 298). Washington, D.C.: U.S. Government Printing Office, 1976.

Westinghouse Learning Corporation and Westat Research, Inc. *Day care survey, 1970.* Washington, D.C.: U.S. Office of Economic Opportunity, 1971.

PART II: ROLES OF PROFESSIONALS

AN EXPANDED ROLE FOR EVALUATION IN IMPROVING THE QUALITY OF EDUCATIONAL PROGRAMS FOR YOUNG CHILDREN

Melvin Shelly

Rosalind Charlesworth

INTRODUCTION

Evaluation as an independent discipline is relatively recent within the field of education. In the past, evaluation was tied into research and tended to be viewed from a rather narrow perspective. Educators are beginning to see that evaluation has a multitude of forms and is not necessarily limited to the traditional research design parameters. Parallel to the development

Advances in Early Education and Day Care, Volume 1, pages 105–135
Copyright © 1980 by JAI Press Inc.
All rights of reproduction in any form reserved.
ISBN: 0-89232-127-X

of educational evaluation as a field of study, "early childhood," as an area of education, grew as a focus for national attention. During the 1960s, many different program approaches were developed for early childhood with a strong emphasis on compensatory education (Abbott et al., 1976; Bronfenbrenner, 1975; Coleman, 1977; Day & Parker, 1977; Fallon, 1973; Ryan, 1974; Stanley, 1972). As the Head Start and Follow Through programs were established, a number of these early childhood program models were included in the planned variation experiments (Rivlin & Timpane, 1975). Officially, there have been national evaluations of Head Start, Follow Through, and these program models, with severe criticisms leveled against the programs and the evaluations.

Examining the problems which plagued these evaluations, particularly the controversy surrounding the recent Follow Through evaluation by Abt Associates (House et al., 1978), can be instructive for our purposes. Due to budget restrictions in its first year, Follow Through was forced to become an experiment in curriculum comparison, rather than a massive service delivery system. Sponsors (the early childhood education program developers of the 1960s) managed projects in various locations. The sponsors were encouraged to conduct their own model evaluations. One large-scale national evaluation was to be used as the ultimate estimate of success or failure of the program and of the idea of planned variation in curricula. Although the popular press has seized on the summary findings that basic skills approaches (Behavior Analysis, Direct Instruction) were most successful, the major findings of the study according to its authors (Anderson, St. Pierre, Proper, and Stebbins, 1978) were the wide variability in effects from site to site within program models, and the essentially small differences on outcome measures between Follow Through and non-Follow Through groups. During and after the evaluation there have been critiques of the research design, data analysis techniques (Hodges & Sheehan, 1978; House et al., 1978; Porter & Chibucos, 1975), and various attempts to reanalyze and reinterpret the data (e.g., Kennedy, 1978a). Apparently, one real dissatisfaction with the national Follow Through evaluation is that it gave no clear answers to important questions such as: Did a program model have the kind and quality of impact that its program description promised? Was the variability between projects (successes and failures of the same model) due to lack of implementation or interaction of instruction with student, teacher, or project characteristics? What, if anything, in the daily process provided the link between the program conception and student outcomes?

Note that questions of this kind have not frequently been addressed in published evaluations. The traditional view of evaluation, with its typical concerns has been restated by Ambron (1977):

> Evaluations attempt to provide evidence for making judgments about the value of educational programs. Questions like the following are asked: Did the program accomplish its objectives? Was the program a good investment? Should the program be cut back, refunded, or expanded? The ideal is to provide totally unbiased evidence for answers to these questions, but in reality this is rarely possible. (p. 210)

The national evaluation of Follow Through did address these more typical kinds of questions and did focus on bias (validity in design and analysis), but failed to satisfy early childhood educators. This chapter will argue for an expanded view of evaluation which will emphasize the less frequently asked questions relating to conceptual frameworks and adequate descriptions of programs, useful process-product linkages, and explication of the expected outcomes and underlying psychological processes.

The equivocal answers to traditional evaluation questions and the significant number of unaddressed conceptual questions in previous Head Start evaluations and the national Follow Through evaluation have added to other negative research findings on the effectiveness of early childhood programs. To a great extent, early education has been portrayed as in no way fulfilling its initial promise of improving the status of young children. The result has been a national "putdown" of educational programs for young children and a lack of positive support and practical evaluation guidelines for use in local, state, and national evaluations. Before early childhood education is put in the trash as a has-been national priority, it is essential that early childhood evaluation be reexamined and placed in perspective.

Much has been learned about evaluation during and since the growth spurts of the sixties and early seventies. At the Minnesota Round Table on Early Childhood Education II the freshly blossoming concepts of the new educational evaluation were discussed as they might apply to programs for young children. The organizers of Round Table II strongly believed that the work of early education evaluators needed to be viewed in the context of developments within the mainstream of educational evaluation. Admittedly, there have been reciprocal relationships among evaluators of programs for young children and evaluators of educational programs for children at other stages of development. Yet evaluation of early education programs has only recently reflected the influence of those who affirm the values of criterion- or domain-referenced assessment, formative evaluation, the use of measures of cognitive style and other process variables, an aptitude-by-treatment model, and other developments which have evolved within the mainstream of educational program evaluation (Weinberg & Moore, 1975, p. 3).

The ideas discussed at the Minnesota Round Table II are beginning to surface in early education. Virginia Shipman of Educational Testing Service has recently reported on the ETS Head Start study.[1] In the late 1960s, ETS identified, 1875 three and one-half year old Head Start children for an intensive study of normal development. The ETS study was neither a program development study nor an evaluation study in the traditional sense. In the new view it represented one of the many possible approaches to evaluation: the *descriptive approach*. Shipman has described in great detail the school, family, community experiences, and environment of the children studied (Shipman et al., 1976). This study explored expected outcomes (what the competent Head Start graduate might become) and the process which leads to the actual outcomes. Another example is some work being done at High/Scope Educational Research Foundation where researchers are developing process measures of children's communicative competence. High/Scope's curriculum emphasizes children's productive language in the program description and in the actual classroom interaction (Stallings, 1977a). As part of the sponsor evaluation of Follow Through, Bond (1976) and his associates have designed the Productive Language Assessment Tasks, an instrument which uses student-generated text, reports, and stories to assess the cognitive complexity of student language. This study emphasized the link between curriculum conception, daily practice, and measured outcomes.

At Huron Institute, Yurchak, Haney, and Bryk[2] are attempting to set in motion the ideas of the expanded views of evaluation into practical, user-oriented models for early childhood educators. Following the earlier work on Title I evaluation models (Horst, Tallmadge, & Wood, 1975; Tallmadge & Horst, 1976), they hope to offer the practitioner examples of design, analysis, and measurement techniques which will maximize the potential of future local early childhood evaluation. Their goal is for evaluations to address and to answer more questions related to developmental process and program process rather than a current narrow focus on short-term impact.

The purpose of this chapter is to summarize current thinking on educational evaluation, to pull together some of the lessons that have come out of past mistakes, and to show, through examples of qualitatively good evaluation, that there are means for evaluating programs for young children that will aid in the discovery of characteristics that single out programs and evaluations of high quality. The suggestions presented might be applied to any evaluation whether developed for a day care home, a nursery school, or a multidisciplinary child development center or for programs for infants, toddlers, preschoolers, kindergarteners or primary age children. Our premise is that quality evaluation can offer support to quality educational programs for young children.

THEORETICAL ISSUES OF EVALUATION

Definitions of Evaluation

The traditional view of evaluation, the definitions that have guided most evaluations of early education, have appeared again recently in the early childhood literature as the following quotations indicate. The first reflects the basic concepts discussed by Stake (1967). The second is from Stufflebeam (1968), and the final one from Scriven (1973).

> Evaluation includes both the description and judgment of school programs and children's attainment. Central to this process is a consideration of the goals of education and whether they are achieved (Spodek, 1978, p. 369).

> Evaluation is an attempt to use social science research methods to gather evidence for decision making (Ambron, 1977, p. 206).

> Essentially evaluation is a way of helping people who run programs understand whether or not they are succeeding, and how they might better achieve their goals (Huntington, 1973, p. 94).

Although evaluation studies of early education are becoming increasingly more sophisticated, these definitions and conceptions of evaluation reflect a ten-year-old perspective.

Evaluation is a process of attributing value or determining worth. Informally, in everyday life, it always includes a subjective personal value component. Social scientists are acknowledging the use and potential of subjective involvement of the researcher (or evaluator) in the describing, judging, or deciding process (Stake, 1978). Since evaluation theory has grown and expanded its definitions and conceptions over the last decade in a parallel fashion to early childhood curriculum development, it is appropriate that current and future early childhood program evaluators expand their conception.

In a review of *The Handbook of Evaluation Research,* a mid-1970s compendium of evaluation theory, Ross and Cronbach (1976) provide an analogy for traditional and expanded views of evaluation. The program is pictured as a train. The traditional evaluator begins as the train does, runs alongside observing and collecting data, and abruptly stops at the end of the line, or perhaps is left behind. In an expanded approach, evaluators do more. They board the program train, influencing personnel and passengers. They are free to observe any event on the train, and pay special attention to the interaction in progress.

The suggestions attached to issues discussed later in this chapter push toward this expanded view. What emerges is an eclectic approach with a number of potential directions. Running through these suggestions is the notion that values, internal and external, play a necessary and facilitating role in evaluation, and ought to be made explicit. An informal phenomenological view of this topic is discussed by Stone (1978). A more formal approach based on Bayesian statistics, including a way to incorporate values into numerical estimates is provided by Edwards and Guttentag (1975). For the early childhood educator, evaluation should be a process of estimating, in the best possible ways, the value of the educator's self-chosen commitment of time and resources. It makes great sense to assemble as much relevant information as possible in assessing the value of our personal investments.

Evaluation as Information

There is some logical minimum of information necessary for determining worth. A thorough description of the program, the daily process, the rationale, and the expected outcomes or benefits to children are required. As Fein and Clarke-Stewart (1973) point out, evaluation should be more than a yes or no question. Rather, more substantive questions must be asked, such as:

1. How do day care programs differ from one another with respect to intention and implementation?
2. How do these differences influence communities, families, and children?
3. How can the relations between "inputs" and "outputs" be interpreted?

The answers, for day care, might come from two in-progress descriptive evaluations of naturally occurring variations in programs, the National Day Care Study by Abt Associates, and the National Day Care Home Study conducted by Westat and Abt. Along with adequate descriptions, evaluations need clear conceptions of the program models, the theoretical base for expectations concerning process and impact. Zimiles (1977) has commented on this lack of attention to developmental descriptive studies which flesh out these conceptual frameworks as the most pressing and relevant problem for early childhood evaluation.

Beyond the necessary information, the underlying psychological and developmental processes ought to be a target for evaluations in early childhood. Evaluations whose primary or even secondary purpose is to describe and interpret developmental phenomena are rare (Anderson & Ball, 1978). This is not bootlegged research, but an area of prime concern for early childhood educators. For example, the concept of *valued-added analysis,* a model of differential growth rates for children (Bryk & Weisberg, 1976, 1977), was developed during the Head Start Planned Variation Study. Originally a technique for information reduction and data analysis, it enabled the evaluators to speculate about, and conceptualize alternative notions of growth trends in preschool-aged children.

Useful information in evaluation is that which is instrumental or strategic. If the process observation portion of an evaluation reveals characteristic goal defeating patterns of interaction and alternative facilitative patterns, the teachers (producers, administrators) can use it to alter and improve the quality of the program. Applications of ethnography to education (Gearing et al., 1975) and previously developed classroom observation techniques (Weinberg & Wood, 1975) illustrate this potential. Regarding impacts, if measures of outcomes are conceptually close to the goals of the program, patterns of student performance can also be used in a diagnostic fashion for individual child or program wide strategic replanning (Borich, 1977; Levin, 1976).

Focus

The expanded view of evaluation has a broad and multilevel focus. The individual child has typically been the unit of analysis in evaluations, but results and interpretations were commonly based on classroom groups. Depending on the program's conception, individual assessment and description of change might be particularly informative in understanding the underlying growth process. Classroom level or teacher level evaluation provides the foundation for some generalizability. Focus on the daily interaction or conduct of the program answers such basic questions as: Is there a program? Does it match its description? Does it provide the process link between conception and expected impact? Finally, a focus on the descriptive-conceptual information gathered on the program allows a logical and psychological analysis of the program philosophy in action. Smith, Neisworth, & Greer (1978) have suggested a total-environment approach focusing on all of these levels with various methodologies (checklists, observations, tests) as a way to get a comprehensive estimate of the worth and the values involved in an educational program.

Spodek (1978) illustrated a possible expanded view of evaluation in practice in a local school system, focusing on multiple levels and acquiring considerable information. Spodek suggested that the choice of programs should be evaluated carefully in order to find one based on values congruent with the values of the school and the teachers who will use it. He gave examples of two checklists, one for selecting reading programs and one for selecting social science programs, that can be used by teachers for comparative purposes. This type of program evaluation is done before the program is even tried out by a particular center or school. Once the program is chosen the teacher then can find out if it really works in practice. Through classroom observation it can be discovered whether or not the program is being implemented as designed. Spodek used Jones's (n.d.) classroom dimensions evaluation as an example of a tool teachers themselves can use. Another tool he suggested is a checklist of activities provided in the classroom which teachers can use for self evaluation. He offered one way that a single teacher might evaluate the interaction that took place. Self-analysis could be done by writing down a summary of some aspect of the day and studying what happened and what might be done in the way of improvement. In this way, the teacher can assess both the potential benefit to the child and the degree to which the child actually benefits from instruction. Not only can teachers expand their methodological repertoire but also evaluate at different levels of program impact. Very broad general assessments might be made at one level, such as whether or not children and staff are smiling and happy, whether or not parents are involved, or if comprehensive services are being used. Gradually evaluators could work down to more precise and detailed measurement as they search for that which makes a difference in programming quality for children.

PRACTICAL ASPECTS OF EVALUATION

The Audience

Evaluations produce reports, some oral, most written. The audience is the logical first consideration of any evaluator. The audience determines how or if the evaluation results will be used (Bracht, 1975). A recent American Educational Research Association (AERA) symposium on the impact of evaluations clearly illustrated this point (Granville et al., 1978). In introducing the participants, Raizen, of the National Institute of Education, directed the listeners' focus to the recurring theme of audience problems. The symposium participants, all researchers from High/Scope Educational Research Foundation, discussed rather typical, but frequently unanticipated problems in presenting evaluation information to multiple audiences with divergent information needs, differing levels of theoretical or professional sophistication, and distinct and potentially competing value preferences.

Many evaluations are commissioned, making the commissioner, usually the funding source, the primary audience. The values theme discussed earlier is relevant here. Whereas some value positions are explicit and easy for the evaluator to respond to, frequently there are latent decision criteria (Granville et al., 1978). Strong concerns and questions in the minds of the commissioners which are not always made public frequently make it difficult for the evaluator to be responsive to the audience.

The audience issue is clearly a question of both power politics and personal values. If the evaluators expect their information to be useful, they must accommodate their reporting style to the appropriate level of sophistication, technical expertise, and reading ability of their audience. When more than one audience is intended, the High/Scope researchers suggested multiple or alternative reporting formats, exemplified by their efforts on the Home Start study final report for the contracting officers (Love et al., 1976) and the manuscript for parents and educators (Hewett et al., 1978).

Sources of Direction

Purpose is a strong controlling factor in evaluations. Anderson and Ball (1978) listed six typical purposes for evaluations, making contributions to: (1) decisions about program installation, (2) expansion or certification, (3) program modification, (4) evidence of support or (5) opposition evidence, (6) understanding the psychological process. The first two purposes can be considered diagnostic or *descriptive* evaluation, including front-end analysis (Datta, 1978), needs-assessment, and conceptual framework evaluation. Purpose 6 also falls in the descriptive category at a deeper level. Purpose 3 is the popular notion of *formative* evaluation (Scriven, 1967), feedback of evaluation data for quality improvement. Purposes 4 and 5 are similar to *summative* evaluation, Scriven's notion of post-treatment judgment of outcomes. Assembling evaluative data for support or opposition to a program is typically summative in nature. It can also involve the *comparative* evaluation approach, using the traditional alternative treatments or alternative products assessment. Purpose ties closely to conceptual framework and influences the choice of evaluation model, research design, and criterion measures. Ambron (1977) and Day (1977) discuss recent examples of different purposes in evaluations of early childhood programs and the application of these purposes (formative, summative) to the evaluations. Several authors cautioned against premature summative evaluation in developing or recently implemented programs (Rivlin et al., 1975; Ball, 1975). Bracht (1975) and Weikart & Banet (1975) provided suggestions for stages of evaluations including pilot studies, implementation assessment, formative evaluation, and summative or comparative evaluation in true field experiments.

The issue of time span also directs the evaluation. One of the strengths of the early childhood model programs developed in the 1960s has been the longitudinal nature of the evaluations. The consortium on Developmental Continuity (Lazar et al., 1977) has summarized data from fourteen follow-up evaluations of compensatory preschool programs. There are persistent positive effects on achievement, and some unanticipated positive consequences such as less special education placement and retention. Although relatively few evaluations of early childhood programs are designed to continue into the elementary years, some conception of short- and long-term developmental change ought to interact with the primary purposes of the evaluation, and guide the information gathering process (e.g., without certain baseline and treatment process data, the consortium's summary analyses would not have been possible).

Most evaluations of preschool programs have not aimed and probably could not aim at broad generalizability. However, there is usually a concern for breadth, some balance of children in various blocks of status characteristics (age, sex, ethnic background, etc.). This problem becomes increasingly complex in large-scale evaluations of federal programs. There is an unfortunate trade-off: As breadth increases, the quality and utility of the information decreases. As Kennedy (1978b) notes, "Past evaluations have tended to emphasize breadth more than depth, but a common result has been descriptions of status that lack insight into the reasons for the status" (p. 30). Concerns about breadth ought to be subordinated to concerns about the usefulness of certain in-depth information which matches the evaluation purposes.

Evaluation Models and Research Designs

In the past decade, several well-developed, conceptual models of educational evaluation have been presented. Popham's *Educational Evaluation* (1975) and Worthen and Sanders's *Educational Evaluation: Theory and Practice* (1973) are standard references on these evaluation models. Popham classifies these current conceptual models as goal-attainment models, judgment models, or decision-facilitation models. The standard notion of behavioral objectives, prespecified goals, and evaluative criteria, falls under goal attainment. Scriven's work on formative, summative, and comparative evaluation (1967) is a judgment model. Stufflebeam's (1968) context-input-process-product model is designed for facilitating decisions. Refer to these texts for extensive treatments of these models.

There are some other standard evaluation models which might have particular applicability to early childhood programs. Stake's (1967) *countenance model* focuses on description and judgment. The evaluator attempts to fill a matrix of information categories, including the program rationale, the intents, observations, standards, and judgments of the antecedents, transactions, and outcomes of the program. Through this data collection, the evaluator comes to see the countenance (face) of the program, in order to judge its worth. Scriven's later work (1974, 1976) set aside the comparative emphasis and focused on intensive observation. This *modus operandi* model requires the evaluator to look for outcomes, generate a list of probable causes, identify the presence of causes, and look for complete causal chains. Scriven's goal free evaluation model has the evaluator, without knowledge of program intentions, looking for any and all possible consequences, positive or negative, intended or unintended, in order to assess program effects in an unbiased fashion. Provus' (1971) discrepancy evaluation model is a constant comparative model used for decision making. The developer/evaluator defines standards for some aspect of the program. Performance is assessed. If there is a discrepancy, either the program or the standard is modified. Performance is again assessed. This model works by internal comparisons and feedback. It can be applied to individual children or to a single experimental group, without comparison children, as long as there are normative standards or ways in which to estimate expected and desired performance (e.g., Strenio, Bryk, & Weisberg, 1977).

Researchers at RMC Research Corporation have developed combination evaluation model/research design guidebooks for use in local Title I evaluations (Horst et al., 1975). These guidebooks address typical problems of evaluation of intact groups, with nonequivalent controls, or no possible comparison groups. Current efforts at the Huron Institute may produce similar guidelines and model applications for early education programs. This work is attempting to reconcile evaluation theory, constraints of research design, and practical concerns of early educators.

For the most part, the evaluation models discussed here do not force the choice of a particular research design. Is a true experimental design necessary or possible? Perhaps. But there is a continuing debate about the necessity or feasibility of true, random experiments in evaluation (Bennett & Lumsdaine, 1975). The strongest reasons for a true experimental design, with random assignment to treatment and control groups, is to control for sources of bias which might systematically invalidate the results of the evaluation, and to promote the generalizability of the findings. National evaluations are particularly susceptible to those problems. But, in a local evaluation, it may be possible to intensively observe process in such a way as to rule out other competing causes of effects. And, specificity for a particular program and/or group, rather than broad generalizability, might be more desirable and appropriate.

Campbell and Stanley's (1966) book has been used as the standard work on research design flaws and alternatives focusing on threats to internal and external validity. But, depending on purpose and choice of evaluation model, the early childhood educator might opt for "soft" evaluation (Ball, 1975), discrepancy evaluation, or the detective-like approach of the *modus operandi* method. The evaluator or program administrator should consider information needs, focus, audience, and purpose when selecting an evaluation model and choosing a complimentary research design which will answer useful questions. In a revision of the earlier work on experimental and quasi-experimental designs, Cook and Campbell (1976) introduce the important new notion of conclusion validity, which focuses on the probable causal interpretation one can derive from data collection and analysis. Perhaps if the descriptive, conceptual, and process information are complete, and expected impacts are clearly identified, then appropriate and acceptable conclusions might be drawn from evaluations, despite threats to internal validity created by the lack of a true experimental design.

The Conceptual Framework

The working conception of the program ought to be the most valuable information available to the evaluator. Unfortunately, conceptual frameworks are frequently elusive. The evaluator needs to ask the program developer about the notions which form the basis for the program's expected benefits and outcomes and the conduct of daily interaction. These notions may be goals, behavioral objectives in a skills-oriented program, or less specific concepts, such as the development of choice and responsibility or the enhancement of positive learning attitudes.

Historically, psychological theory has been a major source for the formulation of conceptual frameworks for early education. For example, adaptations based on a learning theory approach have been made by Bushell (1973) directly and by Bereiter-Engelmann-Becker (Bereiter & Engelmann, 1973) indirectly. Bushell and his associates have developed their approach from operant conditioning theory. The B-E-B approach is congruent with reinforcement theory in that small increments in learning are used and immediate reward in terms of praise and accomplishment is given to each child. Kamii & DeVries (1977) have also inspired educational program design. The High/Scope Cognitively Oriented Curriculum (Hohman et al., 1978) and the Kamii & DeVries (1977) approaches are conceptualized using Piagetian theory, although the interpretations are quite different in practice. Biber (1977) described a program with its conceptual roots lodged in psychoanalytic and Gestalt psychology. Stallings (1975) presented examples of classroom interaction patterns which clearly indicate the influence of these conceptual frameworks on the actions and interactions in a typical program day.

Another way of developing a conceptual framework has come from the work of Cronbach and Snow (1977) concerning attribute/treatment interactions. From this point of view, the individual learner and his or her characteristics are considered as they interact with the learning environment and its characteristics. For example, one might ask: What are the characteristics of children who flourish in different types of program models, or what are the characteristics of program models in which certain types of children flourish? This is an empirical approach where the conception of appropriate program match to students is developed through naturalistic and experimental research, not from a prior notion. An example of this approach in Early Childhood Education can be seen in the ETS Longitudinal Study (Shipman, 1976). Shipman took subsamples of children who had specific characteristics and traced their progress through six years of participation in the study. Of particular interest was the phenomenon of children who, though predicted to do well, did poorly; and conversely, those who were predicted to do poorly did well. By following the experiences of these children individually through six years of study, Shipman was able to identify factors in the environment which seemed to play a strong role in the child's eventual success in school, interacting with the capabilities indicated by first year measures. Another example is a study done in the fourth grade of the Montgomery County Maryland Schools (Solomon & Kendall, 1976). With 50 classrooms, and approximately 1,300 students, these researchers attempted to tease out the complex relationships between patterns of student academic and personality characteristics and clusters of teachers/classrooms which were more or less open, more or less warm, more or less structured, etc. The study, while not a typical evaluation, provided evidence for rethinking the match of child to program. In a book on diagnostic-prescriptive teaching, Levin (1976) presented clear and usable models for adapting instruction to student characteristics. Levin's step-by-step models could be used successfully as evaluation guides for observational study and reformulation of a conception of the program.

A third approach to specifying a conceptual framework can simply be called the logical approach. Whimbey's (1975) cognitive therapy is an example. He analyzed the operations necessary for solving IQ-type test problems by listening to high scorers solving problems orally. Then, he logically reasoned that one could teach those steps orally to low scorers. The program conception, teaching technique, and assessment device were linked. In this approach, evaluation is part of the process. Similarly, on a more sophisticated level Browne et al. (1978) described the evaluation of critical thinking skills in college students. The terminal performance, logical analysis of two opposing viewpoints, became their rubric, serving in three capacities, as criteria for evaluating the terminal performance, as the teaching document (a description of the process of the classroom activities), and as the conceptual framework or rationale for the course. This methodology for conceptual frameworks is ultimately very tight. An attempt to develop this form of conceptual framework for young children has been made by Anderson and Messick (1974), who outlined 29 areas of expected and desired social competence in young children. Although the areas were not sufficiently specific (e.g., "control of attention . . . role perception and appreciation"), their thinking did provide a logical base for evaluators of Project Developmental Continuity (Love et al., 1975) to refine competencies (e.g., "recognition of feelings in self and others" . . . "social situation problem solving") and guided the choice of outcome and process measures.

Product (or Impact) versus the Process

Typically, early childhood evaluations have been impact studies, focusing on summative evaluation using school readiness and/or achievement measures. It has been appropriate to some extent, since programs have promised benefits for children at the end of the program. Lack of specificity of products or impacts has been a problem. An extended view of evaluation would suggest that goal-setting, derived from program descriptions and a logically developed conceptual framework, ought to be in the form of expected outcomes. If a program emphasizes interpersonal skills, impact evaluation should be specifically looking for, or assessing evidence of, post-treatment presence of those skills. A serious and common example of an outcome problem is the use of IQ tests as an evaluation device. Zigler (1978) suggests that: ". . . we must repudiate forever the view that higher IQ scores and their close correlate, elementary school grades, are the ultimate goals of the Head Start effort" (p. 6). It is surprising that such a statement is necessary. IQ tests were developed as arbitrarily stable measures, not intended to be useful for analyzing change. There is considerable skepticism about increased IQ scores since such altered scores might no longer hold a strong relationship to school achievement. But, beyond those criticisms, it is difficult to imagine any logical or psychological conceptual framework in a program for young children which would predict, as its primary expected outcome, increase in IQ scores. IQ tests might tap transfer of training from programs emphasizing cognitive skills such as relational concepts or sequential problem solving. But IQ tests measure a higher level goal, laudable but speculative. Too frequently, the specific program-related expected impacts have gone unmeasured. Impact evaluation should start from a list of sensibly expected outcomes.

Future evaluations of early childhood programs focusing solely on outcomes or impacts will be relatively useless. Without concurrent evaluation of the level of implementation or the process of the program in action, it will be impossible to determine what caused any outcomes (Bryk, 1978). Take the case of a project adopting a new curriculum model. Even if the expected outcomes and their measurement link to the program's conception, even with a true experimental design and/or an adequate comparison group, unless the degree of implementation is known, one cannot know whether or not the program is actually operating. Outcome findings (positive or negative) might be attributable to the previously operating curriculum or other factors. The evaluation of Project Developmental Continuity is an attempt to address this problem (Love et al., 1978). A large portion of the evaluation budget, time, and effort in this demonstration study is being spent assessing the presence and development of continuity in educational focus and ancillary services for children, preschool through third grade.

Berk (1976) discussed a comparative, descriptive process study of several center-based early childhood programs. This study started from records of the kind and quality of typical daily service for children, including assessments of the influence of the setting and the complexity of student-teacher interaction. This study exemplified the ecological approach to evaluating early childhood programs (Smith et al., 1978).

Another ecological approach, inspired by the work of Roger Barker and his associates, is that taken by Prescott and Jones and their long, painstaking study of the day care environments provided for young children (Prescott & Jones, 1972; Prescott, 1973, 1978). They have developed observational methods which can be used to study the day care environment and to develop descriptions of the environment. Both adult and child behavior were observed and coded and equipment and space arrangements described and rated. Daily process was examined closely. Product was considered only in a speculative way as "healthy" development. These researchers assume that day care environments which included what they defined as positive characteristics would have positive effects on children. A positive environment was defined as one in which children exhibit many positive behaviors. It is assumed that certain types of adult behavior would support the child through the early stages of development. This approach to evaluation would be the antithesis of the traditional product type of approach in that only process is measured and impact was assumed to be positive on those who experienced the developmentally appropriate environment.

Transactional evaluation, intensive yet informal records of the give-and-take involved in any form of program development and evaluation, is another process alternative. Cicirelli (1973) offered ideas from this perspective on the early Head Start evaluation. The studies done by Joffre (1977) and by Provence et al. (1977) are examples of descriptions of process and outcomes using anecdotal and case study type materials. Each contains an in-depth description of transactions within two different early childhood settings. The descriptions are used as the basis for evaluation of the impact and efficacy of the programs. Many of the lessons learned from evaluating early childhood programs have depended on some sort of process information to support their interpretations (Granville et al., 1978).

This approach to evaluation is more expensive initially but pays off in the resulting value of the information obtained. As Hilliard (1978) notes:

> Unfortunately, we have restricted too much professional inquiry to a look at those things for which cheap instrumentation is available. My suspicion is that the kind of evaluation procedures that will yield meaningful information are likely to be labor intensive. The biggest problem is to convince funding agencies to spend resources on something other than the "quick and dirty" in evaluation instruments. However, the rewards will certainly be worth it (p. 13).

This comment leads us logically to a consideration of the choice of criterion measures.

Criterion Measures

The goal of measures or instruments should tie very closely to the goals articulated in the program rationale and description and the expected outcomes derived from the conceptual framework. This might appear to be a return to earlier views of evaluation (e.g., behavioral objectives), but this advice seems justified after a decade of IQ criterion studies. In contrast to the difficulties attached to other late 1960s evaluations, Ball (1975; Anderson and Ball, 1978) noted that the evaluation of Sesame Street and Electric Company were successful partly because actual program goals, well-defined skills, were used as criterion measures. It is also quite possible that the reported successes in certain areas on the Follow Through test battery by the "basic skills" program models were largely a function of the matching of test with program conception and process (Bryk, 1978). In her reinterpretation of that evaluation, Kennedy (1978a) provides additional evidence for this position. Although in the High/Scope model, the Cognitive Curriculum emphasizes productive language, this area is not reflected as a substantial positive impact by the language and reading test results of the national Follow Through test battery. However, Kennedy noted, assessment by the sponsor-developed PLAT (Productive Language Assessment Tasks), a measure which matches the model's conceptual framework, demonstrated identifiable impacts in the language area for certain sites employing this program model.

The concept of criterion-referenced testing is relevant to early childhood evaluations. Although norm-referenced tests are readily available and have been frequently adopted, they often fail to test outcomes of primary interest. Further, norm-referenced tests might or might not be sensitive to program related change during the preschool time period.

Normed typically on a cross-sectional sample of ages, their standardized scores can potentially adjust away program-related differences.

According to Millman (1974), the current notion of criterion-referenced testing refers to specific task performance by a student where the interpretation of the score does not depend on reference to the performance of others. Millman noted that two different forms of criterion-referenced tests, the domain-referenced test, and the criterion-referenced differential assessment device, might be useful in educational evaluations. (The interested reader will find Millman's chapter a complete and readable discussion of these concepts.)

In order to assess implementation, program operation, or to investigate the link between conceptual framework and observed outcomes, some process measures are necessary and appropriate. Classroom observation techniques have been developed with increasing sophistication (e.g., Stallings, 1977a). In spite of the complex problems of validity in process measurement, such measures continue to hold promise for early childhood evaluation. Some positive aspects of the process measures include construct validity for an instrument and internal validity for the research design. For example, classroom observation in the Follow Through evaluation (Stallings, 1975) identified positive links between time spent on reading or math activities, drill and praise, and student achievement. The instrument categories grew out of both sponsor concerns and program conceptions. Differences in program model intentions were captured in action (e.g., children in certain cognitively oriented Follow Through programs asked more in-class questions than non-Follow Through children).

Hindsight is a dreadful excuse in early childhood evaluation. Bronfenbrenner (1975) in his review of early intervention programs, cites several examples of programs which may have altered parents' perception of their role in their child's education. He discussed anecdotal evidence and program directors' interpretation in this direction. Unfortunately, those evaluations did not formally measure those perceptions, before, during, or after. This is not to discount the utility of anecdotal information, but to emphasize the need for a broadened measurement perspective which might capture supporting information.

Often, conclusions are reached regarding gains in academic achievement, substantiated by empirical data, followed by some exciting informal findings which may be equally, if not more valuable. The following is a positive example:

> . . . it was noted that since the beginning of the project, less than 1% of the teaching staff requested transfer as compared to the average request before onset of the PEP-IPI in the same school of 20% of the staff. Another subjective impression of

teacher satisfaction was the effort and organization of the staff at duplicating as much of the PEP-IPI treatment as possible without special funding or administrative direction. Finally, and perhaps most significantly, parent approval of the project and parent change as a result of the project were evidenced from two observations. Parent attendance at school-community functions increased dramatically and successful organization of Follow Through parent groups became a reality (Fesler et al., 1976, p. 184)

Other valuable but not usually obtained information would be data regarding changes in family support from public funds to employment or increase in educational level by parents through obtaining high school equivalency diplomas and through post secondary educational programs. A positive attempt in examining family variables has been made by Shipman and her colleagues (Shipman et al., 1976).

Careful front-end analysis will be crucial in future early childhood evaluation (see Anderson et al., 1978; Datta, 1978). Some measurement scheme should be chosen for all important potentially expected outcomes. Home teaching programs are an illustrative case. If the program will deal with mothers and their children, separately and together in the home, some criterion measures, process or outcome, ought to be included for mothers, children, and their interaction. In the Ypsilanti–Carnegie Infant Education Project, a *Language Scale* and the *Bayley Scales* were used with children at age two. A concurrent *Verbal Interaction Record* of a mother-teaching-child session was also included. In the longitudinal follow-up evaluation (Epstein, 1978), in addition to child ability and achievement measures, a complex mother-child interaction task has been developed, the Mutual Problem Solving Task (Epstein et al., 1977). This instrument is an interaction observation system attached to a cookie-baking session with mother and child. It is an outcome measure which allows the evaluators to trace predictions from the program's conceptual framework and earlier process assessments.

Even with extensive front-end analysis, it is still possible to fail to measure or to evaluate important outcomes. Scriven (1974, 1976) advanced the notion of goal-free evaluation. As a supplement to goal-based evaluation he suggested that an external evaluator with no knowledge of the program description or conception be brought in to observe any and all outcomes, positive or negative. Scriven assumed that this might be used to control for bias and self-fulfilling prophecies, and potentially to capture unintended positive outcomes. Within the context of expected outcomes and criterion measures chosen in advance, there is another possibility for expanding the evaluation to net valuable information. McClelland (1973) made the distinction between respondent and operant samples of behavior in measurement situations. Respondent tests are typically objective-type, closed-ended, potentially complex but narrowly defined. Reading comprehension and IQ tests are examples. Operant tests are assessments of competence requiring the student to produce or generate the specifics and structure of the performance. A driving test might be an example. Both the Productive Language Assessment Tasks and the Mutual Problem Solving Task are operant behavior samples. A final examination in a critical thinking course which asks the students to analyze and evaluate the relative merits of opposing viewpoints on a social controversy is an operant test (Browne et al., 1978). Although the expected outcome criteria are specified, there are expanded possibilities for learning more about the effectiveness of the program or the underlying developmental processes.

The selection of criteria and the obtaining of instruments to acquire the needed raw data is, of course, critical to the evaluation process. Resource guides are available (e.g., Johnson & Bommarito, 1971; Walker, 1973) but decision making is not easy. The evaluator must look at not only the goals, objectives, and processes which must be measured but also at the practical resources available in terms of money and training level of personnel. Some measures are designed to be used by highly trained measurement experts only, while others are designed to be used by teachers, and still others by parents or other non-professionals. Some instruments require long, intensive training periods before they can be used and others are simple and straightforward and require little prior practice. In this chapter we will present just a few examples in order to give the reader a more specific idea regarding the types of resources available. Resources for observational systems, checklists, child performance objectives with related interview tasks, adult competencies, questionnaires, and for developmental research will be discussed.

Many types of observational systems are available for data collection (e.g., Boyer, Simon & Karafin, 1974; Irwin & Bushnell in press; Prescott, 1973; Stallings, 1977a; Montes & Risley, 1975). They may involve structured time or event samplings and simple or complex coding systems. They may involve collection of anecdotal material or frequency counts. Observation systems have been developed to look for behaviors of competent adults such as those devised for the Child Development Consortium assessment system (Washington, 1975; Ward, 1976) and for competent children and parents such as the Harvard Preschool project research (Carew, 1975; Carew et al., 1976; White et al., 1973; White et al., 1978). Checklists are available and useful. Most often they call for a decision on the presence or absence of some criteria. Checklists may list criteria for use in any early childhood setting (Mattick & Perkins, 1973; Prescott, 1973; Smith & Giesy, 1972) or in specific ones such as a day care home (*Evaluating Home,* 1971) a home visit setting (Gordon et al., 1977) or for infant caregivers (Honig & Lally, 1975). In other instances criteria are listed which may be developed into a checklist or observational system. Current examples include a list of competencies for teachers of Chicano preschool children (Castillo & Cruz, 1974); a list of criteria for an open type classroom (Marshall, 1972); criteria for infant day care (Jacobson, 1978) and for early childhood environments (Kritchevsky et al., 1969). Very useful evaluational resources, especially for teachers, are lists of developmentally sequenced objectives with accompanying assessment tasks and activities for developing the child's competencies (Charlesworth & Radeloff, 1978; Schirmer, 1976). Questionnaires might provide valuable data, especially on family and environmental variables (e.g., Shipman et al., 1976). Developmental research can offer clues to areas for data collection. In evaluating an infant-toddler program the evaluator might get some good ideas by looking at current research on infant and toddler social behavior (Moore, 1978). The evaluator should be carefully guided by outcome expectations derived from the conceptual framework in selecting measurement devices. Otherwise, the available variety of resources can soon become overpowering and the task will become unmanageable. The evaluator has a responsibility to become acquainted with some of the past efforts at evaluation and give them a critical look before plunging in. Well known studies were done by Caldwell and her colleagues (Caldwell & Richmond, 1968; Caldwell et al., 1970; Schwartz et al., 1973) and by Keister (1970); Keyserling (1972); Miller and Dyer (1975); Robinson & Robinson (1971); and Stallings (1975).

Developmental Issues

In this section, the authors are capitalizing on the multiple meanings of the word "developmental." Early childhood educators are intensely concerned with the developmental processes of preschool-aged children. Early childhood program evaluators are becoming increasingly concerned with methodology which might enable them to capture and describe these developmental processes in the context of their evaluation studies. In addition, both groups are seeking strategies of evaluation which are developmental in the sense of improving the quality of both program operation and useful evaluative information.

There are still gaps in the existing knowledge of child development. What is normal or typical development for the young child at the time of or just prior to entering school? How does educational experience at this time interact with normal maturation? This lack of knowledge is problematic, particularly for evaluators of early childhood compensatory education programs. What are the standards, in terms of outcomes or growth rates, against which such programs should be compared? In many ways, the most informative and useful evaluations in the next few years will be those which focus on typical day care and preschool programs serving middle class or mainstream children (e.g., Kagan et al., 1977). If studies are appropriately designed to reveal information about the normal developmental process, outcomes and along-the-line interactions with instruction, they might provide the basis for deriving expectations about the socially competent preschool-aged child. The authors also recognize and applaud alternative conceptions of child development in a multicultural context. The recent work of the National Black Child Development Institute (Coleman, 1977) provides some direction for studies of normal developmental processes from a differing perspective which might be equally informative for standard setting and outcome expectations.

Sigel (1975) noted certain peculiar measurement problems for early childhood evaluators. Most tests, meeting the traditional psychometric properties of reliability and validity, have not been developed to confront a measurement situation where the particular characteristic and indicators of that characteristic are constantly changing. Rather than focusing on normative measurement, he urged an ipsative analysis strategy. A useful, individually focused approach based on a changing growth model of children's development has been proposed by researchers at Huron Institute (Bryk & Weisberg, 1977; Strenio et al., 1977). *Value-added analysis* allows the evaluator to make predictions about individual growth rates, taking into account empirical relationships among the criterion measure and background characteristics in pretest or cross-sectional data. Predictions or expectations for individuals or groups can be estimated, and the value added by the educational program can be determined. This strategy might be coupled with Provus' discrepancy evaluation model (1971), potentially eliminating the need for a comparison group.

Recent writing on formative evaluation (Baker, 1978; Sanders & Cunningham, 1974) has emphasized the flexibility and multilevel potential of this conception. These writers, along with Bryk (1978) urged careful planning and choice of evaluation methodologies which might capture the information needed at highly specific points in the development, implementation, and refinement of an educational program. The development of evaluative strategies can interact with the development of the program and the children's developmental processes. In such uses, evaluation becomes a clarifying rather than a judgmental process. Kennedy (1978b) described the rich complexity of such developmental evaluation activities in explaining the multi-purpose, multi-faceted, multiple strategy evaluation plan for public law 94-142, the Education of All Handicapped Children. Her report detailed extensive feedback and interaction as evaluations and educational agencies begin to realize the intent of this new federal legislation.

Most broadly, evaluation can be seen as a means for the generation of new knowledge. Hodges and Sheehan (1978) noted a number of useful areas where the planned variation evaluations have expanded useful information. New data on such issues as structure in educational programming, staff training, quality, and efficiency, parental involvement, and the impact of educational philosophies in practice, have been accumulated. Most important, new hypotheses have been generated about the direction of effects of educational models, and important variables which might facilitate those effects. In this light, if we return again to the criticisms of the Follow Through evaluation, primarily those unanswered questions, we see that such an evaluation has done an important service in alerting us to more appropriate and potentially more useful questions.

SUMMARY AND CONCLUSIONS

Future Directions

In our discussion of the theoretical issues and practical aspects of evaluation relating to early childhood education programs, we have been primarily concerned with describing the state-of-the-art in evaluation, and suggesting our notions of future directions for early educators. To summarize, we are compelled to become prescriptive on several major points. Professionally and politically, early childhood education cannot afford another eleventh-hour national evaluation of preschool programs which relies on child impact data as the sole criteria for determining program quality. Useful information will not be produced in evaluations where the conceptual framework of the program developers and evaluators is not clearly specified prior to the evaluation. Attempts to confirm the effectiveness of one programmatic approach over another in tone or quasi-experiments are again likely to produce the same equivocal results reported in the Follow Through evaluation, until the prerequisite exploratory studies of currently operating programs are completed.

Cooley (1978) described the current state of affairs. Early childhood educators are seeking to explain how quality programs might bring about, that is, *cause* benefits in the academic and social development areas for young children. As researchers, we have been schooled in the experimental paradigms of science. But, as Cooley noted:

> . . . most of what is known about people and the universe has not been based on experimentation, but on observation. If we are to further our understanding of educational processes, and do so in a way that will allow us to *improve those processes* (italics mine), it is essential that we give more attention to developing methods for conducting explanatory observational studies. (p. 9)

Cooley's term, "explanatory observational studies," corresponds to our notion of descriptive evaluations, or evaluations where the primary purpose is the articulation of the underlying psychological processes, and the exploration of the relationships between process interactions, and expected outcomes. He notes that, although much has been learned from the Follow Through evaluation,

> it illustrates a tendency in education to move prematurely into intervention-type, quasi-experiments before the relationships are established among the major variables currently operating in a particular causal network. Confident descriptions of such networks *prior* to the implementation of quasi-experiments are necessary if we hope to be able to generalize from such manipulations (p. 10–11).

We support Cooley's contention that a carefully specified theoretical model is crucial for useful informative evaluations. Summarizing what is known about the subject area—in this case, child development and early education—enables the evaluator to establish priorities and measure the appropriate independent and dependent variables, and to reflect on, and account for, alternative explanations of developmental phenomena, with or without the trappings of traditional experimental design. At this point, we are and ought to be, in Cooley's terms, in the *exploratory* rather than the *confirmatory* stage of investigation. Statistical methodology is available for exploratory data analysis (e.g., Kennedy, 1978a). It is our reluctance to reflect upon, and intensively commit ourselves to process evaluations in one setting or one program that hinders our advances in determining program effectiveness and improving program quality.

With these considerations in mind, we propose a framework for a local evaluation to be used by a program developer:

1. Develop a conceptual framework for the program and the evaluation. Specify expected outcomes and necessary teacher-student process activities.
2. Select from available program approaches those which best fit the conceptual framework.
3. Develop and specify the program objectives and the program description.
4. Choose pretest process and outcome measures which are congruent with the conceptual framework, operationalized objectives, and notions of daily interaction.
5. Choose an evaluation model, research design, and data analyses strategy which will allow for capturing all potentially useful information, keeping in mind the information needs of the intended audiences.
6. Monitor (measure) the implementation and formative development of the program. Analyze and summarize these data for possible use by decision makers (program continuation/termination).

7. Collect and analyze impact data. Evaluate the program, relating process and outcome data to the conceptual framework.
8. Prepare reports in a style and manner appropriate for the intended audiences. Relate what has been discovered to that which was previously known.

The program developer might plug into the sequence at a later, more appropriate stage. However, in our view, no later entrance point is appropriate if the conceptual framework has not been developed.

A final recurring theme of this chapter has been measurement considerations. IQ tests and other typically available standardized instruments might be quite inappropriate considering the program's conceptual framework. It is unlikely that the best expectation predicted by the program developer's conception is a minor alteration in relative scoring on a single test of school-related ability.

Regarding outcomes of program quality, it makes sense to recognize that a person is not valued for a high IQ score, but for the ability to solve problems in a variety of contexts and settings. Evaluators should measure valued and expected process and outcome variables for young children, that is, actual ongoing daily interaction and demonstrations of child competence in single or multiple contexts.

Research Needed

Authors typically use this section to note gaps in existing knowledge and offer research paradigm suggestions. We have mentioned the serious hole in our understanding of the interaction of normal child development and preschool instruction. However, we will not list more of such specific areas nor offer restrictive research design considerations.

Instead, we propose a learning-from-evaluations gap, a need for more well-planned evaluations, at all levels, of all forms of early education programs. The Center for Research on the Utilization of Scientific Knowledge (CRUSK) at the Institute for Social Research, University of Michigan, can serve as an example. CRUSK operates as a contract research shop for, among other things, surveys, organizational development, and program evaluations. While doing an evaluation for a client, the CRUSK evaluators are gathering their primary purpose information about models and research designs in evaluation, underlying psychological processes in the program and the evaluation, and decision making and other information utilization in the client organization. Similarly, early childhood education needs more, expanded evaluations by evaluators curious about these potentially rich sources of data.

Within the context of national evaluations, evaluators could go beyond the current efforts on alternative data analysis strategies to a comparison of evaluation models and parallel research designs. The focus would move away from "best comparative method" or the most effective treatment to an estimation of the most generally informative evaluation methodology.

Quality

Evaluations do not directly define the meaning of quality within the context of a program. However, there is a strong link between the process of evaluation and the presence of quality in an early childhood program. The link is values. An expanded view of evaluation requires explicitly stated value preferences in the form of conceptual frameworks and expected outcomes. Formative evaluation and interaction process assessment encourage monitoring and improvement of quality, essentially realigning the program with the developer's values. Summative and comparative evaluations allow for public appraisal of quality. A well executed evaluation provides the appropriate information for others, beyond the program staff to determine the quality and value of the program.

With the growing implementation of PL 94-142 (Abeson & Zettel, 1977) at the state and local level, evaluation will be increasingly mandated and will most likely involve parents, teachers, and specialized personnel (such as school psychologists, speech and language therapists, physical therapists, nurses and physicians) as well as the traditional professional evaluators. Evaluation can be put in a context that can be understood and implemented by all of the people involved in the educational milieu of the young child. An evaluation addressing questions of daily process, involving a clearly developed conceptual framework and program description, and a number of different criterion measures which cover the scope of intended, expected, or possible impacts, can communicate valuable information to each of these program participants. The Home Start evaluation study (Love et al., 1978) is an excellent final example. The evaluation was planned in conjunction with the program. Case studies of the home visit process were conducted concurrently with the impact study. The interim reports in the study were influential as formative evaluation guides, assisting in refocusing the program operation and specifying future guidelines (Granville et al., 1978). Perhaps the most telling indication of the broad potential impact of this evaluation on the quality of early education is the current strong demand from practitioners for copies of the final report and a book about the Home Start process (Hewett et al., 1978).

FOOTNOTES

1. Shipman, V. *ETS Head Start longitudinal study.* Paper presented at the Minnesota Roundtable V, Minneapolis, May 1978.
2. Yurchak, M. J. Personal communication. Huron Institute, June 1978.

REFERENCES

Abbott, G., Granger, R. C., & Klein, B. L. *Alternative approaches to educating young children.* Atlanta: Humanics Press, 1976.

Abeson, A., & Zeffel, J. The end of the quiet revolution: The Education of All Handicapped Children Act of 1975. *Exceptional Children,* 1977, *44,* 115–128.

Ambron, S. R. A comparison of infant and parent education programs. In M. C. Day & R. K. Parker (Eds.), *The preschool in action* (2nd ed.). Boston: Allyn & Bacon, 1977.

Anderson, R. B., St. Pierre, R. G., Proper, E. C., & Stebbins, L. B. Pardon us, but what was the question again?: A response to the critique of the Follow Through evaluation. *Harvard Educational Review,* 1978, *48,* 161–170.

Anderson, S. B., & Ball, S. (Eds.). *The profession and practice of program evaluation.* San Francisco: Jossey-Bass, 1978.

Anderson, S. B., & Messick, S. Social competency in young children. *Developmental Psychology,* 1974, *10,* 282–293.

Baker, E. L. Evaluation dimensions for program development improvement. *New Directions in Program Evaluation,* 1978, *1,* 59–73.

Ball, S. Problems in evaluating early education programs. In R. A. Weinberg & S. Moore (Eds.), *Evaluation of educational programs for young children.* Washington, D.C.: Child Development Associate Consortium, 1975.

Becker, W. C. Teaching reading and language to the disadvantaged. *Harvard Educational Review,* 1977, *47,* 518–544.

Bennett, C. A., & Lumsdaine, A. A. (Eds.). *Evaluation and experiment.* New York: Academic Press, 1975.

Bereiter, C., & Engelmann, S. Observations on the use of direct instruction with young disadvantaged children. In B. Spodek (Ed.), *Early childhood education.* Englewood Cliffs, N.J.: Prentice-Hall, 1973.

Berk, L. E. How well do classroom practices reflect teacher goals? *Young Children,* 1976, *32*(1), 64–81.

Biber, B. A developmental-interaction approach: Bank Street College of Education. In M. C. Day & R. K. Parker (Eds.), *The preschool in action* (2nd ed.). Boston: Allyn & Bacon, 1977.

Bond, J. T. Research report: The Productive Language Assessment Tasks. *Bulletin of the High/Scope Educational Research Foundation,* Winter 1976, 1–8.

Borich, G. D. *The appraisal of teaching: concepts and process.* Reading, Ma.: Addison-Wesley, 1977.

Boyer, E. G., Simon, A., & Karafin, G. R. (Eds.). *Measures of maturation* (3 vols.). Philadelphia, Pa.: Research for Better Schools, 1974.

Bracht, G. H. Planning evaluation studies. In R. A. Weinberg & S. Moore (Eds.), *Evaluation of educational programs for young children.* Washington, D.C.: Child Development Associate Consortium, 1975.

Bronfenbrenner, U. Is early intervention effective? In M. Guttentag & E. L. Struening (Eds.), *Handbook of evaluation research* (Vol. 2). Beverly Hills, Ca.: Sage Publications, 1975.

Browne, M. N., Haas, P. F., & Keeley, S. Measuring critical thinking skills in college. *Educational Forum,* 1978, *42,* 219–226.

Bryk, A. S. Evaluating program impact: A time to cast stones away, a time to gather stones together. *New Directions in Program Evaluation,* 1978, *1,* 31–59.

Bryk, A. S., & Weisberg, H. I. Value-added analysis: A dynamic approach to the estimation of treatment effects. *Journal of Educational Statistics,* 1976, *1,* 127–155.

Bryk, A. S., & Weisberg, H. I. Use of the nonequivalent control group design when subjects are growing. *Psychological Bulletin,* 1977, *84,* 950–962.

Bushell, D., Jr. The behavior analysis classroom. In B. Spodek (Ed.), *Early childhood education*. Englewood Cliffs, N.J.: Prentice-Hall, 1973.

Caldwell, B. M., & Richmond, J. B. The Children's Center in Syracuse, New York. In L. L. Dittman (Ed.), *Early child care: The new perspectives*. New York: Atherton Press, 1968.

Caldwell, B. M., Wright, C. M., Honig, A. S., & Tannenbaum, J. Infant day care and attachment. *American Journal of Orthopsychiatry*, 1970, *40*, 397–412.

Campbell, D. T., & Stanley, J. C. *Experimental and quasi-experimental designs for research*. Chicago: Rand McNally, 1968.

Carew, J. Understanding intellectual experiences in young children. In R. A. Weinberg & S. G. Moore (Eds.), *Evaluation of educational programs for young children*. Washington, D.C.: Child Development Associate Consortium, 1975.

Carew, J., Chan, I., & Halfar, C. *Observing intelligence in young children*. Englewood Cliffs, N.J.: Prentice-Hall, 1976.

Castillo, N., & Cruz, J., Jr. Special competencies for teachers of pre-school Chicano children: Rationale, content and assessment process. *Young Children*, 1974, *34*, 341–347.

Charlesworth, R., & Radeloff, D. *Experiences in math for young children*. Albany, N.Y.: Delmar, 1978.

Cicirelli, V. G. Transactional evaluation in a national study of Head Start. In R. M. Rippey (Ed.), *Studies in transactional evaluation*. Berkeley, Ca.: McCutchan Publishing, 1973.

Coleman, M. (Ed.). *Black children just keep on growing*. Washington, D.C.: National Black Child Development Institute, 1977.

Cook, T. D., & Campbell, D. T. The design and conduct of quasi-experiments in field settings. In M. D. Dunnette and J. P. Campbell (Eds.), *Handbook of industrial and organizational research*. Chicago: Rand McNally, 1976.

Cooley, W. W. Explanatory observational studies. *Educational Researcher*, 1978, *7*, 9–15.

Cronbach, L. J., & Snow, R. E. *Aptitudes and instructional methods: A handbook for research on interactions*. New York: Irvington, 1977.

Datta, L. E. Front-end analysis: Pegasus or Shank's mare? *New Directions for Program Evaluation*, 1978, *1*, 13–30.

Day, M. C., & Parker, R. K. (Eds.). *The preschool in action* (2nd ed.). Boston: Allyn & Bacon, 1977.

Edwards, W., & Guttentag, M. Experiments and evaluation: A reexamination. In C. A. Bennett & A. A. Lumsdaine (Eds.), *Evaluation and experiment*. New York: Academic Press, 1975.

Emlen, A. C., Donoghue, B. A., & Clarkson, Q. D. *The stability of the family day care arrangement: a longitudinal study*. Corvallis, Ore.: Oregon State University, Continuing Education Publications, 1974.

Epstein, A. S. Parent-child interaction and children's learning. *High/Scope Educational Research Foundation Report 1978*. Ypsilanti, Mi.: High/Scope Educational Research Foundation, 1978.

Epstein, A. S., Schwartz, P., & Meece, J. *The Mutual Problem-Solving Task. Development, instrument procedures and reliability*. Ypsilanti, Mi.: High/Scope Educational Research Foundation, 1977.

Evaluating home day care mothers' work with young children. Seattle Community College, Washington, 1971. (ERIC Document Reproduction Service No. ED 055 104)

Fallon, B. J. *40 Innovative programs in early childhood education*. Belmont, Ca.: Lear Siegler/Fearon, 1973.

Fein, G. G., & Clarke-Stewart, A. *Day care in context*. New York: Wiley, 1973.

Fesler, D., Guidubaldi, J., & Kehle, T. J. Effects of follow through model: Primary Education Project—Individually Prescribed Instruction (PEP-IPI) on children's academic competence. *Psychology in the Schools*, 1976, *13*, 181–184.

Gearing, F., Hughes, W., Carroll, T., Precourt, W., & Smith, A. *On observing well: Self-instruction in ethnographic observation for teachers, principals, and supervisors.* Amherst, N.Y.: State University of New York at Buffalo, Center for Studies of Cultural Transmission, 1975.

Gordon, I. J., Ginagh, B., & Jester, R. E. The Florida Parent Education infant and toddler programs. In M. C. Day and R. K. Parker (Eds.), *The preschool in action* (2nd ed.). Boston: Allyn & Bacon, 1977.

Granville, A. C., Love, J. M., Matz, R. D., Schweinhart, L. J., & Smith, A. G. *The impact of evaluation: Lessons drawn from the evaluations of five early childhood education programs.* Proceedings of a symposium presented at the annual meeting of the American Educational Research Association, Toronto, March 1978.

Hewett, K. D., Jerome, C. M., Nauta, M., Rubin, A. D., & Stein, M. *Partners with parents: The Home Start experience with preschoolers and their families* (U.S. Department of Health, Education, and Welfare Publication No. OHDS 78-31106). Washington, D.C.: U.S. Government Printing Office, 1978.

Hilliard, A. S. How should we assess children's social competence? *Young Children,* 1978, *33* (5), 12–13.

Hodges, W. L., and Sheehan, R. Evaluation: Strategies for generating knowledge. *New Directions in Program Evaluation,* 1978, *2,* 81–93.

Hohman, M., Banet, B., & Weikart, D. P. *Young children in action.* Ypsilanti, Mi.: High/Scope Educational Research Foundation, 1978.

Honig, A. S., & Lally, J. R. How good is your infant program? Use an observation method to find out. *Child Care Quarterly,* 1975, *4,* 194–207.

Horst, D. P., Tallmadge, G. K., & Wood, C. T. *A practical guide to measuring project impact of student achievement* (U.S. Department of Health, Education, and Welfare Office of Education). Washington, D.C.: U.S. Government Printing Office, 1975.

House, E. R., Glass, G. V., McLean, L. D., & Walker, D. F. No simple answer: Critique of the Follow Through evaluation. *Harvard Educational Review,* 1978, *48,* 128–160.

Huntington, D. S. Evaluation of programs. In L. L. Dittman (Ed.), *The infants we care for.* Washington, D.C.: National Association for the Education of Young Children, 1973.

Irwin, D. M., & Bushnell, M. *Observational strategies for children.* New York: Holt, Rinehart & Winston, in press.

Jacobson, A. L. Infant day care: toward a more human environment. *Young Children,* 1978, *33* (5), 14–21.

Joffe, C. E. *Friendly intruders: Child care professionals and family life.* Berkeley, Ca.: University of California Press, 1977.

Johnson, O. G., & Bommarito, J. W. *Tests and measurements in child development: A handbook.* San Francisco: Jossey-Bass, 1971.

Jones, E. *Dimensions of teaching-learning environment.* Pasadena, Ca.: Pacific Oaks College, n.d.

Kagan, J., Kearsley, R. B., & Zelazo, P. R. The effects of infant day care on psychological development. *Evaluation Quarterly,* 1977, *1,* 109–142.

Kamii, C., & DeVries, R. Piaget for early education. In M. C. Day & R. K. Parker (Eds.), *The preschool in action* (2nd ed.). Boston: Allyn & Bacon, 1977.

Keister, M. E. *"The good life" for infants and toddlers.* Washington, D.C.: National Association for the Education of Young Children, 1970.

Kennedy, M. M. Findings from the Follow Through Planned Variation Study. *Educational Researcher,* 1978, *7,* 3–11. (a)

Kennedy, M. M. Developing an evaluation plan for Public Law 94-142. *New Directions in Program Evaluation,* 1978, *2,* 19–39. (b)

Keyserling, M. D. *Windows on day care.* New York: National Council of Jewish Women, 1972.

Kritchevsky, S., Prescott, E., & Walling, L. *Planning environments for young children: Physical space.* Washington, D.C.: National Association for the Education of Young Children, 1969.

Lazar, I., Hubbell, V. R., Murray, H., Rosche, M., & Royce, J. *The persistence of preschool effects* (U.S. Department of Health, Education, and Welfare Publication No. OHDS 78-30130). Washington, D.C.: U.S. Government Printing Office, 1977.

Levin, J. *Learner differences: Diagnosis and prescription.* New York: Holt, Rinehart & Winston, 1976.

Love, J. M., Granville, A. C., & Smith, A. *A process evaluation of Project Developmental Continuity: Final report of the PDC feasibility study, 1974-1977.* Ypsilanti, Mi.: High/Scope Educational Research Foundation, 1978.

Love, J. M., Nauta, M. J., Coelen, C. G., Hewett, K., & Ruopp, R. R. *National Home Start evaluation: Final report findings and implications.* Ypsilanti, Mi.: High/Scope Educational Research Foundation, 1976.

Love, J. M., Wacker, S., & Meece, J. *A .process evaluation of Project Developmental Continuity. Interim report II, part b: Recommendations for measuring program impact.* Ypsilanti, Mi.: High/Scope Educational Research Foundation, 1975.

McClelland, D. C. Testing for competence rather than "intelligence." *American Psychologist,* 1973, *28,* 1-14.

Marshall, H. H. Criteria for an open classroom. *Young Children,* 1972, *28* (1), 13-19.

Mattick, I., & Perkins, F. J. *Guidelines for observation and assessment: An approach to evaluating the learning environment of a day care center.* Washington, D.C.: Day Care and Child Development Council of America, 1973.

Miller, L., & Dyer, J. L. Four preschool programs: Their dimensions and effects. *Monograph of the Society for Research in Child Development,* 1975, *40* (5-6, Serial No. 162).

Millman, J. Criterion-referenced measurement. In W. J. Popham (Ed.), *Evaluation in education: Current applications.* Berkeley, Ca.: McCutchan, 1974.

Montes, F., & Risley, T. Evaluating traditional day care practices: An empirical approach. *Child Care Quarterly,* 1975, *4,* 208-215.

Moore, S. Research in review: Child-child interactions of infants and toddlers. *Young Children,* 1978, *33* (2), 64-69.

Popham, W. J. *Educational evaluation.* Englewood Cliffs, N.J.: Prentice-Hall, 1975.

Porter, A. C., & Chibucos, T. R. Common problems of design and analysis in evaluative research. *Sociological Methods and Research,* 1975, *3,* 235-257.

Prescott, E., & Jones, E. *Day care as a child rearing environment* (Vol. 2). Washington, D.C.: National Association for the Education of Young Children, 1972.

Prescott, E. *A comparison of three types of day care and nursery home care,* 1973. (ERIC Document Reproduction Service No. ED 078 910).

Prescott, E. Is day care as good as a good home? *Young Children,* 1978, *33* (2), 13-19.

Provence, S., Naylor, A., & Patterson, J. *The challenge of day care.* New Haven, Ct.: Yale University Press, 1977.

Provus, M. *Discrepancy evaluation.* Berkeley, Ca.: McCutchan, 1971.

Raizen, S., & Bobrow, S. B. *Design for a national evaluation of social competence in Head Start children.* Santa Monica, Ca.: Rand Corporation, 1974.

Rivlin, A. M., & Timpane, P. M. (Eds.). *Planned variation in education: Should we give up or try harder?* Washington, D.C.: Brookings Institution, 1975.

Robinson, H. B., & Robinson, N. M. Longitudinal development of very young children in a comprehensive day care program: The first two years. *Child Development,* 1971, *42,* 1673-1683.

Ross, L., & Cronbach, L. J. Handbook of evaluation research: Essay review. *Educational Researcher,* 1974, *5,* 9-19.

Ryan, S. (Ed.). *A report on longitudinal evaluations of preschool programs* (DHEW Publication No. OHD 74-24). Washington, D.C.: U.S. Department of Health, Education, and Welfare Children's Bureau, 1974.

Sanders, J. R., & Cunningham, D. J. Formative evaluation: Selecting techniques and procedures. In G. D. Borich (Ed.), *Evaluating educational programs and products.* Englewood Cliffs, N.J.: Educational Technology Publications, 1974.

Schirmer, G. *Performance objectives for preschool children.* Sioux Falls, S.D.: Adapt Press, 1976.

Schwartz, J. C., Korlick, G., & Strickland, R. G. Effects of early day care experience on adjustment to a new environment. *American Journal of Orthopsychiatry,* 1973, *43,* 340–346.

Scriven, M. The methodology of evaluation. In R. W. Tyler (Ed.), *Perspectives of curriculum evaluation.* Chicago: Rand McNally, 1967.

Scriven, M. Pros and cons about goal-free evaluation. In W. J. Popham (Ed.), *Evaluation in education: Current perspectives.* Berkeley, Ca.: McCutchan, 1974.

Scriven, M. Evaluation bias and its control. In G. Blass (Ed.), *Evaluation studies review annual* (Vol. 1). Beverly Hills, Ca.: Sage, 1976.

Shipman, V. C. *Notable early characteristics of high and low achieving black low-SES children.* Princeton, N.J.: Educational Testing Service, 1976.

Shipman, V., McKee, J. D., & Bridgeman, B. *Stability and change in family status, situational and process variables and their relationship to children's cognitive performance.* Princeton, N.J.: Educational Testing Service, 1976.

Sigel, I. E. The search for validity or the evaluator's nightmare. In R. A. Weinberg & S. Moore (Eds.), *Evaluation of educational programs for young children.* Washington, D.C.: Child Development Associate Consortium, 1975.

Smith, M., & Giesy, R. A guide for collecting and organizing information on early childhood programs. *Young Children,* 1972, *28,* 264–271.

Smith, R. M., Neisworth, J. T., & Greer, J. G. *Evaluating educational environments.* Columbus, Oh.: Charles E. Merrill, 1978.

Snow, R. E. Individual differences and instructional theory. *Educational Researcher,* 1977, *6,* 11–15.

Solomon, D., & Kendall, A. J. *Final report: Individual characteristics and children's performance in varied educational settings.* Rockville, Md.: Montgomery County Public Schools, 1976.

Spodek, B. *Teaching in the early years* (2nd ed.). Englewood Cliffs, N.J.: Prentice-Hall, 1978.

Stake, R. E. The countenance of educational evaluation. *Teachers College Record,* 1967, *68,* 523–540.

Stake, R. E. The case study method in social inquiry. *Educational Researcher,* 1978, *1,* 5–8.

Stallings, J. Implementation and child effects of teaching practices in follow through classrooms. *Monograph of the Society for Research in Child Development,* 1975, *40* (7–8, Serial No. 163).

Stallings, J. A. *Learning to look.* Belmont, Ca.: Wadsworth, 1977. (a)

Stallings, J. How instructional processes related to child outcomes. In G. D. Borich (Ed.), *The appraisal of teaching.* Reading, Ma.: Addison-Wesley, 1977. (b)

Stanley, J. C. (Ed.). *Preschool programs for the disadvantaged.* Baltimore: Johns Hopkins University Press, 1972.

Stone, J. C. E-VALUE-ation. *New Directions for Program Evaluation,* 1978, *1,* 73–82.

Strenio, J. F., Bryk, A. S., and Weisberg, H. I. *An individual growth model perspective for evaluating educational programs.* Paper presented at the annual meeting of The American Statistical Association, Chicago, September 1977.

Stufflebeam, D. L. *Evaluation as enlightenment for decision making.* Columbus, Oh.: Ohio State University Evaluation Center, 1968.

Tallmadge, G. K., & Horst, D. P. *A procedural guide for validating achievement gains in educational projects* (U.S. Department of Health, Education, and Welfare Office of Education). Washington, D.C.: U.S. Government Printing Office, 1976.

Walker, D. K. *Socioemotional measures for preschool and kindergarten children.* San Francisco: Jossey-Bass, 1973.

Washington, E. A collaborative approach to early childhood evaluation. In Weinberg, R., & Moore, S. (Eds.), *Evaluation of educational programs for young children.* Washington, D.C.: Child Development Associate Consortium, 1975.

Ward, E. H. The Child Development Associate Consortium's assessment system. In J. D. Andrews (Ed.), *Early childhood education. It's an art? It's a science?* Washington, D.C.: National Association for the Education of Young Children, 1976.

Weikart, D. P., & Banet, B. A. Model design problems in Follow Through. In A. M. Rivlin & P. M. Timpane (Eds.), *Planned variation in education: Should we give up or try harder?* Washington, D.C.: Brookings Institution, 1975.

Weinberg, R. A., & Moore, S. G. (Eds.). *Evaluation of educational programs for young children.* Washington, D.C.: Child Development Associates, 1975.

Weinberg, R. A., & Wood, F. H. (Eds.). *Observation of pupils and teachers in mainstream and special education settings: Alternative strategies.* Minneapolis, Mn.: Leadership Training Institute/Special Education, 1975.

Whimbey, A., & Whimbey, L. S. *Intelligence can be taught.* New York: E. P. Dutton, 1975.

White, B. *The first three years of life.* Englewood Cliffs, N.J.: Prentice-Hall, 1973.

White, B., Watts, J. C., Barnett, B., Kaban, B., Marmor, J., & Shapiro, B. *Experience and environment* (Vol. 1). Englewood Cliffs, N.J.: Prentice-Hall, 1978.

White, B., Kaban, B., Attanucci, J., & Shapiro, B. *Experience and environment* (Vol. 2). Englewood Cliffs, N.J.: Prentice-Hall, 1978.

Worthen, B. R., & Sanders, J. R. (Eds.). *Educational evaluation: Theory and practice.* Worthington, Oh.: Charles A. Jones, 1973.

Wortman, P. M. Evaluation research: A psychological perspective. *American Psychologist,* 1975, *30,* 562–575.

Zigler, E. F. America's Head Start program: An agenda for its second decade. *Young Children,* 1978, *33* (5), 4–11.

Zimiles, H. A radical and regressive solution to the problem of evaluation. In L. Katz (Ed.), *Current topics in early childhood education.* Norwood, N.J.: Ablex, 1977.

ETHICS AND THE QUALITY OF PROGRAMS FOR YOUNG CHILDREN[1]

Lilian G. Katz

INTRODUCTION

One of the characteristic features of a profession is that its practitioners share a code of ethics, usually developed, promoted, and implemented or enforced by one of its professional societies or associations. There is as yet no bona fide professional association to which practitioners in the early childhood education or day care field belong. Nevertheless, the care and education of young children frequently gives rise to the kinds of problems and dilemmas to which codes of ethics are addressed.

The purpose of this chapter is to outline some of the complex ethical issues involved in the daily work of educating and caring for the young. The issues are taken up under four broad headings: (1) problems of definition; (2) sources of ethical pressures; (3) examples of ethical dilemmas, and (4) implications for practice and research.

Advances in Early Education and Day Care, Volume 1, pages 137–151
ISBN: 0-89232-127-X

PROBLEMS OF DEFINITION

Of all the dictionary definitions of ethics available, the one which captures best the domain of interest here is: the system or code of morals of a particular philosopher, religion, group, profession, etc. (Webster, 2nd ed.)

Moore (1970) defines ethics as "private systems of law which are characteristic of all formally constituted organizations." He notes also that these codes "highlight proper relations with clients or others outside the organizations, rather than procedural rules for organizational behavior" (p. 116).

Diener & Crandall (1978) define ethics as "guidelines and principles that help us uphold our values—to decide which goals of research are most important and to reconcile values and goals that are in conflict" (p. 3). However, their definition refers primarily to the functions fulfilled by codes of ethics rather than to their content. Diener & Crandall propose three different types of ethics, called *wisdom* ethics, *content* ethics, and *ethical decisions*, each of which serves distinctive functions and guides actions in different ways. *Wisdom* ethics, they suggest, express the ideals of professional practice (e.g., I shall respect individual differences among all children). *Content* ethics are "explicit rules that state which acts are right and which are wrong" (p. 4), and *ethical decisions* are individual judgments about the practice of the profession, including making choices which involve weighing values implicit in the unique or individual case at hand.

Maurice Levine (1972), in his examination of the complex ethical problems in psychiatry, proposed that ethics can be understood as the ways in which people cope with their temptations. He suggested also that ethics have the function of minimizing the distorting effects of wishful thinking, of limiting or inhibiting one's destructive impulses and behavior. In addition, ethics embody those principles or forces which stand in opposition to self-aggrandizement—especially in cases when self-aggrandizement might be at the expense of others. Similarly, according to Levine, ethics provide guidelines for action in cases of potentially significant damage to others, or potential harm to another's interests. In much the same spirit Eisenberg (1975) proposes the "general law that the more powerful a change agent, or a given treatment, the riskier its application." As the risk increases, so does the necessity of ethical guidelines.

From time to time I have asked students to try their hands at developing codes of ethics for themselves. Invariably they develop sets of statements which are more appropriately defined as goals rather than ethics, although the distinctions are not always easy to make. The statement "I shall impart knowledge and skills" seems to belong in the category of goals. The statement, "I shall respect the child's ethnic background," seems more easily to belong to the category of ethics. The major distinctions seem to be that goals are broad statements about the effects one intends to have. Ethics, on the other hand, are statements about how to conduct oneself in the course of implementing goals.

In summary, a code of ethics can be defined as statements which help to deal with the temptations inherent in our occupations. They also help us to act in terms of that which we believe to be right rather than expedient—especially when doing what is right carries risks. Situations in which doing what is right carries a high probability of getting a reward do not require ethical principles. But situations which carry the risk of losing a job, a license to practice, facing professional black-listing, or even harsher consequences are those to which codes of ethics are addressed. Codes of ethics are statements about the right or good ways to conduct ourselves in the course of implementing our goals. They are statements which encourage, i.e., give us the courage to act in accordance with our professional judgment of what is best for the client, even when the client may not agree; they give us the courage to act in terms of what is in the best interests of the client rather than in terms of what will make our clients like us. Needless to say, ethics in the code reflect the group's position on what is valuable and worthwhile in society in general.

For the purposes of this chapter, the major features of codes of ethics considered are the group's beliefs about:

1. what is right rather than expedient
2. what is good rather than simply practical
3. acts in which members must never engage or condone, even if those acts would *work* or if members could *get away* with them, or
4. acts to which members must never be accomplices, bystanders, or contributors.

SOURCES OF ETHICAL PRESSURE IN PROGRAMS FOR YOUNG CHILDREN

The discussion of various definitions of the term "ethics" and of "codes of ethics" suggests some of the sources of ethical dilemmas and strains in professional practice in general. In this section, we will explore some of the sources of pressure for ethical decision making and ethical choices for people who work with young children.

Client Power

As a point of departure, it is taken to be a general principle that in any given profession, the more powerless the client, the more important the practitioner's ethics are. That is to say, the greater the power of the professional vis-à-vis the client, the greater the necessity for internalized restraints against abusing that power.

Teachers who work with young children have great power over them, especially those who work the long day of child care center programming. Teachers' superior physical power is obvious. But in addition, adults have virtually total power over the psychological "goods and resources" of value to the young in their care. The young child's power to modify teachers' behavior is unlikely to be under conscious control. Obviously children cannot organize strikes or boycotts, call the police or report a day care center to the Better Business Bureau. Children may occasionally report what they perceive to be abusive teacher behavior to a parent, but their credibility is limited. I know of a case in which a five-year-old told his mother that he had been given only one plain slice of bread during his whole day at the center as punishment for being a "bad boy." His mother responded to his complaint by saying, "Then tomorrow, behave yourself."

It is neither possible nor desirable to monitor teachers daily to ensure that such abuses do not occur. Since there are no "other experts watching," as Moore (1970) puts it, and since the child's self-protective repertoire is limited, a code of ethics, internalized as commitments to "right" conduct, may help to strengthen resistance to occupational temptations.

Working daily with young and relatively powerless clients is likely to carry with it many temptations to abuse that power. Practitioners may be tempted at one time or another to regiment the children, to treat them all alike, to intimidate them into conformity to adult demands, to reject unattractive children, or to become deeply attached to some children, possibly at the expense of the psychological comfort of others. Thus the hortatory literature addressed to preschool and day care practitioners reminds them to respect individual differences, to be accepting of children, to use positive guidance, and to treat children with dignity. It seems reasonable to suggest that most such exhortations should be part of a code of ethics.

Practitioner Status

Another aspect of the work of preschool and day care practitioners which seems to give rise to ethical considerations is the relatively low status of their occupation. Parents seem far more likely to make demands on personnel for given kinds of practices in preschool and day care centers than, for example, they are to demand specific medical procedures from pediatricians.

A case in point is an incident concerning a young mother who brought her four-year-old son to the day care center every morning at 7:30 and picked him up again every evening around 5:30. She gave the staff strict instructions that under no circumstances was the child to nap during the day. She explained that when she took her son home in the evenings she was tired from her own long day, and needed to be able to feed him and have him tucked away for the night as soon as possible. It is not difficult to picture the difficulties encountered by the staff of this proprietary day care center. By the middle of the afternoon this child was unmanageable.

The state regulations under which the center was licensed specified a daily rest period for all children. Sensitivity and responsiveness to parental preferences, however, were also main tenets of the center's philosophy. Although staff members attempted to talk to the mother about the child's fatigue and intractability, she had little regard for the staff's expertise or judgment, and total disregard for the licensing standards and regulations.

In the situation just described, the staff was frustrated and angered by the mother and the child, and felt victimized by both. Could they put the child down for a nap and get away with it? A real temptation! Would that work? But would it be right? It might be better to ask the mother to place her child in a different center. But such a suggestion has risks: a proprietary day care center is financially dependent on maintaining a full enrollment. Also, in some communities, alternative placements simply are not available.

Accumulated experience suggests that four-year-olds thrive best with adequate rest periods during the day, and a state regulation requiring such a provision is unlikely to be controversial. The problem outlined above could have been solved by invoking the state's regulations. But state agencies are too understaffed to enforce them except in cases of extreme violations. Why should this particular regulation be honored and others overlooked?

Multiplicity of Client Groups
Another potential source of pressure for ethical decisions is multiplicity of clients served by early childhood workers. Most teachers, when asked, "Who is your client?" usually respond without hesitation, "The child." But it is probably more realistic to acknowledge that teachers in preschool settings have a multiplicity of clients. If the clients are placed into a hierarchy of groups to whom the teacher is accountable, the order probably is: parents, children, employer, and the larger community (Bersoff, 1975). Parental expectations may at times countervail children's demands, and both sets of demands may be in conflict with agency demands, and so forth.

Another type of setting which presents client-group problems is the laboratory nursery school or campus day care center. Not only are parents, children, agencies, and society at large client groups, but in such situations two more client groups become involved: students who are enrolled in courses or practica in the laboratory school classes, and the instructors of those courses. Sometimes the children's welfare is jeopardized by the students' experimental approaches to teaching. Sometimes the student teachers are in need of particular pedagogical experiences even though the children's interests and development might suggest that other experiences should be provided for them at a given time. Occasionally, staff members at a center feel pressured by instructors whose students they are working with in the center to conform to expectations which may violate their own relationships with the children and/or their parents. Who is the primary client in laboratory settings? Which client groups' interest should come first? A code of ethics should clarify the positions of each client group in the hierarchy, and provide guidelines on the resolution of questions concerning which group has the best claim to practitioners' consideration.

Ambiguity of the Data Base

Many conflicts over potential courses of action of practitioners cannot be resolved on the basis of either legal requirements or a reliable body of evidence. It is taken as a general proposition that weakness in the data base of a profession may cause a vacuum which might be filled by ideologies. The field of early childhood education is one which seems to qualify as ideology-bound (Katz, 1975) and its' practitioners face special temptations because of it. The uncertainty and/or unavailability of reliable "facts" about the long-term developmental consequences of early experiences tempts practitioners (as well as their leaders) to develop orthodoxies, as well as to become doctrinaire in their collective statements. Such orthodoxies and doctrines may be functional in that they provide practitioners with the sense of conviction and confidence necessary for action. However such conviction may be accompanied by rejection and denial of alternative methods and whatever data or "facts" might be available. A code of ethics should encourage practitioners to maintain an optimum balance between skepticism toward their own ideas and those of experts, and the conviction required in order to practice with confidence.

Role Ambiguity

Research and development activities of recent years have been accompanied by emphasis on the primacy of the developmental and stimulus functions of day care and preschool practitioners over their more traditional custodial and guidance functions. In addition, recent policies related to early childhood emphasize parental involvement on all levels of programming as well as concern for nutrition, health screening, and relevant social services. These pressures and policies add to and aggravate a long-standing problem of role ambiguity for preschool workers. The central source of ambiguity stems from the general proposition that the younger the child served, the wider the range of his functioning for which adults must assume responsibility. Day care and preschool practitioners cannot limit their concerns only to children's academic progress and "pupil role" socialization. The immaturity of the client presses the practitioner into responding to almost all of his needs and behavior. Responsibility for the "whole child" may be thought to lead to ambiguity over role boundaries, as for example in cases of disagreement with parents over methods of discipline, toilet-training, sex role socialization, and so on.

A code of ethics should include guidelines concerning those cases in which practitioners may want to "take a stand" as to what types of acts they will refuse to perform, contribute or be accomplices to. Clarification of the boundaries of their roles and/or the limits of their expertise should also be reflected in the code.

In summary, five aspects of the role of day care and preschool workers seem to imply the necessity for a code of ethics: high power, low status, multiplicity of client groups, ambiguity of the data base, and of role boundaries. It seems reasonable to suggest that the actual problems encountered in the course of daily practice typically reflect combinations of several of these aspects of the practitioners' role.

EXAMPLES OF ETHICAL PROBLEMS

Some examples of situations which seem to call upon preschool practitioners to make ethical choices are outlined below. The examples are discussed in terms of relationship with major client groups: with parents, with children, and with colleagues and employers.

Ethical Issues in Relations with Parents

Perhaps the most persistent ethical problems faced by preschool practitioners are those encountered in their relations with parents. One common source of problems stems from the fact that practitioners generally reflect and cherish so-called middle-class values and tend to confuse what is conventional behavior with what is normal development. Practitioners' self-consciousness about being middle class has increased in the last dozen or so years, which in turn seems to have increased ambiguity and hesitancy in taking a stand in controversies with parents.

Within any given group of parents, preferences and values may vary widely reflecting their membership in several cultural, ethnic as well as socioeconomic groups. A practitioner may, for example, prefer to reinforce children's development into conventional sex role stereotypes. But one or more parents in the client group may prefer what has come to be called an "alternative life style." Or parents may demand of their child's caretaker that she/he not allow their son to play with dolls, even though the caretaker may prefer not to discourage such play. When practitioners are committed to respect and respond to parental values and "input," they may be faced with having to choose between what is "right" and what is "right." What data base or pedagogical principles can be brought to bear on such choices?

Similar types of parent-staff ethical conflicts issue from cases of discrepancies between parental and practitioner preferences with respect to curriculum goals and methods. For example, practitioners often prefer informal, "open," or so-called child-centered curriculum goals and methods. If parents are the primary clients of the staff, what posture should the staff take when such discrepancies in preferences occur? Let us take a more specific case of such differences in preferences. Suppose a child in such an informal setting produced a piece of art work which might appear to his/her parents to be nothing more than scribbles. On the other hand, the caregiver respected the work as the child's attempts at self-expression and also valued the kinds of fine motor skill development such a product supports. Let us suppose further that the practitioner knows that such a product might cause a parent to make disparaging remarks to the child, or even scold him/her. Suppose the caretaker knows that if the child brought home work which can be seen clearly by the parent as evidence that he is mastering the Three R's, his parents would complement and reward him/her for it. How should caretakers resolve the conflict between their pedagogical preferences and the child's home demands? What choice would be in the best interests of the child? It is unlikely that such issues can be settled on the basis of available evidence (Spodek, 1977a).

Disagreements between practitioners and parents as to which child behaviors should be permitted, modified, or punished are legion. Some of the disagreements are a function of differences between the referent baselines of the two groups. Practitioners tend to assess and evaluate behavior against a baseline derived from experience with hundreds of children in the age group concerned. Thus their concepts of the range of what is normal or typical behavior for the age group are apt to be much wider than parents'. As a result, practitioner's tolerance for children's behavior (such as thumb-sucking, crying, masturbation, using "dirty words," aggression, sexual and sex role experimentation, etc.) is likely to be greater than the majority of parents'. Parents do not universally accept the wisdom that comes from practitioners' experience, and not infrequently instruct them to prohibit what practitioners themselves accept as normal behavior. How can practitioners respect parental preferences and their own expertise as well?

In the course of their daily work, preschool practitioners often encounter a parent who involves them in his or her total life problems. For example, a parent may spill all his or her own personal problems to the child's preschool teacher. In such cases the practitioner may find him- or herself with information she/he would prefer not to have. Two kinds of ethical issues emerge from such cases. First, the parent may be seeking advice on matters which lie outside of the practitioner's training and expertise. In addition, the practitioner may want to refer the parent to specialized counseling or treatment. Are there risks in making such referrals? What about the possibility that the unwanted information implies to the practitioner that the child might be in psychological danger, and the parent rejects the recommendation for specialized help? Ethically, what are the limits of the practitioner's responsibility to the "whole child"? Secondly, such cases are representative of many other occupational situations which require confidentiality and sensitivity in handling information about clients' private lives. A code of ethics should address issues concerning the limits of expertise and the confidentiality of information.

Another example of ethical issues in practitioner-parent relations concerns the risks and limits of truthfulness in sharing information with parents and colleagues. For example, parents often ask caregivers and preschool teachers about their children's behavior. In some cases a parent wants to know whether or not the child is persisting in undesirable behavior. If the practitioner knows that a truthful report will lead to severe punishment of the child, how should she or he reply? Similarly, in filling out reports on children's progress for use by others, practitioners often worry as to whether a truthful portrayal of a given child will result in prejudicial and damaging treatment in the subsequent setting receiving the report. Withholding information is a type of "playing God," which causes considerable anxiety in teachers generally. In a similar way, let us suppose that a practitioner had good reason to believe that making a positive report to a parent about a child's behavior (even through the report might be untrue or exaggerated) would improve relations between the child and the parents. Even if the ploy had a high probability of "working," would it be ethically defensible?

In summary, day care and preschool practitioners face constant ethical dilemmas in their relations with parents. Today's emphasis on greater involvement and participation of parents in their children's education and care is likely to increase and intensify these problems. A code of ethics cannot solve the problems encountered by preschool practitioners. But it might provide a basis upon which staff members and their clients could, together, confront and think through their common and separate responsibilities, concerns, and ideas about what they believe to be right.

Ethical Issues in Relations with Children

One of the problems encountered by preschool workers stems from the fact that the young child has not yet been socialized into the role of pupil. A ten-year-old has been socialized to know very well that some things are not discussed with teachers at school. The preschooler does not yet have a sense of the boundaries between home and school, and what one should or should not tell caretakers and teachers. Children often inform practitioners about activities they would rather not know. For instance, children sometimes report on illegal activities going on at home. Furthermore, the reliability of the report is difficult to assess. Similarly, asking leading follow-up questions may encourage a child to "tell too much." What should a practitioner do with information of that sort? Also, young children often inadvertently violate their parents' right to privacy by telling too much. Practitioners sometimes find themselves at a loss for words in such situations (Rosenberg & Ehrgott, 1977).

Another type of problem with ethical implications stems from the temptation to provide activities simply because the children appear to like them. Certainly children's liking for activities should be considered in program planning. But this attribute of an activity is not sufficient to justify its inclusion. For example, children like to watch television, but they are not good judges of which programs are worthwhile. This type of problem involves complex pedagogical and psychological as well as ethical issues (Peters, 1966). Sometimes such problems are confounded by a caregiver's wish to be loved, accepted, or appreciated by the children. Children's affection and respect for caregivers and preschool teachers is one useful indicator of their effectiveness. But such positive child responses should be consequences of right action rather than the motives underlying practitioners' choices and decisions.

Preschool practitioners are increasingly under pressure to teach children academic skills. On the whole, practitioners appear to resist such pressures, not only on the basis of the possible prematurity of such skill learning, but also as part of a general rejection of so-called "structured" or traditional schooling. Occasionally, however, the pressure may be so great as to tempt practitioners into giving their charges "crash courses" on the test items, thereby minimizing the likelihood of a poor showing on standardized tests. Even if practitioners can "get away with" such tactics, should they be ethically constrained against doing so? Should a code of ethics address questions of the stand to take on the uses and potential abuses of tests for assessing achievement, for screening, and for labeling children?

In summary, only a few examples have been outlined. Many more examples should be described in the process of developing a comprehensive code of ethics.

Problems in Relations with Colleagues and Employing Agencies

One of the most common sources of conflict between co-workers in preschool settings centers around divergent views on how to treat children. Staff meetings conducted by supervisors, or supervisory intervention and assistance on a one-to-one basis, are appropriate strategies for resolving such conflicts. But when a parent complains to one adversary about the other, how should the recipient of the complaint respond? Such cases seem to offer a real temptation to side with the complainant. But would that response be "right"? Perhaps one guideline which may be relevant to such intrastaff conflicts would be for the individual practitioners to ask themselves (and other appropriate resource people) whether the objectionable practice is actually harmful. If the answer is clearly "yes," then the appropriate authority must put a stop to the harmful practice. But the state of the art of day care and preschool education does not yet quite lend itself to definitive answers to questions of "clear and present danger" to children. If the practices are objectionable merely on the grounds of taste, ideological persuasion, or orthodoxy, then practitioners should resist the temptation to indulge in feuds among themselves and alliances with parents against each other.

Examples of ethical dilemmas facing practitioners in their relations with employers are those in which they are aware of violations of state or local regulations, misrepresentations of operating procedures in reports to licensing authorities, and occasionally instances of an owner's misrepresentation of the nature of the program and services offered to clients. To what extent should practitioners contribute, even passively, to such violations? Most day care and preschool personnel work without contracts, and thus risk losing their jobs if they give evidence or information which might threaten the operating license of their employing agency. Should employees be silent bystanders in such situations? Silence would be practical!

Another type of dilemma confronts practitioners when agencies providing services require declarations of income from parents in order to determine fees. One such case concerned a welfare mother who finally got a job and realized that the fees corresponding to her income would cause her actual earnings to amount to only a few more dollars than she had been receiving on welfare—and she really wanted to work! Her child's caregiver advised her not to tell the agency that she was employed, and to wait for the authorities to bring up the matter first. It is easy to see that the practitioner in this situation was an active agent in violating agency and state regulations. But she also knew that alternative arrangements for child care were unavailable to this mother, and that the child had just begun to feel at home and to thrive in the day care center. The practitioner judged the whole family's best interests to be undermined by the income-fee regulations. Could a code of ethics address such an issue?

IMPLICATIONS FOR PRACTICE AND RESEARCH

Discussions about codes of ethics inevitably include questions concerning their effectiveness. It is difficult to ascertain the effects of such codes on the behavior of practitioners of well-established professions. While early childhood workers belong to a few specialized organizations, people in other roles (e.g., parents, students, government officials, etc.) also belong to these same organizations, and no qualifications are required for membership in them. For example, the National Association for the Education of Young Children (NAEYC) welcomes members from any segment of society, from any role, or workers from any relevant setting. As Spodek (1977b) points out, the diversity of the membership raises questions about whether the development of a single code of ethics could be appropriate or relevant to the members. Spodek's concerns are amply justified when the Code of Ethical Conduct Responsibilities adopted by the Minnesota Association for the Education of Young Children in 1976 is inspected. The code ennumerates 34 principles, divided into three categories: (1) General Principles for all members, (2) Additional Principles for Members who Serve Children in a Specific Capacity, and (3) Members Who Serve Through Ancillary Services such as Training, Licensing, etc. The latter category contains 19 principles and is further delineated into four sub-categories for members whose concerns are training, licensing, relations with parents, and supervision and administration.

Many of the principles listed correspond to suggestions made throughout this chapter. However, a number of the principles might be more appropriate for a job description than a code of ethics (e.g., principle 29 for supervisors: "Should provide regular in-service training to further staff development and to meet licensing requirements when appropriate"). Three of the principles are addressed to members who are parents. Since the parents are clients rather than practitioners, the appropriateness of including them in a practitioners' code of ethics is doubtful.

Even though the Code of Ethical Conduct Responsibilities adopted by the Minnesota Association may be too comprehensive, it provides an excellent point of departure for further refinement and development of a code for practitioners.

In a penetrating discussion of why codes of ethics fail, Bersoff (1975) points out that such codes typically represent "the professional group's view and are rarely developed with the help of the consumers (sic) who receive the professional's services" (p. 372). Because of this "ethnocentrism," as he calls it, clients rarely share and seldom understand the honorable intentions of the professional. This "ethnocentrism" may leave the professional vulnerable to strong counterpressures, attacks, and confrontations. Bersoff also criticizes the typically high level of abstraction of most codes, suggesting that practitioners are left with insufficient guidance for specific applications of the code. Discussing the practice of psychology in particular, he points out that it is a field which does not yet "offer universally-accepted, systematically-developed, scientifically-grounded solutions to practical problems" (p. 373). Practitioners of child care and preschool education work in contexts of similar ambiguity and divergence of views. Using somewhat strong language, Bersoff asserts that

> As long as it appears to courts and to the public that psychology is a cacaphony of competing claims to workable procedures, the judgement of its members, regardless of the profession's high-minded ethical standards, will be open to challenge (p. 373).

However, remedial measures suggested by Bersoff should be considered. He recommends inclusion of client groups in the membership of ethics committees and regular publication of the reports of cases heard by ethics committees. These reports should be designed to sharpen understanding and awareness of the relationships between the code and specific implementations of it.

It is relatively easy to dismiss codes of ethics as lists of ideals generated by the high-minded with philosophical predilections. It is all too obvious that business and professional ethics are often violated. If they were not violated, their observance would represent the *norms* of business and professional conduct, and would therefore be redundant to include in a code.

A rationale for the potential power of a code of ethics may come from contemporary research on social comparison processes (Suls & Miller, 1977). It has been shown fairly convincingly that individuals evaluate their own attitudes, opinions, abilities, and behavior by comparing them to relevant others'. Individuals tend to ask themselves, "Is my way of feeling, behaving, responding, etc., in this kind of situation the same as others'?" If the individual's answer to the question "Is this response normal or typical?" is "yes," then the evaluation is positive and self-permission is granted. If the answer is "no," then the evaluation is negative, probably giving rise to anxiety. These questions are attempts to locate oneself on a distribution of possible responses. It may be that a formal code of ethics adopted by an occupational group could be cited, used as reference points in answering those kinds of questions. In other words, members of the occupational group might be able to believe that their colleagues who subscribe to the code would back them up and support them in facing the risks attendant upon an ethical response. A code of ethics may be a device by which groups hope to elevate their norms of conduct. The process of elevation may be laborious and slow, but imperceptibly sure, over time.

Research which would address some questions related to ethical issues in early childhood education and care would be very welcome. A point of departure in such research might be to ascertain the most frequent and most severe ethical conflicts confronted by practitioners. Are conflicts reported by day care workers different from those reported by persons working in nursery or preschools? What is the incidence of ethical dilemmas with different client groups? What are the typical ways of resolving them? How are the pros and cons of possible actions weighted? Do practitioners believe their colleagues would back them up in ethical stands? Who are the reference groups with whom individual practitioners compare themselves? Baseline data in answer to these questions might provide a starting point for extensive study of the issues. Levine (1972) refers to the self-scrutinizing function of a group's efforts to define its own ethics. The procedures may be arduous but ultimately should help practitioners to live with the ever-present ambiguities inherent in their work, and thus improve the quality of the care they provide.

FOOTNOTE

1. This chapter is based on the Ethical Issues in Working with Young Children, published in *Ethical Behavior in Early Childhood Education* by L. G. Katz and E. H. Ward. Copyright 1978 by the National Association for the Education of Young Children, 1834 Connecticut Avenue, N.W., Washington, DC 20009. Reprinted by permission.

REFERENCES

Beker, J. Editorial: On defining the child care profession. *Child Care Quarterly,* 1976, *5,* 165–166.

Bersoff, D. Professional ethics and legal responsibilities: On the horns of a dilemma. *Journal of School Psychology,* 1975, *13,* 359–376.

Code of Ethical Conduct Responsibilities. St. Paul, Mn.: Minnesota Association for the Education of Young Children, 1976.

Diener, E., & Crandall, R. *Ethics in social and behavioral research.* Chicago: University of Chicago Press, 1978.

Eisenberg, L. The ethics of intervention: Acting amidst ambiguity. *Journal of Child Psychiatry,* 1975, *16,* 93–104.

Katz, L. G. Early childhood education and ideological disputes. *Educational Forum,* 1975, *3,* 267–271.

Levine, M. *Psychiatry and ethics.* New York: George Braziller, 1972.

Moore, W. *The professions: Roles and roles.* New York: Russell Sage, 1970.

Peters, R. S. *Ethics and education.* Glenview, Il.: Scott, Foresman & Company, 1966.

Rosenberg, H., & Ehrgott, R. H. Games teachers play. *School Review,* 1977, *85,* 433–437.

Spodek, B. Curriculum construction in early childhood education. In B. Spodek & H. J. Walberg (Eds.), *Early childhood education.* Berkeley, Ca.: McCutchan, 1977. (a)

Spodek, B. From the president. *Young Children,* 1977, *32* (4), 2–3. (b)

Suls, J. M., & Miller, R. L. *Social comparison processes.* Washington, D.C.: Hemisphere, 1977.

PART III: ROLES OF PARENTS

THE INFORMED PARENT

Greta G. Fein

Two moods—often in conflict—characterize stances toward the role of parents in the rearing of young children. One mood, nourished by the idea of the "informed parent" is considered by some observers as ". . . the pet educational reform of the 1970s" (Schlossman, 1976).

The other, nourished by the idea of the "informed professional," is currently in a period of decline and disparagement, although it, too, has at times been heralded as the best way to achieve stronger, purer, or smarter people (Keniston, 1977). These ideas are not new and neither is the tension between them.

In the past, the separation between informed parent and informed professional was complete, supported by the tangible boundaries of home and school. The parent was to govern in the home and the professional outside the home, and it was up to the child to manage the transition from one to another. From John Amos Comenius (1592–1670), the "father of education," came the simplifying idea of presenting the transition in developmental terms. Comenius created a systematic pedagogy based on children's changing capacities from birth to adolescence. Taking into account institutional matters, he proposed a sequence of four schools.

Advances in Early Education and Day Care, Volume 1, pages 155–185
Copyright © 1980 by JAI Press Inc.
All rights of reproduction in any form reserved.
ISBN: 0-89232-127-X

The first, the "School of the Mother," covered the first six years of a child's life. The others were roughly equivalent to the contemporary sequence of elementary, secondary, and higher education. In the first handbook for the education and rearing of infants, dedicated to "Godly Christian Parents, Teachers, Guardians, and all who are charged with care of children," Comenius held that most children should remain in the School of the Mother until six years of age for two reasons. First, until that time, children required more personal and individual care than the teacher of a group of children could give, and second, until the brain was "rightly consolidated," it is enough that the child learn "spontaneously . . . in play whatever may be learned at home," (Eller, 1956). In addition, Comenious set forth a set of child-rearing principles to guide the parent in promoting the child's spiritual, physical, and mental health. The infant's education must begin at birth, for "a young sapling, planned for a tree, must be planted, watered, hedged around for protection and propped up" (ibid.). However, "parents are often incompetent to instruct their children, or unable because of duties or family affairs, or deem instruction of trifling importance" (ibid.), in which case children might be handed over for instruction to "righteous, wise, and good persons." With considerable clarity, Comenious outlined the format that guided subsequent reformers: a) parents are to be in charge of rearing children during the period of infancy, b) parents can benefit from guidance in that task, and c) under certain circumstances, the task might be taken over by others. But the persons (parents or others) and the places (home or school), represented separated institutions connected only by the child who traveled from one to another.

These themes have appeared with considerable regularity in discussions of early education since Comenius' time. At different times there emerged reformers who doubted the ability of parents to rear children unaided and who took upon themselves the task of providing such aid. And, at other times, there were reformers who stressed parental incompetence, inaccessibility, or disinterest and who advocated alternative child-rearing arrangements. But the long-standing separation between the informed parent and the informed professional is breaking down.

At one time, the Sunday school, day nursery, nursery school, and day care center were clearly marked "off limits" for parents. And, with a complementary sense of separateness, those who would change the behavior of parents were restricted to public forms: sermons, pamphlets, lectures; informal study groups were promoted by essentially local, voluntary organizations controlled by the mothers themselves. Today, parents are gaining a presence on territory once deemed exclusively professional; concurrently, professionals are gaining unprecedented access to the home. It is the position of this chapter that the interface between parent and professional, family and institution, merits more systematic attention than it has previously received. The issue will be examined from the parents' perspective because it is their invasion of professional turf that marks the most radical departure from previous practice. From the professionals' perspective, it may be advantageous to encourage a parent presence. In view of the increasingly important role out-of-home arrangements are assuming in the care of children under six years of age, an informed parent presence might provide a viable strategy for securing, among other things, increased community support for child development programs. In view of the regulatory problems this increase will pose, informed parents provide a way of monitoring the safety and well-being of children.

The case for parent participation is presented in three parts. First, we trace the history in America of the idea that parents need to be informed, links to assumptions about the education of young children, and the seeming phasic character of the stress on either parent or professional. Second, we discuss the contribution of poverty programs of the 1960s, especially Head Start, to a new conceptualization of the parents' relation to institutions that stressed the idea of the participant parent. Finally, we examine areas in which a stronger parent presence might be encouraged in child care arrangements that occupy a large portion of the child's day.

PARENT AND PROFESSIONAL: AN HISTORICAL OVERVIEW

The ideas of informed parent and informed professional emerged with clarity and force in Europe during the Protestant Reformation of the sixteenth century. As Phillip Aries (1962) demonstrated so well, it was during this period that the family began to acquire many of its contemporary characteristics. It was also during this time that the idea of childhood as a special time of life became a matter of serious discussion. These ideas were compelling extensions of revolutionary religious, political, and moral visions that accompanied pervasive social and economic changes. And so, the ideas of family and child were elaborated and strengthened by a broader intellectual framework into which they fit quite comfortably. Descartes' heresy, "I think, therefore I am," paved the way for new concepts of self, personal consciousness, and individual autonomy and new definitions of child and adult as persons. Shortly thereafter, the empiricists argued that the child comes into the world a *tabula rasa* shaped by experience into an adult human being. These were awesome and thoroughly optimistic visions, opposing in their full philosophical implications but complementary in their practical consequences. On the one hand, the authority of the individual person came to supersede the authority of secular institutions, kingdom, and church. On the other, forms of individuality, consciousness, and knowing were not set out immutably at birth, but rather were molded through experience. Experience, then, was the crucial determinant of mind and character. If so, good experiences could mold good people, an idea one step away from the vision of education as a way of reshaping and saving the world. And, in the eyes of seventeenth-century reformers, it was a world in turmoil, badly in need of saving. The Inquisition, the Thirty Years War in Eastern Europe, religious repression in England had produced martyrs and homeless bands of Protestant refugees who eventually sought asylum in America.

The idea of a self-conscious and responsible individual merged with the idea of education as a means for achieving better individuals. Even though Calvinist doctrine retained the belief in infant depravity, religious leaders argued that careful and vigilant nurture could contain and inhibit the inborn proclivity to evil. To be effective, training had to begin at an early age; the infant's willfulness and passion had to be curbed and never indulged. The educational attitude emerging from this perspective was repressive, intolerant of individual diversity, and aimed ultimately at producing compliant and conforming adults.

Another, more benign concept of nurture and education appeared during this period in the writings of Comenius. Firmly rejecting the Calvinist doctrine of infant depravity, Comenius claimed that children came into the world innocent and unable to discern between good and evil. He proclaimed love as the child's right, "descended from heaven," arguing that "no man" can "dispossess them of this inheritance" for children "come from our own substance" and "deserve to be loved by us, certainly not less than we love ourselves" (Eller, 1956). As if sensitive to the concept of private ownership and the growing materialism of pre-industrial Europe, Comenius took care to distinguish between gold as a transferable possession and children as the "peculiar possession of their parents, divinely assigned."

Comenius offered a radical vision of education. First, he believed that the world was entering a new period of great discoveries in the physical, mathematical, moral, and political sciences. Along with Bacon, his dream was to create a great intellectual center, where those in the forefront of creating this knowledge might come to work, study, and share. Second, he believed that the new knowledge had to be available to each and every individual because a better world could only come about if the minds and characters of individuals were improved. Finally, Comenius believed that this knowledge could be acquired by everyone if a proper pedagogy were available. And this, we noted earlier, is what Comenius set out to design.

We dwell on these ideas because they constituted the intellectual tradition of those who settled in America. There is some evidence that Calvinist doctrines may have been especially influential during the colonial period. But Comenius' views were widely circulated in the Protestant countries of northern Europe, and by members of his own Moravian church who, in 1735, settled in Georgia and later in Pennsylvania and North Carolina. Whatever the content, whether conservative or liberal, ideas about rearing children were disseminated primarily through sermons and occasional religious tracts (cf. Eller, 1956; Sunley, 1955; Wishy, 1972, for discussions of child rearing in early America).

It wasn't until the turn of the eighteenth century that child-rearing ideas came into wider circulation. It was also about that time that reformers in a thriving and liberated nation turned their attention to the children of the poor. Abandoned or neglected by dissolute or incompetent parents, these children desperately needed enlightened training. Sunday schools were expanded to weekdays in order to provide such training. In the words of one enthusiastic Boston supporter writing in 1828, citizens were urged to have "compassion for the . . . poor little ones who have no nursery and no mother deserving the name, and not to rest until every section of the city has its infant school" (Kuhn, 1947).

But then the country discovered public corruption, greed, and immorality in high places. The misdeeds engendered by the spoils system of the Jacksonian presidency became a growing matter of concern. It seemed that the nation had lost the virtues of an earlier time. In the self-scrutiny that followed, there were many who suggested that America's fall from grace had occurred because children were no longer being reared as they ought to be (Wishy, 1972). Pamphlets, tracts, magazines, and sermons on child rearing inundated the public and were purchased by anxious parents. Although mothers interested in child rearing began to form study groups called "Maternal Associations" as early as 1820, these spread throughout the country over the following decade and the first publication for mothers, *Mother's Magazine,* appeared in 1832.

What counsel were mothers receiving in this flood of material? Not surprisingly, it was conflicting. Some writers advised repression and the rod. Others, who soon became the dominant force, recommended firmness and affection, with respect for the child's individual interests. In a perceptive analysis, Wishy (1972) suggested that the more basic conflict was unresolvable. Although vastly transformed from its original philosophical form, Americans had come to believe deeply in the ultimate authority of the individual, the legitimacy of self-interest, and in the idea that social benefits will be gained when self-interest is exercised. Social reciprocity ("one good turn deserves another") was a practical ethic that fit individualism better than the ethic of social responsiblity. Whatever its moral limitations, the spoils system broadened the base of political participation. In time, shock at the discovery of political corruption diminished, and the public came to terms with the ethical unevenness of American society. Although benign nurture, with its emphasis on individual growth and personal expression, did not take issue with the idea of social responsibility, child rearing advice focused on the former with platitudes to accommodate the latter. As memories of the Jacksonian exposés waned, interest in the informed parent waned. By 1850, *Mother's Magazine* had stopped publishing, the mother's associations lost membership, and the first parenting crusade came to an end.

According to some analysts, the parenting movement had its base in small rural communities (Kuhn, 1947), and its demise may, in part, have reflected the rise of cities and the rapid growth of industries. Jobs were in abundance and people came from the American countryside and northern Europe to take them. The participation of women in the work force at the time rose to about 20 percent, and a significant number of these women were mothers. They were also predominantly foreign-born and poor, and they worked in the sweatshops and factories for long hours and low pay. But who took care of the children? Some, of course, worked alongside their parents. Others stayed at home to mind the little ones. These adjustments conflicted with the goals of a new crusade, the Americanization of the foreign born. In the great debate over public education, the major argument for the common school stressed acculturation. How could children go to school and learn English if they were roaming the streets or tending younger siblings? And so again, interest shifted to child rearing by persons other than parents and infant schools became a popular reform (Addams, 1910; Fein & Clarke-Stewart, 1973). These establishments were called "day nurseries," rather than "infant schools," a name change reflecting the young ages of the children, the concern with health and health habits, and the new professional identity of child care workers as "nurses." If Calvinist child rearing had lost out as the preferred way of rearing children at home, it was revived in the new day nurseries. Children were to be clean, orderly, obedient, and compliant. In the institutional child care literature of the period, little attention was paid to the young child's need to explore, discover nature, or play (Fein & Clarke-Stewart, 1973).

These contrasting moods—parent and home or professional and institution—continued to occupy the attention of reformers in alternating fashion until recent times. Rich accounts can be found in Wishy (1972) Schlossman (1976), and Fein and Clarke-Stewart (1973). Perhaps too much ought not to be made of what may be superficial economic and political correlates of these shifts. Surely, day care is linked to the participation of women in large numbers in the work force, and until recently this participation has reflected the immigration of the foreign born and waves of industrial expansion. By contrast, the second great upsurge of popular parent education appeared in the 1880s when the nation was reeling from the scandals of the Grant administration. For the first time, parent education acquired an organizational structure, a recognized national leadership, and, with the active participation of G. Stanley Hall, expert authority derived from the new empirical child study. The Society for the Study of Child Nature (later to become the Child Study Association of America) was formed in 1888, followed in 1897 by the prestigious and influential National Congress of Mothers (later to become the National Congress of Parents and Teachers). This was a grass-roots, voluntary, and essentially middle-class movement. It appealed to mothers who were preoccupied with the task of rearing children in what were becoming increasingly nuclear, isolated, urban households. The strength of the movement came from the local chapters through which mothers could organize study groups that met in one another's homes. The organization provided the spirit of sharing and mutual support. Although the dominant theme was self-improvement, the movement's missionary zeal carried over to societal improvement and, in local communities, the mothers organized political campaigns in behalf of child labor laws, prohibition, pure food and drug acts, housing codes, and so forth.

With the new wave of immigration preceding World War I, interest once again shifted to the institutional care of poor children. Settlement houses and the new social work profession championed the needs of abandoned, neglected, and abused children, achieving national attention in the first White House Conference on Children (1909). The profession also gained a national, organizational structure with the creation of the Children's Bureau under the leadership of Grace Abbot.

By the second decade of the twentieth century, the cleavage between the voluntarism of parent education and the professionalism of institutional care seemed complete. In the former, "experts" played an inspirational, advisory role, providing supposedly scientific information about the development of children and interpretations regarding the child-rearing implications of this information; expert and activist cooperated in the transformation of child development concepts into socially and politically usable forms. In the latter, experts played a different role becoming both conceptualizers and implementers, identifying issues and designing the institutional frameworks needed to address them. If parent education was a populist women's movement, child care became a professional women's movement that increasingly stressed the provision by trained persons of direct services to a relatively passive clientele.

Some signs of compromise between these strands began to appear in the 1930s as middle class mothers discovered the nursery school. For the first time in substantial numbers the young children of middle class families entered secular, institutional environments. Some were professional dominated, some were parent dominated, and some combined parent education and child care (Fein & Clarke-Stewart, 1973; Swift, 1964). In an extension of the voluntaristic, participatory spirit of the mother's movement, there appeared a new form, the parent cooperative nursery school. But ever-present was the theme that parents needed help; the family unaided could not provide an environment adequate to the task of rearing children. The severity of the Great Depression, the pressure on middle-class women to find employment, and the formation of WPA day nurseries contributed further to the participation of middle class families in institutional forms once assigned exclusively to the poor. The industrial mobilization of World War II operated in a similar fashion. At least a barrier in one direction, child care for middle class children, was lowered. However, the participation of parents in these arrangements was not encouraged; the children were there, but parents were not.

Serious attention to the relation between parent and institution did not emerge until the 1960s. Poverty programs of this period attempted to implement a sweeping and, of course, controversial reconceptualization of the informed parent and the informed professional. At the core, was the idea that domains were overlapping and authority reciprocal. The rearing and development of children occurred in a political and economic context that influenced homes and institutions. If the trend in the past was toward a growing separation between home and institution, these new notions set in motion a movement for reunion that merits careful examination.

THE INFORMED PARENT IN PROGRAMS
FOR THE POOR

By the mid-twentieth century, 98 percent of all Americans were literate. At the same time, the economy of the nation had changed. With advanced technology, the need for unskilled workers decreased and, with the growth of massive industrial organizations, the need for skilled managers and technicians grew. Minimal literacy no longer sufficed for employment and a substantial segment of the population became unemployable and unemployed in terms of the new requirements. The change was a pervasive one, extending to rural areas where a new agricultural technology had transformed farming and decreased the need for unskilled workers. In the midst of prosperity, the nation was confronted with a sizable and restless group, the "hard core" unemployed, drifting to urban centers in search of work, settling in the inner cities and surviving on the welfare systems found there. In the East and Midwest, a large percentage were black; in the Southwest, a large percentage were Chicano. But the process of assimilation that had worked in an earlier period could not work now. First, because a century earlier, when unskilled workers were in demand, parents had found work and the public school had absorbed the children. Second, the societal racism facing blacks was an institutionalized aspect of American life with a long history of violent suppression and denial of social and political rights. Third, in the earlier period, the political structures of urban centers were open and new organizational forms based on patronage gave political power to the foreign born. Half a century later, these political structures had solidified; the urban poor were sealed in a breathless, uneasy, chamber.

Reform movements of the 1960s responded to these conditions with demands for civil rights, equal opportunity, and affirmative action. In response to several influential analyses demonstrating widespread school failure, school reform became a major target and the concept of compen satory education was born (cf. Hunt, Note 1). Since school failure became evident in first grade, reformers argued that poor children were ill prepared to make the transition from home to school. A long time ago, Comenius had held parents responsible for this preparation. Evidence appearing in the mid 1960s suggested that poor parents were inept in this respect (Hess & Shipman, 1965). In keeping with tradition, day care, as the transfer of child rearing from parent to professional, was offered as a solution. But when parents are at home, unemployed and unemployable, day care as an intervention model poses too many political and moral issues to receive widespread support. Rather than day care, the middle-class nursery school and the kindergarten became models for compensatory preschool programs. Parents became involved in roles that were new for the poor but similar to those developed by the parent cooperative nursery school and the grass-roots voluntary, community-based mothers' movement. At last, the poor were to experience control and autonomy comparable to that of the middle class. Traditionally, power and autonomy accompanied discretionary income. Now, reformers urged that power and autonomy become available regardless of income. The solution, radical and far reaching, was to mandate the right to participate.

Mandated Participation

Beginning with the Economic Opportunity Act of 1964, relations between parents and social institutions entered a new era of reciprocity and public regulation. At the core of the legislation was the community action program, defined as one

> . . . which is developed, conducted and administered with the maximum feasible participation for the residents of the areas and members of the groups served. . . . (S.2642, Note 2).

What exactly did "maximum feasible participation" mean? Did it mean jobs, consultation, or power? What were the community action programs supposed to do? As one critic put the question, were they supposed to "hire the poor, involve the poor, or be dominated by the poor?" (Moynihan, 1968).

The Economic Opportunity Act provided the philosophy and funds for Head Start, the first large scale program for poor children. Not surprisingly, it had to solve the problem of legislative intention and it did so by touching most of the possibilities. At first, the major emphasis was on the parent as learner, with jobs and ancillary programs designed to enhance and modify parents' child care skills. According to several reviews (Chilman, 1973; Hess et al., 1971; Gordon, Note 3; MIDCO, Note 4) new notions emerged over time and were embodied in program practices. Later, parents were seen as connecting links between the program and the community, as a public relations group which could generate support for the program from the families it served as well as from the local political leadership. It was not until 1967, however, that the role of parent as decision maker became clearly enunciated. The 1967 amendment to the Economic Opportunity Act held that

> Head Start . . . will provide for the direct participation of the parents of such children in the development, conduct an overall program direction at the local level (Public Law 90-22, Note 5).

The Head Start manual was subsequently revised (U.S. Office of Economic Opportunity, Note 6) to extend the objectives of parent participation. The new objectives included human development goals for the parents themselves and opportunities for parents to influence the program. By way of implementing these objectives, the term "advisory" was dropped from the description of committees and councils; at higher levels of decision making, parents were given veto power and elected to policy making bodies.

Some Justifications

The participation principle rapidly became a part of the image of early childhood programs developed to alleviate poverty. Its rationale, however, came from strikingly different theoretical and philosophical positions well removed from child development. Inevitably, the principle became realized in different and, perhaps, incompatible ways. Since these positions have been discussed elsewhere in detail (Chilman, 1973; Greenberg, 1962; Harrell, 1972; Hess, Beckum et al., 1971; Hess, Black, 1971; Gordon, 1969; Note 3) they will be summarized here under three main groupings: political, economic, and sociopsychological. Each position was able to call upon a body of social science literature to elaborate one or another aspect of what was often a broader philosophical world view.

Participation in the Democratic Process.   The principle of political participation is entirely consistent with the value system of a democratic society. The principle is incorporated into the Bill of Rights and has been elaborated over time to prevent the systematic exclusion of persons from political, economic, and educational activities. The civil rights movement of the late 1950s and early 1960s applied the principle to a panoply of visible and hidden injustices. In the process, the nation became sensitized as it perhaps had never been before to the subtle and devious ways in which citizens, especially the poor, are effectively blocked from participation in the major institutions of our society.

Quite unexpectedly, the spotlight landed on institutions to which the principle of political participation did not ordinarily apply—hospitals, schools, and welfare agencies, institutions typically organized and administered by white middle-class professionals and dominated by the values and judgments of such professionals. Moreover, the white middle-class community exerted control over the policies of these institutions by their representation on boards and advisory councils. By contrast, the poor were disenfranchised. As a result, there was a discrepancy between the goals, values, and operations of institutions and the life circumstances of the poor which led to dysfunctional intervention and educational strategies. In addition, the programs developed by such institutions tended to be carried out in a paternalistic manner which highlighted the sense of competence and control of the professional and deepened the sense of failure and helplessness of the poor.

The themes became that of power and control in both a political and a psychological sense. Politically, it was held that the poor must enter into the decision-making process to ensure that programs would respond to the needs and sensitivities of the group. Psychologically, and more subtly, political participation would support "an assertive attempt to provide for their children protection against what they (the poor) regard as a noxious social and political environment" (Hess, Beckum et al., 1971). The apathy, self-contempt, and hopelessness of poverty might be remedied if people had an opportunity to learn connections between their activities and social consequences (Cottrell & Foote, 1953; Smith, 1969). It was especially important to enhance the competence—i.e., power and control—of parents. Parents were seen as the primary socializing agents of children. It was they who knew best what their children needed and would provide it were they able. If the confidence and ability of parents were enhanced, if parents learned, for example, how to plan and implement plans, they might transfer these skills to the management of home and children. Presumably, experience in the democratic process—formulating problems and negotiating solutions—would influence relationships in the home. Parental change would come about through the generalization of positive adult experience, rather than through direct training in particular child-rearing skills.

Participation in the Economy.   Another strand which supported the idea of parent participation was concrete and practical. According to many analysts the central cause of social disadvantage was blocked access to economic resources. Although civil rights legislation and the courts might eventually alleviate discriminatory practices, other strategies were needed to alleviate the liabilities of inadequate skills and work know-how. In the spirit of time, it was reasonable to call for the participation of the poor as salaried workers in antipoverty projects. The concepts of career development and career ladders spread rapidly in the area of human services which was expanding under Federal support (Chilman, 1973; Besaw, Note 7).

The concept seemed especially appropriate to early childhood programs. First, it provided incentives and funds to train parents in child development and child care skills which might transfer to the home. Second, it provided an opportunity to staff child care enterprises with personnel who were indigenous to the community, yet had skills and expectations consistent with those of professionals. The "paraprofessional," composite parent, poor and community representative, became an accepted staff member in a wide variety of programs for children; they functioned as classroom aides, parent educators, and community coordinators. According to one report, approximately one-third of the paid staff positions in Head Start were filled by parents and another third was filled by parent volunteers (Note 8). The enterprise ultimately forced a reexamination of the skills and training needed to rear children, with a chain of associated implications: What (and who) is a child care professional? If indigenous people (parents) can acquire the skills needed to rear effective children, is there a need for elaborate training programs and costly preschool institutions? Exactly what must a person know and do in order to support and enhance the development of children? Special certification-training programs (cf. U.S. Department of Health, Education and Welfare, 1973) were developed in response to the uncertainties of definitions and boundaries.

These questions became crucial with the passage of the 1967 amendments to the Social Security Act which established the Work Incentive Program (WIN). The legislation emphasized the employment of welfare mothers, with provisions for training, counseling, placement, and child care. At the present time, there is little evidence that the program was successful [The percentage of employed AFDC mothers was 14.3 percent in 1961 and only 16.2 percent in 1973 (Leviton & Aldemans, 1975).] Developing marketable skills and stable employment for mothers who did not do well in school settings, who were responsible for maintaining a home and caring for children proved to be no simple task. Moreover, the program required the creation of surrogate care situations, which again posed the problem of standards and how standards were to be met. The WIN program actually ran counter to the parent participation tide by separating parent from child for substantial parts of the day under circumstances which made it difficult for the mother to maintain any but the most superficial contact with the child care situation.

Participation in a Learning Experience. The third major strand of parent participation stressed two issues. The first was that the family is and will continue to be the major socializing and protecting agent for young children. The second was that if a preschool program is to benefit the child over the long term, opportunities offered to the child must be sustained at home.

Clearly the notion of the parent as a learner who, with help, can create a more beneficial home environment for the child, implies that the parent lacks skills or competencies. A rather large research literature documents social class differences in how children are reared, differences presumably linked to the difficulties poor children face in acquiring the skills needed to do well in school or to gain access to employment opportunities (Bayley & Shaefer, 1960; Deutsch, 1973; Garfield & Helper, 1962; Hess & Shipman, 1965; Scheinfeld et al., 1970; White, 1957). However, the evidence is correlational and thereby does not warrant the conclusion that child rearing behaviors "cause" children's difficulties or that parent change is possible without more basic changes in social and economic conditions (Hess et al., 1965; MIDCO, Note 4).

Programmatic Provisions

Head Start, more than any other poverty program for young children, translated the various justifications for parent participation into detailed program guidelines. These guidelines were in accord with the more general notion of child-rearing as occurring in a "socialization community." For example, Lippitt (1968) suggested that such a community could be characterized by two primary forms of collaboration and coordination. Vertical collaboration is that which occurs *within* an institution; it is represented by communication and planning across hierarchically organized levels of decision-making and authority (e.g., the relationship between federal and state agencies, a local governing board, executive director, staff, and children). In contrast, horizontal collaboration refers to collaboration *between* institutions (family and school, parent and teacher).

Vertical Collaboration. As we indicated earlier, by 1970 Head Start policies began to stress parent participation in decision-making functions. The parent involvement workbook (Draper, 1969) offered a formula for parent participation at all operational levels: (a) at the classroom level, there was to be a parent committee composed entirely of parents; (b) at the center level, there was to be an advisory committee of whom no less than 50 percent were to be parents; (c) and (d) at the delegate agency and at the grantee level, parent representation was to be no less than 50 percent. Moreover, parents were to be elected to committee slots.

In the 1970 revision of the Head Start Manual (U.S. Office of Economic Opportunity, Note 6) the role of parents was further strengthened. At the center level, the committee was to be made up entirely of parents; at other levels, parents were given veto power; the word advisory was dropped and committees and councils became policy bodies. By 1970, Head Start policy committees were empowered to deal with the following functions: goals, location of centers, use of community resources, recruitment of children, the composition and selection of the policy group, services delegated to Head Start by the Delegate Agency, personnel policies, hiring and firing the Start director, requests for funds and programs, and budget. The councils were also to be consulted in identifying children's needs and in ensuring that operational standards, such as space, equipment, were met.

It is evident that the organizational structure introduced under parent participation provisions represented intrainstitutional collaboration only in the special sense that it gave the children, through their guardians, a voice in the power structure. To the extent that staff at all levels of operation were not systematically included, it did not address the more general problem of integrating roles and functions within the institution by admitting into the decision-making process those who must translate policy into daily happenings.

Unfortunately, there is relatively little evidence regarding whether recommendations in the manual were actually implemented. As measured by positions on boards and committees and attendance at meetings, parent participation was extensive, far more so than in centers not funded under Federal guidelines (Westinghouse Learning Corporation, Note 9). The Kirschner survey suggested a relation between parent participation in Head Start and parent participation in other community activities associated with the welfare of children. Informal descriptive accounts by professionals tend to stress parents' inexperience and the role of the agency in guiding, training, and containing parent activities (Auerbach,

1975). As yet, there are no data on how parental participation in decision-making bodies influenced the quality of programs or the home lives of children (Chapman & Lazar, Note 10; MIDCO, Note 4; Stearns, Note 11). There is some evidence that parent participation in elementary school programs was positively associated with a number of quality indicators and with child gains (White et al., 1973), but distressingly little is known about the elements of parent participation that contributed most to parent change or children's development.

Horizontal Collaboration.   Among Head Start's programmatic standards was a heavy stress upon the ongoing exchange between parents and staff. The 1967 *Head Start Policies Manual* states that there are at least four major areas of parent participation in Head Start. Three of these provide opportunities for ongoing contact between parents and staff: a) participation in the classroom as paid employees, volunteers, or observers; b) educational activities for the parents which they have helped to develop; and c) welcoming center staff into their homes for discussion of ways a parent can contribute to the child's development at home.

One criticism of the horizontal concept as implemented in Head Start was that the exchange was one way, from "expert" to the less capable parent (Hess et al., 1971; Gordon, Note 3). Later the notion of "partnership" and reciprocal exchange began to emerge, especially in programs explicitly designed to modify parenting skills (Weikart, 1971; Weikart & Lambie, 1969; Kessen & Fein, Note 12). This issue merits far more attention than it has received. Some aspects are fairly evident. Comenius observed that children grow at different rates and drew the conclusion that his handbook should be used as a guide rather than a prescription; parents must apply the principles of child rearing appropriately to their own children. Other aspects, less evident, pertain to implicit value assumptions. For example, an especially sensitive issue concerns the degree to which children are encouraged to accept gender-based stereotypes. These are likely to be anathema to middle-class program developers, but cherished values to some parents. In defining the role of parent in the classroom and teacher in the home, some attention must be paid to value conflicts and their resolution. If the teacher's values are to reign in the classroom and the parent's in the home, how can fragmentation for the child be avoided? If teachers are to be chosen or programs developed to maintain value congruence, how can social class or ethnic segregation be avoided? And, if segregation is encouraged, what are the likely social consequences? To complicate matters, working with children in groups involves different skills and, most likely, different principles than working with children individually at home.

A number of experimental programs were developed during this period to assess the relative benefits of parent-oriented and child-oriented programs [cf. Fein & Clarke-Stewart (1973) for a review of studies and findings]. The findings of two studies are especially provocative. In one, the investigator examined diffusion effects within the family (Miller, 1968). Three program orientations were compared: one focused on training the parents of four-year-old children and the other two focused on training the children either in a group setting or in the home. Then, the investigator studied the effects on younger siblings. Siblings benefited most when the program involved parents. In another program, the investigators compared an exclusively parent focus, an exclusively child focus, and one that combined preschool for the child and home visits for the parent (Karnes et al., Note 13). Combining preschool and parent education failed to increase program effectiveness over one or the other separately. In accounting for these results, the investigators make a distinction between the parent cast in the secondary role of teacher's aide, and the parent encouraged to function as the primary educational agent. In the latter, the parent will assume an active and initiating role. These distinctions are useful because parent education strategies must come to grips with the larger issue of coopting parents, reducing parental authority, and transforming the home into a subsidiary of larger, more powerful public institutions (Faber & Lewis, 1975).

For the most part, horizontal involvement attracted far more evaluative research attempts than did vertical involvement. Although Head Start efforts were not always what they could have been (Payne, Mercer, Payne, & Davidson, 1973), the current consensus seems to be that:

1. The more intensive the parents' involvement, the more noticeable the difference in child performance (Bronfenbrenner, 1974; Stearns, Note 11; Westinghouse Learning Corporation & Westat Research, Inc., Note 9).

2. The more the parent's self-perception is that of the primary educator of the child, the stronger the effect on the child's intellectual development (Bronfenbrenner, 1974; Hunt, Note 1; Stearns, Note 11).

3. Although parent employment as a child care worker seems to have beneficial effects on the child's intellectual development, little is known about the impact of such employment on the family constellation (Chapman et al., Note 10; Stearns, Note 11).

Parent Education. Compensatory educational programs of the 1960s stressed change. The goal, agreed upon by both parent and professional, was the child's success in school. Although boundaries between parent and professional were substantially reduced during this period, it was generally agreed that it was the professional, not the parent, who knew how to prepare children for school. Although there was some discussion of informational reciprocity and although the qualifications of professionals were challenged, professionals retained their status as experts. If professionals shared what they knew, parents could acquire the skills needed to rear and educate children who would succeed in school. Moreover, there was some evidence that parent education might be an effective substitute for group programs and, if so, Comenius' vision of the School of the Mother might be realized. Indeed, Gordon (Gordon & Jester, Note 14) and Levenstein (Levenstein & Sunley, 1968) offered evidence that parent education for the poor could be successfully delivered in the home by people trained by professionals but who themselves were poor. The parent retained exclusive control over the child's experiences; the home visitor was a guest in the home.

Parent education seemed especially appropriate for infants. In the influential report of the President's Task Force on Early Child Development (Hunt, Note 1), the concept of the Parent-Child Center (PCC) was advanced to serve this purpose. Although initially the plan was to fund a few experimental efforts, almost 40 operational programs were funded by 1969. But the idea was a new one; few professionals outside the medical profession had been involved in infant care and even fewer in infant education. Into the gap flowed an enormous variety of interpretations concerning the definition and structure of the new programs, and with the variety, considerable uncertainty concerning how programs were to be assessed (Kirschner Association, Note 15).

In an attempt to bring order to a chaotic situation, a special group of research centers were created. These centers, called Parent-Child Development Centers (PCDC), were charged with the task of defining program goals, treatments, and developing appropriate evaluation strategies and instruments (Robinson et al., Note 16). If these programs produced successful and adequately evaluated models, they were then to become a part of a systematic dissemination effort. Programs located in three cities (Birmingham, Alabama; New Orleans, Louisiana; and Houston, Texas) survived the first phase. These programs were able to demonstrate parent change and child gains on a variety of measures (Robinson et al., Note 16). Of equal importance was preliminary evidence that parents involved in these programs acquired relevant employment skills and began to enter the labor force when their children were older.

Of course, there were skeptics and critics. When the parents of infants under two years of age were involved in well-organized programs, the children made striking gains on tests of social, cognitive, and language skills (Gordon et al., 1969a; Robinson et al., Note 16). Moreover there is evidence that center-based programs produced changes in the mother's effectiveness as parent and adult (Robinson et al., Note 16). In the PCDC's these latter changes were especially striking since the parents were drawn from the most impoverished groups. But how long will these effects endure? There is some evidence that the effects were evident when the children enter school, two years after the parents' involvement in the program terminated. However, the programs have not been in existence long enough for long-term effects to be examined in sufficiently large numbers of parents and children.

Skeptics also question the costliness of the PCDC's relative to more modest programs. The PCDC's operate within a center setting that provides a large array of services and learning opportunities for parents. Although the roles of professionals—nurse, consumer economist, social worker, or early childhood educator, are nontraditional (e.g., the focus is on training parents to identify and obtain social or medical services in the community, to provide basic health care and first aid in the home, to shop wisely), the involvement of such persons increases costs. On the other hand, program sponsors point out that parents as poor as those in these programs cannot become effective child-rearing agents if their lives as adults are chaotic and if the parents feel hopeless and out of control. Adult support systems are viewed as program elements that are essential in freeing the emotional reserves required in effective child care.

With respect to parent education, critics have raised other issues concerning the intrusion of institutions into the home. Schaefer (Note 17), for example, has developed a program in which the parent serves as a teacher's aide. The goal of the program is explicitly focused on school learning and the parent is mobilized to transmit school expectations and curriculum into the home. Programs such as Schaefer's raise the issue of coopting parents by changing parents into teachers; the more serious danger of reducing the status of the parent in the eyes of the child as the parent in the home functions in the shadow of the teacher's authority in school (Faber et al., 1975).

There are really two issues here. One concerns the "hidden curriculum" of middle-class homes and evidence that middle-class parents in countless ways teach the school curriculum and reinforce school expectations at home. When poor parents are given an opportunity to express themselves on such matters, they typically come out on the side of the "hidden curriculum" and practices associated with the middle class. Unfortunately, the degree to which middle-class parents function as "child advocates" as well as "teachers" has not been studied. The second issue involves the child's perception of the parent's authority and concern that the parent's status will diminish if the parent is cast in the role of teacher assistant. There is, however, little evidence pertaining to this concern. Most likely, the act of school attendance of itself dilutes parental authority, or so research seems to suggest (Fein & Clarke-Stewart, 1973). As discussed earlier, home and school have traditionally maintained a separateness, and the power of the school, the resources, and status it commands far outweigh the resources and status of families. Certainly, one may present a case for the alternative outcome, namely, that parent status will be enhanced through contact with the school. In the absence of evidence, these plausible alternatives cannot be assessed.

Of course, infant programs do not present a comparable issue. First, in the most carefully designed programs, those who work with parents are members of the community in which the family lives; the young child perceives the mother interacting with someone more like a neighbor than a teacher. In center-based programs such as the PCDC's, paraprofessionals have a central role. On the one hand, paraprofessionals and parents may control the curriculum and, on the other, they may become allies of the institution. Moreover, in keeping with guidelines governing parent participation on decision-making bodies, parents have some measure of control over program policies.

THE INFORMED AND PARTICIPATING PARENT

In sum, reviewers have concluded that the most successful compensatory educational programs tended to have a strong parent focus and a strong parent participation component. But, in addition, these programs had a clear sense of purpose and displayed high levels of managerial, interpersonal, and intellectual skills. One might surmise that the programs which best supported change were those that were able to modify institutional social structures enough to encourage the kind of parent participation that enhanced parent confidence, skills, and the skills of children.

In the poverty programs of the 1960s, the concept of the informed parent was extended to the role of parents outside the home. Parent education and preschool programs, once available only to the affluent, became available to the poor, and day care, as the preferred intervention for poor children, became a minor theme. In several respects, the customary relation between social status and recommended intervention was altered. The data seem to suggest that if skills related to school success is a primary intervention goal, means other than a separation of child from parent are available.

Unfortunately, the innovations of this period have not received the systematic, in-depth analysis they merit. Although several components of parent participation were identified and undoubtedly implemented in varying degrees, little is known about problems and processes, or linkages between adult experiences and children's development. The role of parent as decision maker is likely to create uneasiness among professionals and, in the case of early childhood enterprises, it is likely to threaten a barely formed professional identity. For these reasons, it would be useful to know something about the parents who tend to enter this role, the nature of the parent-professional relationship, and the impact on program quality. Under what circumstances do parents make an independent, active contribution, and what kinds of resources are needed to enhance the effectiveness of this contribution? It is likely that a relatively small proportion of parents actually participate in a decision-making role, but it is also likely that there are diffusion effects to nonparticipating parents. Finally, what are the consequences of direct participation with respect to parent functioning in other life arenas and with respect to the development of their children? The important hypothesis that participating parents would experience an enhanced sense of personal control has yet to be assessed.

The notions of parent as worker and parent as learner were designed, in part, to provide parents with a legitimate role in the day-to-day operations of Head Start programs. Again, there are countless unanswered questions about how these roles were implemented, by whom, and with what outcomes. Although experimental studies focusing on parent education have yielded promising outcomes, they tend to be detached from the overall institutional context created by Head Start. Much remains to be learned about the influence of participatory roles on the interface between home and institution, on the network of relationships within the family and between the family and other social units. Although the danger of usurping the parent role in the name of strengthening it is always present, the lack of data permits but a dutiful nod of concern.

The forms of parent participation pioneered in the poverty programs of the 1960s were aimed at altering traditional relationships between the family and extrafamilial institutions. Some, but not all of these forms, with modification, might apply to day care. In the following section we examine areas of overlap and areas in which day care, as currently constituted, poses special problems.

THE INFORMED PARENT AND DAY CARE

The statistics are familiar. Almost six million children under six years of age have working mothers and of these about 2,500,000 are infants. Between 1961 and 1973, the labor force participation of married mothers with children under three years of age increased from 15.3 to 29.4 percent. Moreover, a major part of the increase occurred in families where the husband earned over $5,000 per year, and most dramatically (from 10 to 27 percent) in families where the husband earned over $10,000 a year (Levitan & Alderman, 1975). There is little evidence that the upward trend leveled off during the recession of 1974–1975 although the unem-

ployment rate of women was higher than that of men. In two-parent
families, a large proportion of fathers (20 percent) care for the children
while the mother works, an arrangement usually dependent on nonover-
lapping work schedules (Woolsey, 1977).

Although some mothers may decide to work or not work, according to
the availability of child care resources, the evidence indicates that such
resources are created by the parents themselves regardless of supportive
governmental policies. Most often both single and married parents make
informal arrangements with relatives, friends, and neighbors to provide
child care in the child's own home (Fein & Clarke-Stewart, 1973;
Woolsey, 1977). Two distinctive trends appeared between 1965 and 1971
among non-Caucasian mothers (Woolsey, 1977). First, child care in the
home by a combination of family and nonfamily members increased (44
percent to 61 percent), and, second, child care in group-care centers also
increased (6 to 15 percent). The use of center care by Caucasian mothers
increased slightly (6 to 8 percent). Although for both groups of mothers,
care in another person's home decreased (28 to 18 percent and 42 to 17
percent, respectively), almost 1,200,000 children continue to receive care
in such homes.

According to a recent survey (Abt Associates, 1978), approximately
915,000 children are enrolled in 18,300 licensed day care centers. Of
these, 400,000 children are enrolled in 8,000 centers which receive federal
funds and are subject to federal regulation. The remainder are in centers
subject to state licensing codes which tend to set minimal standards of
care. Of the over one million children receiving care in other persons'
homes, only a small percentage are in settings subject to any kind of
regulation.

The importance of these figures is twofold. First, they help highlight
differences between Head Start and day care that are consequential with
respect to the concept of the informed parent. Head Start is a federally
initiated, professionally conceptualized, organizationally structured, and
visible program that has developed strong, focused political support from
the people it was designed to serve. Of course, the master concept is
translated into diverse forms of varying effectiveness in the field, but
Head Start has developed a management style of negotiating, cajoling,
training, experimenting, and politicking around matters of funding and
quality. By contrast, day care today is a grass-roots, individually initiated,
largely invisible, consumer phenomenon. Professionals are on the
periphery, federal support (e.g., tax credits) follows but does not create
public demand and, in keeping with the above, much of the support is
distributed directly to individuals rather than through institutional channels. At any rate, to the degree that day care is largely a matter of private
arrangements, the parent becomes a key figure in the enterprise.

Second, the figures reflect how hard it is to upgrade the quality of child care and protect children from harm. To the degree that parents who initiate child care arrangements are naive, unassertive, or uninformed, their children are vulnerable. As the distance between the parent and the care providing situation increases, the parent becomes less able to exercise control over the child's well-being in the situation. In the absence of an effective public monitoring system the responsibility falls to the parent, but an uninformed parent cannot do the job. The above suggests a need to conceptualize new roles for parents as informed consumers and, on a day-to-day basis, as informed supervisors of their child's well-being. In the following sections we briefly discuss these roles and, in a final section, the more political role of parents as informed citizens.

Parent Roles
Parents as Informed Consumers. It is well known that parents and caregivers often differ markedly in their values and expectations regarding the development of children (Robinson et al., 1973; Sjolund, 1973). To the extent that a parent is informed about the policies and practices of a child care arrangement, the parent can protest, negotiate, or choose an alternative arrangement. Ideally, the parent as consumer would know what is best for the child and would be able to ascertain when that standard was met. The problem has been clearly posed by Nelson & Krashinsky (Note 18):

> In the traditional theory of consumer behavior the consumer is assumed to be expert at knowing what he likes—sweet juicy oranges—and the alternative goods and services are assumed to be displayed in a way that quality characteristics are evident as well as price.
>   . . . But what if the appropriate conditions are not met? Even for oranges the consumer has little information as to whether they are picked early or late (which may effect their sweetness) or the extent to which color is influenced by dyes rather than sunlight, etc.
>   . . . Since day care service is provided when the parent is not there, there is a severe problem of reliable display. How does a parent really know what kind of day care a child is getting at a day care center (pp. 36–37).

The question can be divided into two parts. First, when setting out to find a day care arrangement, how does a parent assess the various possibilities? There is some evidence that convenience is a major selection criterion, but, generally, research in this area is weak. As Douglas Powell discusses in Chapter 10 of this volume, it is likely that informal informational networks play a decisive role in such decisions, but little is known about how such networks operate. Of course, the criteria parents use reflect what they know about suitable child environments. If child development or program information is limited, decisions are likely to be made on other grounds.

Professionals have had a surprisingly limited role in helping parents make such decisions. When traveling in unfamiliar territory, AAA or Michelin guides are immensely useful. When purchasing a car or appliance, *Consumer Reports* are equally so. These are popular and well-accepted devices for minimizing poor choices. Comparable guides are not available for child care services. When it comes to such services, professionals are reluctant to make public judgments of quality, as if to do so would constitute a breech of intraprofessional solidarity. And yet, as Endsley & Bradbard discuss in Chapter 9, professionals form such judgments privately and agree with one another when they do so. Moreover, these investigators demonstrate that parents, with relatively little training, can successfully use professional criteria in rating child care centers. The strategy outlined by these researchers offers a promising approach to the problem of choice.

Second, when a child is in day care arrangement, how does the parent know what kind of care the child is getting? Often, parents are encouraged by centers to drop their child and run. More alarming is the increasing tendency of centers to provide transportation for the child, which means that parents may have no regular contact with the day care setting. Many centers explicitly restrict the hours parents may visit, and some do not allow parents into the classroom. Whatever the reason, limited evidence indicates that parents have little contact with the day care centers attended by their children (Abt, 1978; Powell, Note 19), and that most of the contact occurs when children are dropped off or picked up. Since most parents are working, these findings are not surprising. They lead, however, to questions about the nature of the communication between parents and day care providers during those brief times when an opportunity for communication occurs.

Parents as Informed Monitors. If the parent doesn't know about the child's life in a child care arrangement, the parent's ability to monitor the child's well-being is severely limited. As Powell notes in his chapter, the monitoring function touches broad issues involving continuity and stability in children's lives. Powell's findings indicate that for many children, the discontinuity is considerable, and thereby verify the worst fears of those who see day care as having a negative influence on the family's exercise of authority and influence over the rearing of young children. More optimistically, there is considerable variation in the depth and frequency of parent-staff communication. Discontinuity is seemingly not inevitable. Exactly how discontinuity or different patterns of communication influence child behavior has not been examined and strategies for reducing discontinuity have not been developed or tested.

Mandated Horizontal Collaboration.   Poverty programs of the 1960s promoted policies that departed from traditional practices. By mandate, parents gained a presence in the institution and, by negotiation, professionals gained a presence in the home. The mandate was explicitly extended to the use of federal funds for day care in the Federal Interagency Day Care Requirements (1968). The mandate was modified to take into account the use of day care by parents who were working or for other reasons unavailable to care for their children. In the FIDCR (1968) horizontal collaboration took the following cryptic form:

> Opportunities must be provided parents at times convenient to them to work with the program and, whenever possible, observe their children in the day care facility (p. 14).

It may well be that horizontal collaboration is not amenable to regulation, but in a draft revision proposed in 1972 some attempt was made to formulate a goal and a statement of the practices likely to serve that goal (White et al., 1973). The revision proposed the goal of "ensuring continuity with home and school" (p. 16). Toward that end, day care activities must "complement and supplement the child's experiences at home and in school" and "reflect respect and understanding of the parents' desires for the care and development of their children" (ibid.). Evidence of satisfactory compliance would be provided by specific practices involving communications between caregivers and parents, parental presence, and ethnic diversity.

Unfortunately, there is no evidence of whether centers governed by the FIDCR show a higher level of ongoing daily exchange between parents and caregivers than other centers. Generally, the relationship between parents and caregivers is treated as a peripheral issue, covered by a few questions slipped into a comprehensive parent interview (Abt Associates, 1978). Although mandated opportunities to participate may serve largely symbolic purposes, they can provide a point of departure for research, program development, and training.

Parents as Informed Citizens.   One of the most alarming aspects of out-of-home care for young children is that parental unavailability and public apathy combine to privatize a consumer service. Even when facilities meet licensing requirements, they need not permit professionals or interested citizens access to the premises (Keyserling, 1972) and, as we indicated earlier, parent access may be subtly or overtly discouraged.

Of equal concern is that the quality of child care rarely becomes a matter of public debate or newspaper headlines. Although nursing home improprieties were topics of intensive investigative reporting, equally outrageous malpractices in day care have been ignored. A case in point is the New York scandal in which 171 direct-lease day care centers yielded windfall profits for center landlords at a cost estimated at $19 million to the city (*The Village Voice,* June 14, 1976). Although the direct lease arrangement and the possibility of political collusion was reported by the Bank Street Day Care Consultation Service six years earlier, there were no formal mechanisms through which the public interest could be protected.

Perhaps the most radical departure from traditional practice pioneered by Head Start was the involvement of parents in the decision-making process. Again, in modified form, this type of involvement was incorporated into the FIDCR (1968) in the following provisions:

> Parents must have the opportunity to become involved themselves in the making of decisions concerning the nature and operation of the day care facility (p. 14).

However, "decision making" was to be advisory in nature, covering areas such as program development, funding applications, director and staff hiring, channeling complaints and organizing parent activities. In contrast with the policies developed for Head Start, the type of program information that was to be made available to these bodies was never specified, although the requirements implied that parents were to have access to budgets, staff credentials, and other crucial elements of program operation. Importantly, the resources required for the successful operation of such bodies were not specified, although if they were to function autonomously, they would require an appropriate budget providing staff support and other amenities. Once again, evidence regarding parent roles on day care advisory committees is limited, consisting for the most part of loose, descriptive accounts of how such committees worked in particular agencies (Auerbach, 1975). Data from the National Day Care Study (Abt Associates, 1978) indicates that only one percent of the parents who were interviewed participated in decision-making activities, but they were more likely to do so if the center was receiving federal funds. Clearly, parent participation in such activities is not currently an established day care practice. However, 81 percent of the parents considered parent participation in hiring the center director an important aspect of day care. The Abt report of parent participation merits critical scrutiny since the instrument upon which this information hinges is weak, the presentation of the data unclear, and the interpretation inconsistent. Accurate information and sound interpretation is especially important since parent participation in administrative matters is a political issue with significant consequences.

In addition, the policy role of parents outlined in the FIDCR may need elaboration. These issues are discussed in more detail elsewhere (Fein, Note 20). The monitoring of administering and regulating agencies concerned with the provision of human services is a persisting, unsolved problem of considerable importance. Since parents have a strong investment in services for children, they might, with proper support, strengthen traditionally ineffective monitoring agencies. Unfortunately, there is little reliable information about how parent councils have operated in the past and, as far as we know, there has been no attempt to develop systematically participation models around monitoring or other functions.

The Parent in Day Care

Although concerns for discontinuity in the lives of children and the dwindling authority of the family are long standing, these concerns have yet to be translated into systematic research and program policies. In the preceding section, the concept of the informed and participating parent was extended to day care. The day care parent is faced with problems of choice and supervision. Ideally, the parent would choose a child care arrangement on the basis of the best possible information. Having made a choice, parents would be able to monitor the arrangement on a daily basis. Preliminary evidence indicates that current practices depart considerably from the ideal. Most parents are only dimly aware of possible arrangements and the differences between them. Often, communication between parents and child care providers is limited and parents are insulated from the day-to-day experiences of their children. Not only do parents lose authority as monitors and, if need be, as child advocates, but they also may lose a sense of closeness, sharing, and pleasure in their child's developmental achievements. The lack of research and program development in this area is striking. Little is known about the perceptions and behavior of parents and children as child care arrangements are made and maintained. Moreover, little is known about the effects on quality day care of parents who function as discriminating consumers.

The participation of parents on policy bodies raises an additional set of political, administrative, and psychological issues. On the one hand, day care has lacked a coherent constituency of parents and professionals. In addition, there is a need for the public monitoring of public services. On the other hand, a parent-professional constituency is likely to alarm established political structures and, in the past, monitoring was viewed as a professional task. These issues require more attention than they have received. As with other forms of informed and participating parenting, little is known about the possibilities or the difficulties.

SUMMARY AND CONCLUSIONS

In the present paper, the concept of informed parent was discussed in a social and historical perspective. In the past, whether affluent or poor, parents were held responsible for their children's faults. Stress upon this responsibility varied with changes in the economic and social organization of American life, but the idea was tied to the larger assumption that successful child rearing was a matter of individual willingness and personal skill regardless of social and economic circumstances.

Although parental inadequacies were a consistent theme, remedial strategies depended on the economic or cultural status of the family. Parent education was advocated for middle class parents and institutionalized rearing was advocated for the children of the poor. In the past the division was fairly straightforward: affluent mothers were to stay home and rear children whereas poor mothers were to demonstrate their industry and usefulness by working. For the latter group, separation was viewed by reformers as a way of Americanizing the children of immigrant parents. For the former group, togetherness was viewed as a way of promoting the child's individuality and independence.

These alignments began to crumble in the early nursery school movement of the twentieth century. Middle-class parents were advised to send their children to nursery school because many of the basic needs of young children could not be satisfied even in affluent homes. Three parent-professional arrangements emerged during this period: one in which the parent was detached from the school, another in which the parent came to the school to learn about proper child rearing, and a third, the parent cooperative, in which parents controlled the institutional structure. The new nursery school incorporated the new nurture of the previous century in its attention to play and individuality. In the 1960s, previously middle-class prerogatives were extended to the poor. The idea of informed, participating, and even governing parents was built into child development programs such as Head Start and the Parent-Child Center. Although the idea was intended in part to support the role and authority of parents, much research is needed to trace the social consequences of these innovations. On the one hand, the emphasis on school-related skills was in keeping with earlier themes in programs for the poor, but, on the other, the emphasis on poor parents as the teachers of such skills was distinctly new. Parents may have controlled the delivery of the curriculum, but they also may have become allies of the institution.

By the 1970s, substantial numbers of nonpoor, American-born mothers were entering the labor force and day care arrangements for their children became a pressing issue. In some families, parents and relatives shared child care responsibilities, and the children remained in their own homes.

In other families, the children spent large portions of the waking day with persons whom the parents barely knew, in settings often strikingly different from the home. It is with respect to these latter settings that the most serious questions have been raised about discontinuities for the child and the authority and sustained involvement of the parent in the rearing of the child. Informed and participating parenting acquired special significance under these circumstances.

In the present paper, we examined three aspects of the informational requirements of parents whose children receive care outside the home. First, parents as consumers require information to judge the adequacy of child care environments. Second, parents require ongoing and enriched contact with those who provide care. Finally, parents require a public and political mechanism for monitoring institutional practices. Although the FIDCR is a consequential statement of policy, innovative practices will have to be developed, tested, and disseminated to parents and professionals through training programs, systematic replication, and the media. We noted that evidence regarding the interface between families and institutions, parents and caregivers, and the development of children is lacking. Little is known about how Head Start policies influenced parents and children, and surprisingly, little is known about the influence of somewhat similar policies incorporated into the FIDCR. Sophisticated studies designed to address the influence of overlapping institutional contexts on children's development have not emerged. Finally, there has not been a sustained and systematic effort to develop parent information—participation program models that deal with parent choice, influence, parent-caregiver relations, and child development outcomes. Until these issues receive the careful and sustained scrutiny they merit, child development theories will lack the scope required to address practical issues, and those responsible for practical decision making will lack the conceptual framework required to design and evaluate useful innovations.

REFERENCE NOTES

1. Hunt, J. Mc.V. (Ed.). *A bill of rights for children*. Report of the President's Task Force on Early Child Development. Unpublished manuscript, University of Illinois, Urbana, 1967.
2. Economic Opportunity Act of 1964. S. 2642, Section 202(a) (3).
3. Gordon, I. J. *Early child stimulation through parent education*. Final report submitted to U.S. Department of Health, Education, and Welfare Children's Bureau and Social and Rehabilitation Service, PHS-R-306 (01), June 30, 1969.
4. MIDCO. *Perspectives on parent participation in Head Start: An analysis and critique* (Contract No. HEW-05-72-45). Washington, D.C.: U.S. Department of Health, Education, and Welfare, Project Head Start, Office of Child Development, November 1, 1972.
5. Public Law 90–92, Part B, Section 222(1) (B). December 23, 1967.

6. U.S. Office of Economic Opportunity, *Head Start manual*. Instruction 1–30, Section B2. Washington D.C.: Office of Economic Opportunity, August 10, 1970.

7. Besaw, V. E. (Ed.). Proceedings of the national conference on child care. Mimeographed paper, Pittsburgh, May 1969.

8. Bates, B. D. *Project Head Start 1969–1970: A descriptive report of programs and participants*. Washington, D.C.: U.S. Department of Health, Education, and Welfare, Office of Child Development, 1972.

9. Westinghouse Learning Corporation and Westat Research, Inc. *Day care survey — 1970 Summary report and basic analysis*. Washington, D.C.: Office of Economic Opportunity, Evaluation Division, 1971.

10. Chapman, J. E., & Lazar, J. D. *A review of the present status and future needs in day care research*. Prepared for the Interagency Panel on Early Childhood Research & Development. Washington, D.C.: U.S. Department of Health, Education, and Welfare, 1971.

11. Stearns, M. S. *Report on preschool programs: The effects of pre-school programs on disadvantaged children and their families*. Washington, D.C.: U.S. Department of Health, Education, and Welfare, Office of Child Development, 1971.

12. Kessen, W., & Fein, G. *Variations in home-based infant education: Language, play and social development*. Final report to the Office of Child Development. Washington, D.C.: U.S. Department of Health, Education, and Welfare, August, 1975.

13. Karnes, M. S., Hodgins, A. S., Teska, J. A., & Kirk, S. *A research and development program on preschool disadvantaged children*. Unpublished manuscript, University of Illinois, Urbana, 1969.

14. Gordon, I. J., & Jester, R. E. *Instructional Strategies in Infant Stimulation*. Final report submitted to the U.S. Department of Health, Education, and Welfare, National Institute of Mental Health, 5-R01-MH-17347-02, May 1972.

15. Kirschner Associates. *A national survey of the Parent-Child Center program*. (Contract No. B89-4557) Report prepared for the U.S. Department of Health, Education, and Welfare, Office of Child Development, Project Head Start, March 1970.

16. Robinson, M., Johnson, D., Weisberg, P., & Weiner, G. Symposium presented at the biennial meeting of the Society for Research in Child Development, Philadelphia, 1973.

17. Schaefer, E. S. Parent-teacher interaction and parent involvement: Realities and responsibilities. Paper presented at biennial meeting of the Society for Research in Child Development, New Orleans, 1977.

18. Nelson, R., & Krashinsky, M. *Some questions of optimal organization: The case of day care for the children* (Working paper 1205-2). Washington, D.C.: The Urban Institute, 1971.

19. Powell, D. *Day care and the family: A study of interactions and congruency*. Final research report of the Parent-Caregiver Project. Detroit: The Merrill-Palmer Institute, 1977.

20. Fein, G. *Infant day care and the family: Regulatory strategies to ensure parent participation*. Report prepared for the Office of the Assistant Secretary for Planning and Evaluation, Department of Health, Education, and Welfare, Contract No. SA-7354-76. Washington, D.C., 1976.

REFERENCES

Abt Associates. *National day care study second annual report*. Cambridge, Ma.: Abt, 1977.

Abt Associates. *National day care study: Preliminary findings and their implications*. Cambridge, Ma.: Abt, 1978.

Addams, J. *Twenty Years at Hull House*. New York: New American Library, 1910.

Aries, P. *Centuries of childhood: A social history of family life* (R. Baldick, Trans.). New York: Random House, 1962.

Auerbach, A. B. Parents' role in day care. In D. L. Peters (Ed.), *Day care: Problems, process, prospects*. New York: Human Sciences Press, 1975.

Bayley, N., & Schaefer, E. S. Relationships between socioeconomic variables and the behavior of mothers toward young children. *Journal of Genetic Psychology*, 1960, *96*, 61–77.

Brim, O., Jr. *Education for child rearing*. New York: Russell Sage Foundation, 1959.

Bronfenbrenner, U. Is early intervention effective? *Teachers College Record*, 1974, *76*, 279–303.

Caldwell, B. The fourth dimension in early childhood education. In R. Hess & R. Bear (Eds.), *Early Education*. Chicago: Aldine-Atherton, 1968.

Chilman, C. S. Programs for disadvantaged parents: Some major trends and related research. In B. M. Caldwell & H. N. Ricciuti (Eds.), *Review of Child Development Research* (Vol. 3). Chicago: University of Chicago Press, 1973.

Cloward, R. A., & Epstein, I. Private social welfare's disengagement from the poor: The case of family adjustment agencies. In G. A. Brager & F. P. Purchell (Eds.), *Community action against poverty*. New Haven: Yale University Press, 1967.

Cottrell, L., & Foote, N. N. *Identity and interpersonal competence*. Chicago: The University of Chicago Press, 1955.

Demos, J. *A little commonwealth*. London: Oxford University, 1970.

Draper, B. *Parent involvement: A workbook of training tips for Head Start staff* (Pamphlet No. 6108-12). Washington, D.C.: Office of Economic Opportunity, 1969.

Deutsch, C. P. Social class and child development. In B. M. Caldwell & H. N. Ricciuti (Eds.), *Review of Child Development Research* (Vol. 3). Chicago: The University of Chicago Press, 1973.

Eller, E. M. (Ed.). *The school of infancy by John Amos Comenius*. Chapel Hill, N.C.: University of North Carolina, 1956.

Faber, B., & Lewis, M. The symbolic use of parents. *Journal of Research and Development in Education*, 1975, *8*, 29–43.

Federal Interagency Day Care Requirements 1968. U.S. Department of Health, Education, and Welfare, U.S. Office of Economic Opportunity, U.S. Department of Labor (Publication No. 033-665). Washington, D.C.: U.S. Government Printing Office, 1969.

Fein, G., & Clarke-Stewart, A. *Day care in context*. New York: Wiley, 1973.

Garfield, S. L., & Helper, M. M. Parental attitudes and socioeconomic status. *Journal of Clinical Psychology*, 1962, *18*, 171–175.

Gordon, I. J. Developing parent power. In E. Grotberg (Ed.), *Critical issues in research related to disadvantaged children*. Princeton, N.J.: Educational Testing Service, 1969.

Greenberg, P. CDGM . . . An experiment in preschool for the poor—by the poor. *Young Children*, 1969, *22*, 307–315.

Harrell, J. A. (Ed.). *Selected readings in the issues of day care*. Washington, D.C.: Day Care and Child Development Council of America, 1972.

Hess, R. D., Beckum, L., Knowles, R. T., & Miller, R. Parent-training programs and community involvement in day care. In E. H. Grotberg (Ed.), *Day care: Resources for decisions*. Washington, D.C.: Office of Economic Opportunity, 1971.

Hess, R. D., Bloch, M., Costello, J., Knowles, R. T., & Largay, D. Parent involvement in early education. In E. H. Grotberg (Ed.), *Day care: Resources for decisions*. Washington, D.C.: Office of Economic Opportunity, 1971.

Hess, R. D., & Shipman, V. C. Early experience and the socialization of cognitive modes in children. *Child Development*, 1965, *34*, 869–886.

Keniston, K. (Ed.). *All our children*. New York: Harcourt, Brace & Jovanovich, 1977.

Keyserling, M. D. *Windows on day care.* New York: National Council of Jewish Women, 1972.

Kuhn, A. L. *The mother's role in childhood education. New England concepts, 1830–1860.* New Haven, Ct.: Yale University Press, 1947.

Levenstein, P., & Sunley, R. An effect of stimulating verbal interaction between mothers and children around play materials. *American Journal of Orthopsychiatry,* 1968, *38,* 116–121.

Levitan, S. A., & Alderman, K. C. *Child Care & ABC's too.* Baltimore, Md.: Johns Hopkins Press, 1975.

Lippitt, R. Improving the socialization process. In J. A. Clausen (Ed.), *Socialization and society.* Boston, Ma.: Little, Brown, 1968.

Madden, J., Levenstein, P., & Levenstein, S. Longitudinal IQ outcomes of the Mother-Child Home Programs. *Child Development,* 1976, *47,* 1015–1025.

Miller, J. O. *Diffusion of intervention effects in disadvantaged families.* Urbana, Il.: ERIC, 1968.

Moynihan, D. P. The crisis in welfare. *The Public Interest,* 1968, *10,* 3 29.

Payne, J. S., Mercer, C. D., Payne, R. A., & Davidson, R. G. *Head-Start: A tragicomedy with epilogue.* New York: Behavioral Publications, 1973.

Robinson, H. B., Robinson, N. M., Wolins, M., Bronfenbrenner, U., & Richmond, J. B. *Early Child Care in the United States of America,* New York: Gordon and Breach, 1973.

Scheinfeld, D. R., Bowles, D., Tuck, S., & Gold, R. Parents, values, family networks, and family development. *American Journal of Orthopsychiatry,* 1970, *40,* 413–425.

Schlossman, S. L. Before Home Start: Notes toward a history of parent education in America, 1897–1929. *Harvard Educational Review,* 1976, *46,* 436–467.

Sjolund, A. *Day care institutions and children's development.* Lexington, Ma.: Heath, 1973.

Smith, M. B. Competence and socialization. In J. Clausen (Ed.), *Socialization and society.* Boston: Little, Brown, 1968.

Sunley, R. Early nineteenth-century American literature on child rearing. In M. Mead & M. Wolfenstein (Eds.), *Childhood in contemporary cultures.* Chicago: University of Chicago Press, 1955.

Swift, J. W. Effects of early group experiences: The nursery school and day nursery. In M. L. Hoffman & L. W. Hoffman (Eds.), *Review of child development research* (Vol. 1). New York: Russell Sage Foundation, 1964.

U.S. Department of Health, Education, and Welfare, *The CDA Program: The Child Development Associate training guide* (DHEW Publication No. OCD 73-1065). Washington, D.C.: U.S. Department of Health, Education, and Welfare, 1973.

Weikart, D. P. Learning through parents: Lessons for teachers. *Childhood Education,* 1971, *11,* 119–236.

Weikart, D. P., & Lambie, D. Z. *Ypsilanti-Carnegie Infant Education. Project progress report.* Ypsilanti, Mi.: Ypsilanti Public Schools Department of Research and Development, September 1969.

White, M. S. Social class, child rearing and child behavior. *American Sociological Review,* 1957, *22,* 704–712.

White, S. H., Day, M. C., Freeman, P. K., Hautman, S. A., & Messenger, K. P. *Federal programs for young children: Review and recommendations. Vol. III: Recommendations for Federal program planning* (Publication No. 0574-103). Washington, D.C.: U.S. Government Printing Office, 1973.

Wishy, B. *The child and the republic.* Philadelphia: University of Pennsylvania, 1972.

Woolsey, S. M. Pied Piper politics and the child care debate. *Daedalus,* 1977, *106,* 127–146.

THE IMPORTANCE OF EDUCATING PARENTS TO BE DISCRIMINATING DAY CARE CONSUMERS

Marilyn Bradbard

Richard Endsley

QUALITY DAY CARE—WHO IS RESPONSIBLE?

The increasing number of children receiving out-of-home day care services poses a problem for both parents and professionals who value family life. The problem is how family life can be strengthened when an increasing portion of the child's day is spent away from the family. The economic and psychological needs for parents to work outside of the home encourage them to resolve the problem by relying on mechanisms that purport to offer child care services as good as (or even better than) they might have been able to provide for their own children. The economic and psy-

Advances in Early Education and Day Care, Volume 1, pages 187–201
ISBN: 0-89232-127-X

chological needs of professionals encourage them to resolve the problem by developing mechanisms for insuring quality day care services with which parents feel comfortable and secure.

However, until recently the overwhelming time, energy, and resources devoted by our society to insuring quality day care services have not involved parents (Stevens, 1978). While the reasons for this are undoubtedly complex, one overriding factor for parents concerns the limited time that they have available to participate with their children in day care when they work all day (Hess et al., 1971). On the other hand, child care professionals, whether they be caregivers, licensers, researchers, or policy makers, are typically not trained to work with and to understand the complexities of whole families. Indeed, the present volume is a testimony to the current activities of professionals in the day care field. Seven chapters are devoted to professional influence and government regulation of day care quality, while only three focus on parents' roles in insuring quality.

Further, when examining the limited material on parent involvement, virtually all of it concerns the role parents can play *after* they have enrolled their children in the program. (See the Fein chapter in this volume for an overview.) The point to be emphasized in the present chapter is that parents can play a crucial role in insuring quality day care *before* they place their child in a program.

Specifically, we have argued that, regardless of existing regulations, day care programs vary, and will continue to vary, substantially in quality above some minimum level set by licensing (Bradbard & Endsley, 1978a,b,c). Further, since parents rather than professionals select programs for children, in a direct sense, the parents' choices determine the quality of services their children will ultimately receive. Therefore, it follows that the delivery of quality day care services will be enhanced by educating parents to be more discriminating day care consumers.

Unfortunately, parents have few resources available to help them become more discriminating consumers of quality care. The scarcity of resources was evident in the comments of parents we interviewed in our own community.[1] Most of the parents indicated that they were unaware of what information they needed to choose quality day care, or if in fact such information existed. They also stated that having such information would enable them to choose a program with more confidence and less guilt.

HOW SOME PARENTS CHOOSE DAY CARE

Specifically, we telephone-interviewed 45 white, well-educated, middle-class mothers in our community who had already selected a day care program for their preschool children. We asked these mothers to respond to a series of (a) demographic questions [e.g., age, marital status, educational level of respondent and spouse] and (b) questions designed to get at the sources of information parents seek before making a day care decision [e.g., "How did you first learn about the day care center in which your child is currently enrolled?" "What were the specific steps you took or contacts you made when you first decided you needed a day care program for your child?"].

The interviews revealed a number of methods by which these parents chose day care for their children. Some of the methods involved using "secondhand" sources of information (e.g., advice of friends) while others involved "firsthand" sources (e.g., observing in a center). Regardless of the method or combination of methods, the problems associated with them strengthen our position that more professional energy and resources should be devoted to helping parents make effective day care choices.

Secondhand Methods and Their Problems

In this section, selected interview accounts with parents will be used to exemplify how some parents choose day care programs for their children without ever visiting and/or observing the programs. The problems with using these secondhand methods of day care selection (including the *Yellow Pages*, newspaper ads, talking with friends, neighbors, professionals, and contacting the local day care licenser) are then discussed in more detail.

> . . . I picked up the phone book and turned to the *Yellow Pages*. Would you believe there were over 30 day care centers listed! But, they all sounded like what I was looking for—"sound nutritional program," "tender loving care," "planned pre-school instruction," and "that special peace of mind that only a satisfied parent can know." And, the names of the centers sounded like so much fun—Candy Cane, Mother Goose, Sugar & Spice, and Kiddie Land. One sounded as good as another. . . .

> . . . I simply opened up the *Yellow Pages* to the day care section, closed my eyes and "let my fingers do the walking . . ."

> . . . I went across the street to my neighbor and asked if she knew anything about day care. She said that her sister had used one center in town but was never very happy with it—the teachers weren't very friendly and her son's clothing kept getting lost. My neighbor suggested that I ask my child's doctor about day care . . . maybe he would know what some of his mothers did. The doctor's only suggestion was not to use day care! He said that little children get too sick when they are around large groups of children. He suggested that if I really had to work that I should place my child in a family home or with a babysitter. I didn't want to do that again . . . babysitters are so unreliable . . . my boss would probably fire me if I had to miss any more work. . . .

. . . A friend suggested I call the State Welfare Department. She had an idea that day care centers are licensed, and before anyone could get a license they had to have a good program. So I called them, and guess what—welfare workers can't say anything about which centers are better than others—they can only say which centers have a license. We pay those people with our tax money, and they can't even give us a straight answer. . . .

These mothers' comments provide us with a number of secondhand methods used to select day care. Let's examine each of these methods and its potential for helping select quality programs.

The Yellow Pages.   One can turn to the "day nurseries," "nursery school," or "day care" sections of the *Yellow Pages* in any phone directory in the country and find a list of day care center names similar to these: Drop-A-Tot, Kiddie Koral, Hansel and Gretel, Lollipop Lane, Stork Resort, or Pied Piper. Obviously, the intent of these names is for parents to conjure up images of fun, convenience, and playtime activity. It may be less obvious to parents that little can be learned about the quality of a day care program from reading the names and descriptions of centers in the *Yellow Pages.* Yet television commercials encourage the consumer to think that quality services result if they trust the *Yellow Pages.* Parents do not know that *Yellow Pages* advertisers are not required to show proof that their ads are truthful, nor do telephone company officials check information for truth before ads are published.

Thus, the unknowing parent can thumb through the *Yellow Pages* and find numerous day care programs offering attractive services and "extras" such as a large fenced play yard, central air conditioning, music, art, dramatics, and special field trips that are not really extras, but are essentials for a quality program. A combination of these "selling points" tended to make a program sound so attractive that some parents were apparently willing to choose a day care program over the phone.

We do not want to belabor the point, but an interesting article concerning the problems of using the *Yellow Pages* was reported in the consumer newspaper, *Media and Consumer* (Wright, 1974). Consumer reporter Susan Wright (KPRC-TV, Houston) studied the notion of "Yellow Page Peril"—the idea that many consumers use and trust the *Yellow Pages* as a main resource for selecting goods and services, including day care. The reporter was appalled to find that many day care centers described in the *Yellow Pages* as "state licensed" were actually unlicensed. When she questioned one unlicensed day care proprietor as to why a false licensing statement appeared in her *Yellow Pages* ad, the proprietor said, "I had a girl who worked for me who stayed drunk about half the time and sometimes I was gone. Anybody who would come here with something to sign my name, she would sign it . . . ."

Newspaper Advertisements.   While centers usually advertise in the *Yellow Pages*, family day care providers often use the want ad section of the local newspaper. However, the same basic problem that we discussed for the *Yellow Pages* holds true of newspaper ads. What can a parent tell about day care or any other type of child care arrangement from a newspaper ad? To find out, one of the authors recently answered an ad in a local newspaper:

> CHILD CARE: Will care for children in my home. Experienced and reliable. Planned activities and individual attention for your child. Large fenced-in play area. Nutritious lunches.

The telephone conversation she had with the caretaker was pleasant, and she made an appointment to visit her the following day. When she arrived, the caretaker was not at home. Three children, approximately three, four, and five, were home alone making peanut-butter sandwiches. One of them said Mrs. X had gone across the street to borrow some coffee from a neighbor. When she returned five minutes later, she scolded the children for playing in peanut butter and proceeded to show us around. Mrs. X pointed out the children's play room, a 9 × 12-foot bedroom containing only a few toys, most of which were on high shelves out of the children's reach. She mentioned that if the children did not want to play in the bedroom, they could always watch television or play in the backyard. The backyard was fenced in just as the ad stated, but had no play equipment except for a sandbox and a few trucks. The charge was $25 a week—five dollars less than the best and most expensive center in town.

While this is only one example, many similar situations can be found over and over again in both day care homes like the one we visited and in large centers. The point is clear. A parent (or highly trained professional, for that matter) cannot evaluate the quality of a child care arrangement by simply examining the wording of a newspaper ad. Visiting and observing the situation are necessities.

Friends, Neighbors, Professionals.   Talking to friends, neighbors, or even doctors and other professionals who are knowledgeable about preschool children is another way that parents typically obtain information on the local day care situation.[2] However, before taking their advice too seriously, a parent should determine how expert these people actually are. Our interviews suggested that most parents talk to friends and neighbors about choosing a program. However, their friends' "expertise" is questionable; at best it may be based on firsthand contact with the one program in which they had enrolled their child.

Parents are lucky if their next-door neighbor happens to be a pediatrician who spends time volunteering and consulting in local day care centers. Such neighbors are truly rare. Amazingly, few people including pediatricians, teachers, social workers, and others who might be viewed as experts, have ever visited even one center. Fewer still are familiar with all or even several local programs and are able to provide parents with an unbiased comparison of what these programs can offer their children.

To dramatize the relatively small number of day care experts that are likely to be available to parents, we searched the "experts" in our community, a university town of approximately 50,000 people which includes scores of highly educated persons in child-related professions (Bradbard & Endsley, 1978a,b,c). To our surprise, after a thorough investigation, we found only five people whom we considered to be "experts." That is, besides being trained in a child-related profession, they had actually visited at least three-fourths of the local day care programs within the preceding year.

Day Care Licensers.   Our interviews revealed that a few parents call their local day care licensing office for advice and recommendations about day care programs. Consequently, we recently conducted a nationwide survey of the executive directors of state day care licensing agencies in the 50 states and the District of Columbia to determine what they and their licensers say to parents who call them seeking help in selecting a day care program (Bradbard & Endsley, 1979). As indicated in Table 1, Item 1, 48 of the 51 licensing agency directors stated that they and their licensers are not allowed to provide parents with information on the quality of specific day care centers (e.g., which centers are high in quality and which are low in quality). Generally, the agency responsible for day care licensing (most frequently the State Welfare Department) is only allowed to reveal a list of all local day care centers that are licensed, as well as to provide the guidelines that are the basis for issuing the license (see Table 1, Items 2 and 3). In some cases they also provided booklets for parents or referred them to other sources such as the local Community Coordinated Child Care (4-C) agency (see Table 1). However, they cannot single out specific centers as being better or worse than others. From this general list, therefore, parents are still left with making their own decision on day care quality.

Knowing which local programs are licensed could be of benefit to parents to the extent that it decreases the likelihood of choosing an unlicensed program. Unfortunately, many parents assume that all licensed programs are good programs. Yet, as has been detailed elsewhere (*A Survey,* 1971), a license sets only a "floor" on day care quality—the minimum standard below which centers are not allowed to operate.[3] Thus, the license in no way provides a tool that parents can use

Table 1.   Summary of Questionnaire Information

Questionnaire Items	Yes	No	No Answer
Item 1: Are licensers allowed to provide parents with information on the quality of specific day care centers?	3[a]	48	0
Item 2: Are licensers allowed to provide parents with a list of licensed centers?	50	1[b]	0
Item 3: Are licensers allowed to provide parents with a copy of state licensing guidelines?	51	0	0
Item 4: Are licensers encouraged to suggest additional sources of information to parents?	38	10[c]	3[d]

[a] Florida, Vermont, and Washington
[b] Tennessee
[c] Georgia, Louisiana, Maine, Nebraska, Nevada, Oklahoma, Oregon, Texas, Vermont, West Virginia
[d] Maryland, Missouri, Rhode Island

Note. From "What Do Licensers Say to Parents Who Ask Their Help With Selecting Quality Day Care," by M. R. Bradbard and R. C. Endsley, *Child Care Quarterly*, in press. Copyright 1979 by Human Science Press. Reprinted by permission.

to distinguish centers that barely meet minimum standards from those that go far beyond such standards.

Further, suppose a center is licensed and decides to disregard some of the existing licensing regulations. Licensing laws in many states are extremely difficult to enforce, and often, failure to comply with licensing standards is only a misdemeanor punishable by small fines. In fact, some larger centers have found it cheaper to pay the fines rather than comply with the licensing "red tape" (Breitbart, 1975).

Finally, the licensing field itself has raised questions about the process of selecting and training licensers (*A Survey*, 1971). (See also the chapters by Class and Costin in this volume for more information about the preparation of licensing staff.) New licensers typically have not had specific training in the field of day care licensing before they are hired; rather, they are usually hired from diverse fields, some of which are unrelated to the care and development of young children. Licenser training mostly consists of on-the-job supervision, hopefully by a colleague highly skilled and experienced in licensing work. Further, their training is focused on determining the presence or absence of minimum standards, not on differentiating quality above that minimum level. For these and other reasons many licensers may not be in a position to rate day care quality much better than the average parent trained in a few simple observation techniques.

Special Interest Groups.   The Day Care and Child Development Council of America (DCCDCA), the National Council of Jewish Women (NCJW), the Child Care Task Force of the National Organization of Women

(NOW), and many other groups are now focusing on the day care quality issue. These groups, including spokespersons from local chapters, can often provide excellent reading materials for parents to aid them in day care selection. However, these materials, like most of the methods of selecting day care that we have presented so far, are only a supplement to and not a substitute for firsthand observation in several day care programs. In fact, all of the special interest groups mentioned above strongly recommend observing in local day care programs as an essential step before selecting one.

First-Hand Methods and Their Problems

Several other parents we interviewed mentioned that as they went through the selection process their primary sources of information about the quality of programs in their community were from firsthand encounters with local day care center personnel. Below are a few additional accounts obtained from these parents and a discussion of the problems associated with their selection methods.

> . . . Except for a few problems, I've been pretty happy with the center. I always wondered, though, if I could have done better if I had some more time to see other day care centers. Some of the others might have been better than they sounded over the phone. . . .

> . . . I finally decided I wasn't going to get much help from anyone. I would have to decide for myself which centers are the best. But, I couldn't visit all of them—it would take too much time away from my job. So, I called some of the licensed centers listed in the telephone book and asked some questions on the cost, the hours they stay open, the children's program. One director was very friendly to me over the phone and invited me to the center to visit. I went the next day . . . it looked good . . . I enrolled my child right away. . . .

Phone Calls.   Speaking to the director or staff, a parent can of course obtain specific information about the program (e.g., cost, hours of operation) and an impression of what the staff member is like. However, such information can be misleading. For example, some large day care centers have personnel (typically the director or assistant) who are trained to do public relations work. Consequently, if a parent calls one of these centers she or he may speak to a staff member who is willing to spend unlimited time chatting about the program. On the other hand, if the parent calls a proprietor of a small program, she or he may speak to a staff member who serves as teacher, cook, and secretary and who has limited opportunity to "sell" the program over the phone. In either case, little is learned about the quality of the program.

Observing in Centers without Specific Quality Criteria.   Often parents visit one or more day care programs before enrolling their child. However, because they are uninformed about what to look for in a center, these parents often obtain only basic information on cost, hours of operation, and obvious physical features of the center before ending their visit. Several of the parents we interviewed likened their day care selection process to choosing a house for its beautiful fireplace and finding out too late that the plumbing didn't work. That is, it is not uncommon for parents to enter a day care center without criteria upon which to make a selection, focus on an interesting toy or piece of play equipment, and become convinced that the day care center is the "right" place for their child. However, like the person who buys a house based on the fireplace, parents may learn, often too late, that the internal workings of a day care center are not right. For example, even though a center has many interesting toys and gadgets, parents may learn later that the children are not allowed to play with them, or that these gadgets cannot substitute for warm and sensitive interactions between the child and the caregiver.

The point is that a visit to a day care center is not the same as a close observation. Observation suggests that you know which particular items to focus on when you visit. It is our view that parents need specific guidelines to look for in day care centers before they can be good judges of their quality.

Visiting Centers with Specific Quality Criteria. Recently, several guides to selecting quality day care centers have originated in organizations concerned with the development and welfare of young children (Auerbach & Freedman, 1976; Gold & Bergstrom, 1975). These guides have also been made accessible to parents as a result of their publication in women's magazines (e.g., *Ms, Parents*). While these guides appear to include useful information for parents, they also share several common problems. First, the authors do not report the procedure by which their guides were developed. In fact, we do not know whether these guides were rationally derived from the authors' experiences with day care, whether other professionals in the field were consulted, or whether the authors generated the items for the guides from the empirical literature.

Second, some of the items contained in these guides seem vague and difficult for parents to observe during one brief visit (or even several visits) to a day care center. One example of an item taken from Auerbach & Freedman is: "Are children learning balanced social roles?" We think it is problematical that "balanced social roles" could be operationally defined by either parents or professionals, and if they could, their assessment in a given center would probably require several visits.

Finally, these guides have not been field-tested to show that they can reliably distinguish high-quality centers from those of low quality. Also, these guides have not been evaluated to determine whether or not they improve parents' abilities to select a good program.

Conclusion.   In summary, the methods of day care selection that parents typically say they used had limited utility, particularly when used alone. While we believe that firsthand methods are superior to secondhand methods, the pitfalls of each clearly point to the need to provide parents with additional information to help them become more discriminating day care consumers. In the subsequent section we will describe our research efforts to help parents improve the quality of their day care choices through the use of a tested parent guide.

A GUIDE TO HELP PARENTS BECOME DISCRIMINATING DAY CARE CONSUMERS

In this section we have summarized our efforts to develop and field test a guide designed to help parents become more discriminating day care consumers. The reader who wishes to examine our procedures and results in more detail is invited to read the more complete description of our research (Bradbard & Endsley, 1978a,b,c).

Developing The Guide

Briefly, we went through three major steps in developing the guide. First, based on our review of the child development/day care literature, we generated a set of items consisting of characteristics parents should and could see when visiting a high-quality day care center. These items included health and safety features, adult-child and child-child interactions, program activities, home-center coordination, and physical space of a center. Second, a group of day care/child development professionals, several with national reputations, examined our items in terms of whether they were clearly worded, reflected high quality, and could be observed in a center during a single brief visit. Third, a group of mothers examined the items for their clarity and potential for being observed when visiting a day care center.

The revised guide, which resulted from the development process just described, consisted of 65 items organized in checklist form. Examples of the items are presented in Table 2. The raters who subsequently used the guide were asked to check whether they observed the condition described in the item to be *present* or *absent,* or whether they could not tell from the available information if the item was present or absent.

Field Testing the Guide

The field-testing phase also consisted of three steps. First, a group of five local day care experts independently rated 12 licensed proprietary day care centers on a nine-point quality scale, where *1* represented a "deplorable" program that should not be licensed, *5* an "average" pro-

Table 2. Examples of Items Included In The Guide

1. *Health and Safety*
   a. Floors are carpeted or have a nonskid covering.
   b. The center displays a day care license.
2. *Adult-Child-Peer Interactions*
   a. Enough adults are available so that children can be given individual attention (for example, children can be held, talked to, played with) if they need it.
   b. Adults appear warm and affectionate toward children (for example, children are hugged, smiled at, cuddled, spoken pleasantly to by adults).
3. *Home-Center Coordination*
   a. Lunch and snacktime menus are posted (so that mothers will not duplicate meals at home, and to show balanced meals are being served).
   b. The center director is willing to answer questions or talk about the program.
4. *Materials, Equipment, and Program Activities*
   a. Attractive and well written story and picture books are available for the children.
   b. Adults ask some questions of children that require more than "yes" or "no" answers.
5. *Physical Characteristics of the Center*
   a. The outdoor play area is well drained and covered with *both* a *soft surface* (for example, sand, bark, grass) as well as a *hard surface* for riding toys.
   b. Some of the children's art work (pictures, posters, etc.) is seen in the center.

gram, and 9 a "superior" program with comprehensive services. The experts were in good agreement in their ratings (mean intercorrelation among expert ratings was .82). All programs were rated between 3 and 7 on the 9-point day care quality scale.

Next a group of 26 Caucasian women with an average of three years of college were asked to visit eight centers, four somewhat below average and four somewhat above average in quality as judged by the local experts. Approximately half of these women were mothers of preschool children who were actually in the process of looking for day care services. The women made visits in pairs and returned to some centers a week later in order to provide information both about the consistency of the judgments between raters and the stability of their own ratings over time.

Results from this phase revealed that pairs of women agreed in their guide judgments 75 percent of the time, which was significantly above the 33 percent level they would have achieved had they merely randomly checked the three alternatives for each guide item (present, absent, could not decide). They also agreed with their own judgments of what they saw one week earlier on 80 percent of the items, again significantly above the 33 percent level expected by chance. Finally, and most importantly, they saw 52 of the 65 items more frequently in the above-average centers than in the below-average centers.

The third step in the field-testing phase involved asking 28 women, 22 of whom had preschool children, to visit the same centers. The average educational attainment of these women was also three years of college, and all but one mother were Caucasian. Again, all of these women were potential day care "consumers"; that is, they were actively seeking day care or stated that they planned to continue working when they had a child, and would therefore consider group care arrangements at that time. Each woman rated the centers on the 9-point quality scale used by the local experts. However, only half of the group visited with the guide, while the other half went without the guide or specific knowledge about what to look for in a center.

The results revealed that those women who used the guide made judgments of the centers' quality on the 9-point scale that were very close to those made by the experts. Further, the women who used the guide significantly differentiated the two quality groups of centers, while those women who made judgments without the guide failed to differentiate the two (see Table 3). In fact, the no-guide raters' judgments of quality were virtually the same for the two quality groups of centers.

Conclusion

We were delighted to find that a group of interested, reasonably well-educated women in our community could improve their discrimination of licensed centers that ranged from somewhat below average to somewhat above average in quality. Furthermore, this increased skill was gained by simply reading carefully a set of 52 items that professionals and other mothers had determined would be more characteristic of high-quality centers than of low-quality centers. We are of course unable to state without further field-testing just how useful this or other guides might be for other parents in other communities. However, it seems reasonable that additional development and field-testing of guides and other materials should enhance the competency of parents who are concerned about the quality of day care services their child may receive. This field-testing research and other research needs are discussed more fully in the next section.

Table 3.   Mean Nine-Point Quality-of-Center Ratings of the Above and Below Average Centers by the Guide Users and No Guide Users*

Quality of Centers	Guide Users	No Guide Users
Above Average Centers (rated 6.3 by experts)	6.2	5.5
Below Average Centers (rated 4.1 by experts)	4.4	5.3

* 1 = "deplorable" program, 5 = "average" program, 9 = "superior" program

Note. From "Helping Parents Select Quality Day Care Through the Use of a Guide," by R. C. Endsley and M. R. Bradbard, *The Family Coordinator*, April, 1978, Table 2, p. 171. Copyrighted 1978 by the National Council on Family Relations. Reprinted by permission.

NEEDED RESEARCH TO EVALUATE THE ROLE OF PARENTS AS DAY CARE CONSUMERS

Developing Guides for Other Parents and for Other Types of Day Care Services

As we have suggested, considerably more field-testing is needed with parents, including fathers as well as mothers, and with parents from different ethnic, socioeconomic, and educational backgrounds to determine the utility of guides. The usefulness of the guides for evaluating family day care homes, or even the homes of relatives and other persons who serve as babysitters as well as day care centers also needs further study. The research model used to develop our guide could easily be extended to develop guides for other parents and for other day care situations.

Examining Process by Which Parents Select Day Care

Despite leads from interviews with parents, we still know little about the process that parents go through in choosing day care, or the relative importance of the several elements that are found in the process. For example, what are the typical sources used and their order of usage, and how variable are these patterns of usage for parents of different ethnic and socioeconomic backgrounds? What are the relative effects of various indirect and direct sources of information about day care quality on parents' choice of a program? Detailed interviews with parents who have just been through the process should help answer these and other important questions concerning how parents select day care.

Controlled experiments could also be used as a means of confirming or calling into question the findings obtained by interview. Specifically, parents could be provided with systematically varied information about certain attributes of programs or sources of information about programs, while holding other information constant. As one example, it was our impression that some parents were unduly influenced by their interaction with certain program directors, as a result of the administrators' warmth and charm, and their ability to clarify their program philosophies to parents. It would be possible to vary these attributes using taped conversations and determine their influence on parents' choice of a program. This procedure could be reiterated for other influence sources such as advertising information or advice of friends.

Psychological Impact on Parent and Child of Choosing Good Day Care

Perhaps the most important information we lack regarding parents' choice of day care is its psychological effects on the parent and child.

Studies of the effects of day care on the psychological development of children has only recently been initiated. Though the evidence is far from clear or consistent, there are suggestions that heavily funded and well-staffed programs do have positive benefits for children from low-income families (Belsky & Steinberg, 1978). What have not been demonstrated are the effects of more typical programs likely to be available to most families, particularly middle-income families. Such knowledge would be vastly more significant than simply demonstrating that parents can learn to choose programs like experts, since only then would the claimed benefits for the children be established (or refuted, as the case may be).

For parents, choosing day care is often thought to be associated with the arousal of their anxieties concerning the effects of day care on the children. It is also assumed to arouse guilt among many women who feel that the choice symbolizes an abrogation of their child-rearing responsibilities. Yet, how often are anxiety and guilt aroused among parents choosing day care, and to what extent do these feelings influence the parents' subsequent relationship with their child and with the center? Further, to what extent can knowledge about the effects of day care and skill in selecting good day care moderate these anxieties and guilts? These and other questions concerning the emotional consequences of choosing day care appear answerable through carefully designed field studies.

Evaluating the Use of Parents in the Day Care Licensing and Monitoring Process

Licensers, particularly those in large cities, often state that their excessive case loads make it difficult to monitor systematically even the minimum quality of day care programs. They insist that "grading" quality beyond some minimum standard would surely require increased staff support. We agree with these claims. However, following the model of using parents as paraprofessional teachers in compensatory educational programs (e.g., Head Start), parents might also be used as paraprofessional licensers. Certainly, parents who have children in day care, and consequently have much to lose from poor services, could provide a valuable oversight function as assistants to licensers. Perhaps these "licensers' aides" could be paid contacts who visit local day care programs and subsequently keep licensers informed of their observations and complaints made by other parents. Alternatively, licensers' aides could be volunteer representatives from local service groups who agree to make the rounds of day care programs on a regular basis and submit reports of their findings to licensers.

The fact that hundreds of nonlicensers (e.g., members of the National Council of Jewish Women) could evaluate the quality of day care programs in the way that we propose is documented in Keyserling's (1972) widely cited book, *Windows on Day Care*. Further, we think that the effectiveness of these licensers' aides could be directly assessed by comparing their evaluations of the centers they monitor with those of trained licensers. Similarly, their effectiveness could be evaluated by comparing the day care monitoring process in communities that use licensers' aides as compared to those that do not.

FOOTNOTES

1. Bradbard, M. R., & Endsley, R. C. *The day care selection process*. Unpublished survey.
2. Suelzle, M., Katz, M., & Gans, J. *Child care decision-making: A report to parent participants*. Unpublished paper, 1977.
3. There are indications that a few state day care licensing agencies (e.g., Tennessee, New Hampshire, West Virginia, New Jersey, and California) have or are planning to develop day care "grading" systems. That is, the licensing agency classifies centers by grade or merit beyond the minimum certification for a license so that parents are able to look at a license and obtain information about the relative quality of licensed centers.

REFERENCES

Auerbach, S., & Freedman, L. *Choosing child care: A parent guide*. San Francisco: Parent and Child Care Resources, 1976.

Belsky, J., & Steinberg, L. D. The effects of day care: A critical review. *Child Development*, 1978, *49*, 929–949.

Bradbard, M. R., & Endsley, R. C. Developing a parent guide to quality day care centers. *Child Care Quarterly*, 1978, *7*, 279–288. (a)

Bradbard, M. R., & Endsley, R. C. Field testing a parent guide to quality day care centers. *Child Care Quarterly*, 1978, *7*, 289–294. (b)

Bradbard, M. R., & Endsley, R. C. Improving inexperienced raters' evaluations of day care quality through the use of a guide. *Child Care Quarterly*, 1978, *7*, 295–301. (c)

Bradbard, M. R., & Endsley, R. C. What do licensers say to parents who ask their help with selecting quality day care? *Child Care Quarterly*, 1979, in press.

Breitbart, V. *The day care book: The why, what and how of community day care*. New York: Alfred A. Knopf, 1975.

Gold, J. R., & Bergstrom, J. M. *Checking out child care: A parent guide*. Washington, D.C.: Day Care and Child Development Council of America, 1975.

Hess, R. D., Bloch, M., Costello, J., Knowles, R. T., & Largay, D. Parent involvement in early education. In E. Grotberg (Ed.), *Day care: Resources for decisions*. Washington, D.C.: Office of Economic Opportunity, 1971.

Keyserling, M. D. *Windows on day care*. New York: National Council of Jewish Women, 1972.

Stevens, J. H. Parent education programs: What determines effectiveness? *Young Children*, 1978, *33* (4), 59–67.

A survey of state day care licensing requirements. Washington, D.C.: Day Care and Child Development Council of America, 1971.

Wright, S. The yellow page peril. *Media and Consumer*, 1974, *2*, 4–6.

TOWARD A SOCIOECOLOGICAL PERSPECTIVE OF RELATIONS BETWEEN PARENTS AND CHILD CARE PROGRAMS

Douglas R. Powell

INTRODUCTION

Most child care programs today give at least a rhetorical nod to the importance of "parent involvement," but there is considerable ambiguity concerning the specific ways parents are to relate to program services. The term "parent involvement" conjures up images of parents as program policy makers, as volunteer workers, as consumers and monitors of child care services and, in some cases, parents as recipients of child development information. Empirical evidence dealing with each of these parental roles is beginning to emerge as researchers and program developers attempt to clarify and refine the types of relations that parents and child care programs should and do assume.

Advances in Early Education and Day Care, Volume 1, pages 203–226
Copyright © 1980 by JAI Press Inc.
All rights of reproduction in any form reserved.
ISBN: 0-89232-127-X

A dimension of parent-program relations that typically is not subsumed under the rubric of "parent involvement," and yet may have a significant influence on the quality of a child's experiences, deals with the daily one-to-one interactions between parents and staff of child care programs. Most of the concern for relations between families and child care programs has dealt with the role of parents in the organization and operations of programs, rather than the relatedness of the family and the program. Little research has focused on interactions between family and program from the point of view of respective participants. By posing the problem as one of how families and programs converge to care for young children, the task becomes one of determining the boundaries of the intersection and the roles of parents and caregivers in coordinating relations between family and child care program.

This chapter will review recent research on the nature of relations between parents and child care programs, and suggest major components of a socioecological perspective of day care-family relations by indicating ways in which cultural, organizational, and mediating structural factors may impinge on interactions between family and child care program. The intent is to describe how parents and caregivers manage relations between the two systems, and to identify potentially significant variables that warrant consideration in future studies of parent-staff relations and in efforts to reduce the social distance between family and child care program. Several major reasons for the current interest in parent-staff relations in day care will also be analyzed.

MAJOR DETERMINANTS OF INTEREST IN PARENT-CAREGIVER RELATIONS

Discussions of parent-staff relations in day care can easily reach intense levels of controversy since the main issue here is the degree to which parental authority for child rearing is delegated to nonfamilial persons and institutions. The child-rearing values of this country have dictated that parents and not society control children; that self-sufficient nuclear families are the primary child-rearing units; and that when families need supplementary assistance in caring for children, the extended family is tapped.

Day care disrupts each of these societal norms. Recent profound changes in the role of the American family in child-rearing and the concomitant increase in out-of-home child care create a situation wherein growing numbers of young children spend a lot of time in environments outside the family unit. This raises several critical questions concerning parent-staff relations. What precisely is the role of families in rearing young children? How do parents go about coordinating their child-rearing responsibilities with secondary institutions? How can possible child-rearing dissonance between families and secondary child care agencies be eliminated or reduced?

Family-Child Rearing

The perceived threat of day care to the functions and integrity of the American family is well demonstrated in public policy debates over the role of day care. In this arena the issue of who controls children, parents or the public, is most dramatic. The nature of resistance to two efforts to allocate federal funds for child care services since 1970 tells the story. The 1971 presidential veto of the comprehensive child development bill is a prime example of intense concern over the child-rearing role of the family.

Former President Richard Nixon's veto message stated that the national government should not support "communal approaches to child-rearing" and instead should "cement the family in its rightful position as the keystone of our civilization." Further, "Good public policy requires that we enhance rather than diminish both parental authority and parental involvement with children . . ." (*Congressional Record,* 1971). Similarly, a second example of the perceived threat of day care to the integrity of the family is the successful "smear campaign" conducted in 1975 against the Child and Family Services Bill (O'Neil, 1975). Again the opponents made connections between day care and the future of this country as a democratic civilization.

The central message of these oppositions to federal funds for child care is that the day care weakens and perhaps supplants the family. While presumably the opponents of federally funded child care would prefer that out-of-home child care disappear completely, an outcome of these concerns is an intensified focus on the relationship of existing and proposed day care services to the family.

Coordinative Role

In America a new role for parents is evolving. Increasingly, parents must serve as coordinators of their child's life. They must identify, select, and coordinate the experts and institutions who help rear their children (Keniston, 1977). Much of this coordination is external to the extended family, and for most parents the coordinative role is relatively new and maybe uncomfortable.

How do parents "learn" to coordinate the supplementary caregivers in their child's life? Their own parents, who probably relied on few child-rearing resources and services outside the family network, are inappropriate role models. The coordinative role is a dramatic departure from previous parental responsibilities and reflects a shift in the cultural definitions of adequate families and appropriate parental roles. As society

becomes more heterogeneous, complex, and mobile, a critical social
problem is that of relations between parents and other authority figures
(Smelser, 1965). The pervading newness of the day care coordinative role
in this society may create tension for parents and caregivers. How are the
spheres of influence defined and maintained? How are day care-family
boundaries determined? How does coordination, a relatively neutral
term, translate into legitimate power and authority over caregivers? As
will be discussed later, the tension surrounding these issues may be as
much a part of professional socialization as it is a function of fledgling
societal norms of how parents relate to secondary child care agencies.
The point is that day care is a fairly new social institution for most of the
people who now use formal child care services, and there may be uncertainties as to how parents and caregivers handle the processes of coordination.

Discontinuity

Many of the concerns for parent-staff interaction in group child care
programs are based on a twofold assumption: first, that significant discontinuities between family and child care program have a negative influence
on children and, second, that parent-staff communication helps to alleviate discontinuities.

The potential for discontinuity between family and day care program is
great. These two major social systems maintain their own norms and
values, and serve as key socialization agents in the child's life. Each
system may have a strong influence on shaping the child's development
toward the desired values. The type and intensity of discontinuities vary,
of course, yet the range of areas where discontinuity is likely to occur is of
sufficient breadth to suggest that few children participate in group child
care without experiencing some disparity between home and center. A
review of day care research findings and school-family relations literature
indicates there are five basic areas where the potential for discontinuity
exists.

First, there may be incongruent child-rearing practices between parents
and caregivers. The influence techniques or regulatory strategies that
parents and caregivers employ in interacting with children may be markedly different. The ways in which parents and center staff deal with a
child's curiosity, hostilities, anxieties, unresponsiveness, and fears may
be inconsistent or in conflict with one another. A child's sex play, for
instance, may be handled in far different ways by parents and caregivers
(Prescott, 1965).

Second, it is highly probable that the physical environment of the center
and home will be significantly diverse with respect to freedom of move-

ment, opportunity for privacy, and social and spatial density (Prescott & David, 1976).

A third area of potential discontinuity deals with the scope and affectivity of interpersonal relationships in the family and center. Children occupy a special role within the family; they have a particularistic relationship with parents, siblings, and other relatives. Relationships in a child care center tend to be universalistic. The emphasis is on equalized distribution of attention and universally applied expectations and standards. Universalistic relationships within a child care center enable a rational, predictable, and stable social system that does not experience the chaotic fluctuation of emotions and impulsivity that is found in intimate associations within families (Lightfoot, 1975). Contrasting the primary relationship of parents and children with the secondary relationship of caregivers and children shows the significant differences in the interpersonal relationships of family and center. Research evidence from institutional child care settings suggests that staff mobility and the organization of personnel hinder the development and maintenance of specific adult-child dyads in group care systems (Tizard & Tizard, 1974). (See Getzels, 1974; McPherson, 1972; and Dreeben, 1968, for relevant discussions of school-family differences in affective relations.)

The fourth and fifth areas of possible discontinuity between family and center appear to be considerably pronounced for children from families of low socioeconomic status. Indeed, these discontinuities reflect social class differences. One discontinuity is the language system used by family and center. The verbal environment of the day care center may differ markedly in interaction style, vocabulary, and syntactic structure from that of the child's family. Another possible discontinuity surrounds value codes. Suppose, not unrealistically, a child care center's activities and staff adhere strongly to deferred gratification, emphasis on the future, and the achievement ethic. Imagine the conflicts experienced by a child in this setting whose familial experiences revolve around day-to-day struggles for subsistence (Getzels, 1974).

This range of possible discontinuity suggests, then, that children cannot depend on the norms of interaction in one setting to apply to another setting. For example, the social interaction rules and regulatory systems of the functionally diffuse and particularistic relationships of the family may be most inappropriate for the functionally specific and universalistic relationships of the day care center. Later in this chapter questions will be raised concerning the effects of such discontinuities on children.

The high probability of some type of dissonance between family and child care program gives considerable attention to the role of parents and caregivers in coordinating day care–family relations. The argument here is that the compatibility of two or more social systems depends on the nature of relations between key members of these social systems. Lippitt (1968) has suggested that much of the efficacy of childhood socialization where more than one socialization agency is involved depends on the type of communication and coordination between socialization agents. According to Lippitt, a lack of horizontal collaboration between socialization agents may present the child with incompatible models of appropriate behavior. A description of child care practices in an Israeli kibbutz vividly reflects this assumption. An important belief and practice of the kibbutz is that an optimal condition for a child's development is where the mother and metapelet complement each other; efforts are made to keep the metapelet's relationship with parents "conflict free" at all times (Neubauer, 1965).

RESEARCH ON PARENT-CAREGIVER RELATIONS

What is the nature of relationships between parents and caregivers in day care settings? What factors appear to influence the ways in which parents and caregivers relate to one another?

While the issue of how parents of young children handle relations with other nonfamilial authority figures in their child's life has received little empirical investigation, recent findings provide some answers as to how parents and staff manage relations between family and child care program. Selected findings of a study of the communicative behavior and attitudes of parents and caregivers will be reviewed and discussed here.[1] Research by Powell (1977, 1978a, 1978b) examined the mode, setting, frequency and diversity of parent-caregiver communication and attempted to identify significant predictors of parent-staff communication. The sample consisted of a random one-half of the parents (N = 212) and all caregivers (N = 89) in 12 group child care centers in Detroit. The study was carried out as the first part of a long-term research program at The Merrill-Palmer Institute which seeks to examine the interface between families and child care programs, and how the day care–family intersection influences children.

To supplement discussion of this research, selected findings of a related study by Joffe (1977) will be reviewed. Joffe, a sociologist, conducted a keen investigation of the relationship between parents and school-administered child care programs in Berkeley, California.

The Powell study examined the following dimensions of parent-caregiver communicative behaviors and attitudes: the frequency and diversity of communication; the channels, settings, and modes of communication; attitudes toward discussion of parental child-rearing values, expectations of the child care center, and family-related issues; satisfaction with the current level of communication; parents' perceptions of the child care center as a child-rearing information resource; and preferences for one- and two-way modes of communication.

Communicative Behaviors

With respect to the content of communication, the study found that child-related topics were discussed with much more frequency than parent/family-related topics. The most frequently discussed topic was what the child's day was like at the center. The child's relationships with peers and caregivers was also among the most frequently discussed topics. Within the domain of the parent/family-related topic, the parent's job or school was discussed most often. Parents' friends were almost never the topic of conversation between parents and caregivers.

Most communication between parents and caregivers occurred at the "transition point" when parents leave and pick up their child at the center. For 71 percent of the parent sample and 67 percent of the caregiver sample, there was discussion every week or more between parents and staff when children entered and departed from the center. The telephone was utilized with moderate frequency as a means of communication. One-fourth of the parent sample had never participated in an individual parent-staff conference, and center staff almost never visited parents' homes.

A relationship was found between frequency of communication and the hierarchical arrangement of the center staff. Variations in caregiver communication corresponded to differences in caregiver role status. The higher the status position within the center, the greater the communication frequency and diversity. This means, then, that center directors had the highest frequency and diversity of communication with parents, followed by teachers and assistant administrators, teacher aides, and food personnel.

A strong correlation between communication frequency and diversity (number of topics discussed) was found, suggesting that increases in parent-caregiver interaction correspond to increases in the diversity of discussion. As communication became more frequent, the number of parent/family-related topics discussed increased. Analyses also showed that parent-caregiver communication became more complex as frequency increased. The number of statistically significant relationships among topics within and between the two topic domains increased with communication frequency, suggesting that separations between child- and family-related topic domains diminished as communication frequency grew.

These topic patterns suggest that the core content of communication was clearly child-related and remained so even with increased communication frequency. As frequency increased, though, the content boundaries broadened to encompass parent/family-related information.

A relationship was found between communication frequency and parents' primary source of information about the center. Not unexpectedly, as frequency increased so did the role of center staff members in serving as primary information sources; use of nonstaff information sources (i.e., bulletin boards, newsletter) decreased.

Attitudes and Expectations

The study examined a number of attitudes toward the content boundaries and current level of parent-caregiver communication. First, it was found that caregivers (72 percent) were more dissatisfied with the frequency and content of communication than parents, who were split about evenly in satisfaction. Second, more than one-half of the parents (60 percent) perceived their child care center as a source of information about child development and child rearing, an important indicator of parental perception of staff expertise and knowledge. Third, the vast majority of both parents and caregivers believed discussion of *general* goals for and expectations of the center was an important topic for parent-staff communication, but fewer also concurred that parents and staff should discuss parental suggestions for *specific* caregiver practices. Fourth, most parents (94 percent) perceived the center staff as open to discussion of their child's activities at the center, but fewer parents (61 percent) believed caregivers would be willing to discuss any parent-initiated topic. More than one-half of the caregivers perceived parents as willing to discuss family activities and viewed parents as open to discussion of the home environment. Fifth, a majority of parents (61 percent) believed the center should not be kept informed of family activities on a consistent basis, and about one-half of the sample (51 percent) did not believe family problems should be discussed with center staff. A majority of caregivers (78 percent), however, believed that parents should discuss family problems with caregivers on a regular basis.

Joffe discovered important differences between black and Caucasian parents in expectations of the child care program. Black parents preferred a more formal school atmosphere with respect to discipline, structuring of activity, and academic curriculum, whereas Caucasian parents desired a program emphasizing social, emotional, and intellectual qualities of children. The Caucasian parents' interest in the program dealing with intellectual stimulation was ambiguous; the preference seemed to be for the program to meet the child's intellectual needs but not through a traditional academic program. Joffe observed that the conflict in these differing parental expectations appeared to be resolved through a "symbolic trade-off" where black parents were successful in securing an educational curriculum, but Caucasians' parental preferences dominated the "tone" or interpersonal form of the program, such as no corporal punishment and daily scheduling of activities in spontaneous and informal ways.

Interpersonal Ties

What types of interpersonal ties exist between parents and caregivers? The Powell study found that established parent-caregiver dyads did not exist for nearly one-third of the parent sample. These parents did not communicate consistently with a specific staff person. Communication was spread among two or more caregivers. The remaining parents communicated consistently with a particular teacher (29 percent) or the director of the child care center (32 percent). As frequency increased, parent contact with the child care center staff focused all the more on one particular caregiver. Therefore, increases in communication frequency were associated with a higher probability of a parent and caregiver forming and sustaining a consistent, stable relationship.

The study did uncover indications of some friendship relations between parents and caregivers, and caregiver familiarity with parents prior to center use. Nearly one-third (30 percent) of all caregivers reported knowing parents who used the center where they were employed prior to the parents' enrolling their child(ren) at the center. More than one-fourth (29 percent) of the caregivers reported they considered one or more of the parents using the center to be their friend(s). However, in only two of the 12 research centers did more than one-half of the caregivers consider some parents to be friends. In cases where caregivers did consider some parents to be friends, interaction with parent-friends frequently occurred in settings other than the child care center, and included discussion of job/school, child-rearing issues, family activities and problems, and the child care center at least once a week.

These findings of parent-caregiver friendship bonds were consistent with Joffe's discovery of a child care program "underlife" where staff provided a range of informal services negotiated privately between individual parents and staff members. The network of activity included after-school chauffeuring, after-school "rapping," legal and medical advice, and career counseling. The problems routinely dealt with in the program "underlife" went far beyond the boundaries of school-related matters and yet sometimes utilized the resources of the school to solve problems.

Informal social networks among parents were found in four of the 12 research centers in the Powell study. While small in number (11 percent of the parent sample), members of these friendship networks interacted with three or more parents using the same child care center at least once a week in private homes, at the center, and in other social settings (i.e., church). These parents discussed the child care center, their children, their job/school, and family activities. Many of these parents (71 percent) reported they knew other parents prior to using the center.

A Parent-Caregiver Typology

Variations in communication frequency among parents and caregivers led to the statistical creation of subgroups of parents and caregivers differing in communicative behavior and attitudes. An analysis of differences between these subgroups suggested the following preliminary typology of parent-caregiver relationships.

Three major subgroups of parents were identified. One subgroup, labeled *independent* parents, maintained a significant social distance from the center, with the day care center and family functioning as independent child-rearing systems. Independent parents were characterized by a low frequency of communication with caregivers, almost no discussion of parent/family-related topics, and strongly held attitudes that child-rearing values and family information should not be discussed with caregivers. These parents did not perceive the child care center as a child-rearing/ child development information source. Further, independent parents utilized thier own child and nonstaff sources (i.e., newsletter, bulletin board) as the main channel of communication with the center. They did not communicate with a specific caregiver consistently.

Dependent parents appeared to recognize the dependency relation between family and center, yet did not view the relationship to be reciprocal in terms of information exchange. They perceived the center as a child-rearing information resource, but with one-way communication—from center to parent—characterizing the information flow. Dependent parents discussed some parent/family-related topics with caregivers (i.e., parents' job/school), and mildly believed that child-rearing values and family information should be discussed. Most dependent parents had a stable relationship with a particular staff member.

The behaviors and attitudes of a third subgroup of parents, called *interdependent* parents, reflected considerable intersection between family and center; the two child-rearing systems functioned in an interdependent manner. Interdependent parents had a high frequency of communication with caregivers, discussed parent/family-related information, believed strongly that family information should be shared with caregivers, and that parents and caregivers should discuss child-rearing values.

Caregivers did not fall into the same parent categories. There was one subgroup of independent caregivers whose social distance from parents paralleled the stance of independent parents toward caregivers. There also was a second subgroup of semi-interdependent caregivers. These caregivers related with parents in an interdependent manner except that communication and attitudes toward discussion of family information or child-rearing values did not reach the high levels characteristic of interdependent parents.

The parent and caregiver categories suggested above were based on cross-sectional data and are in need of longitudinal evidence to determine their stability across time and situations.

Predictors of Communication

What factors seem to influence the ways in which parents and caregivers relate to one another? An aim of the study was to identify variables that were predictive of parent and caregiver communication frequency and diversity. In keeping with the exploratory nature of this research, 19 predictor variables were selected for examination based on a review of pertinent research and descriptive day care literature. There has been little empirical investigation of the correlates or determinants of parent-caregiver interaction, and this research sought to identify variables for further in-depth study. (For detailed discussion of this portion of the study, see Powell, 1977, 1978b.)

For parents, analyses revealed more about variables not related to communicative behavior than variables which were predictive of communication. Only four variables were found to be statistically related to parent communication frequency. And collectively these variables accounted for only about 24 percent of the variance in parent communication frequency.

Increases in parent communication frequency were related to the attitude that parents and caregivers should discuss family information, use of the center for six months or less, active participation in an informal social network of parents using the same center, and representing a two-parent family.

Perhaps of greater importance was the list of variables that were not significantly related to parent communication frequency. These included the geographical distance of the center from the parent's home and place of work/school, previous use of a child care center, the number of centers visited prior to selection of the present center, parents' perceptions of the day care center as a child-rearing information resource, and parents' perceptions of the influence of the day care center on their child.

Analyses of the caregiver variables yielded stronger statistical relationships. The significant variables accounted for about 48 percent of the variance in communication frequency. Increases in caregiver communication frequency were related to center role function (i.e., director, teacher), friendship relationships with parents, recent completion of formal education, a child-centered role concept, the attitude that child-rearing values should be discussed with parents, and little formal experience in working with young children.

The relationship between the communication frequency of a center and friendship between parents and caregivers was the highest in centers that had more than one-half of the staff members considering some parents to be their friends. This relationship was consistent with the previously noted finding that caregiver friendship with parents was predictive of caregiver communication frequency and diversity. These centers also were characterized by informal social networks of parents.

The data do not suggest a relationship between center sponsorship (proprietary, nonproprietary) and communication frequency. Centers with high, medium, and low levels of parent-caregiver communication frequency represented varying sponsorship types. Analyses found no real differences between proprietary and nonproprietary centers when examining communicative behavior and attitude variables.

Preliminary Conclusions

What preliminary conclusions about the nature of parent-caregiver relationships may be drawn from these data? The next section of this chapter explores the issue of what determines the nature of parent-staff relations. From a systems continuity perspective, what appears to be the character of parent-staff interaction? The Powell data may be interpreted as follows:

> If [the] findings are used to construct the social worlds of day care children, the image which emerges is one of fragmentation and discontinuity. For many children it appears the boundaries of the child care center and family are sharply defined and narrow in intersection. Evidences of system interdependency are few. The world is a disconnected one, with the child's family, other children's families and the day care center functioning as independent, detached systems (Powell, 1978a).

The flow of information between parents and caregivers suggests minimal attempts to coordinate children's socialization processes. Although for many parents communication was nearly a daily occurrence at the "transition point," interaction surrounding substantive child and family-related topics was infrequent, suggesting that perhaps much exchange between parents and staff was superficial. The brief "how's it going?" exchanges may be important in facilitating interpersonal rapport between parent and staff, but when these messages comprise a significant portion of parent-staff interaction, questions must be raised as to the placement of larger child care issues in the transmission of information between family and center.

The type of information parents and caregivers discussed, and the channels of communication utilized also suggested a detached parent-staff relationship overall. Parent/family-related topics were not often discussed, the child was a main channel of communication for a sizable portion of the sample, and for many parents there was no consistent communication with a particular center staff member.

A SOCIOECOLOGICAL PERSPECTIVE OF PARENT-CAREGIVER RELATIONS

This chapter opened with the observation that much of the research and indeed practitioner interest in parent-staff relations has focused primarily on the roles or involvement of parents *within* the operations of child care programs, with little attention given to the *interrelatedness* of and *interactions* between family and child care center. In this final section of the chapter I wish to demonstrate the importance of viewing day care-family relations as an interactional system by indicating a number of research and program development issues pertaining to parent-staff relations. At the same time I will set forth major dimensions of a socioecological perspective of parent-caregiver relations. The research reviewed above, with other literature, will be used to suggest an ecological framework in which the child's day care center experiences are a partial function of the day care-family interactional system and, in turn, the day care-family system is a function of its cultural and organizational context.

Discontinuity Experienced

Do children really experience dissonance between family and day care center and, if so, how do they cope with discontinuities? An important question for researchers is, What effect, if any, does day care-family discontinuity have on children? Empirical data are not available to answer this question. With respect to child roles in the family and child care center, it appears that the degree of adjustment to the social systems is related to the similarity of roles within the two systems (Magnusson, Dunér & Zetterblom, 1974). But do dissimilar roles have a harmful influence on children? Lightfoot (1975) has argued theoretically that in the case of dissonance between family and school, children become more malleable and responsive to a changing world, whereas absolute homogeneity between family and school would reflect a static society and discourage adaptive development in children. She has submitted that discontinuities between family and school become dysfunctional when they stem from differences in power and status in society, where school-family conflicts are rooted in inequality and racism. Likewise, Deutsch (1964) has suggested that much of the poor academic achievement of children from low-income families is attributable to the discontinuity experienced by these children in middle-class schools.

A study of the effects of multiple-system child rearing would not be complete, however, without concern for the ways in which interactions between systems influence children. Studies are needed to determine the effect of parent-caregiver relations on a child's social experience in dealing with home-center transitions and possible discontinuities. It was tentatively concluded from the data reviewed earlier that the social worlds of many day care children are fragmented and discontinuous. Yet, whether the child perceives and experiences the world in these terms is not known. It is not clear from existing research how a disconnected or more cohesive family-center relationship affects a child's behavior and development. What is the influence of system inconsistencies on children when considering developmental differences and degrees of discontinuity? The theoretical argument that socialization is improved when there is close coordination and communication between socialization agencies needs empirical investigation.

Social Roles
     Day care-family interactions exist at what has been called the mesosystem level of ecological analyses, which comprises interrelations among major settings or social systems (microsystems) in a child's life (Bronfenbrenner, 1976; Brim, 1975). The studies reviewed above provide valuable insights into the ways parents and child care staff relate to one another. While further research is needed on specific dimensions of parent-staff and day care-family interaction, there is a critical need for a more comprehensive empirical understanding of what factors influence the interaction of child care programs and families.
     What variables affect parent-caregiver interaction? Lightfoot (1975) has suggested that the relationship between parents and teachers ("natural enemies") is more a function of assuming roles defined by the social structure of society than it is a function of the dynamics of individual interactions. While not negating the importance of situational and interpersonal determinants of parent-caregiver communication, the Powell study supported Lightfoot's suggestion. The findings indicated social role attributes were more predictive of communication frequency and diversity than interpersonal variables (Powell, 1978b). This raises questions, then, about the efficacy of staff training efforts and program practices which attempt to improve parent-staff interaction through interpersonal skill development only. The idea that social roles significantly influence parent-caregiver relations also raises important questions about the processes and factors which give shape and definition to these roles.
     In the remaining pages of this chapter several possible socioecological determinants of parent-caregiver interaction are discussed. Attention is given to the cultural context of parent-staff relations, which is the macrosystem level of analysis suggested by Brim and which has to do with overarching institutions of the culture such as social and political systems. The ways in which mediating structures might influence parent-staff rela-

tions also are discussed (the exosystem). Lastly, the structural properties of day care centers as organizational systems and the professional socialization of child care workers are suggested as determinants of parent-caregiver relations (microsystem).

Cultural Context

The new coordinative role of parents discussed at the outset of this chapter is a dramatic departure from previous child-rearing practices in this country and is inconsistent with cultural norms of the "ideal" American family. Since the early 1800s the concept of families as self-sufficient, autonomous units has been embedded deeply in the moral, economic, and political fabric of this country. "Adequate" families are those who need no outside help to carry out their functions; those who do need assistance fail to meet conventional widespread standards of familial adequacy and morality. Toward the end of the nineteenth century the ideal family was expected to be not only self-sufficient and independent, but also to have minimal contact and ties with the outside world. Families, especially women and children, were (and, in some cases, still are) to be barricaded and protected from societal pressures and influences (Keniston, 1977). Minturn and Lambert's (1964) cross-cultural study of child-rearing underscored the isolation in which many American mothers raised their children in the 1950s.

Many families have been or are unable to fulfill the self-sufficiency ideal, of course. Families are influenced profoundly by social and economic forces, and the ability to obtain independent, autonomous status often is affected by factors over which families have no control. Nevertheless, as Keniston and the Carnegie Council on Children (1977) have shown, the self-sufficient family ideal continues to prevail in this country, defining the norms of adequate family functioning. Obviously families using day care cannot be totally independent, self-sufficient child-rearing systems, and yet if they are at all sensitive to the ideal of familial autonomy, it would seem to follow that relations with a day care center would be limited in scope and interchange.

It is within a society that subscribes to independence rather than interdependence, then, that relations between families and child care centers are formed and sustained. The cultural context of this value system, and its presumed concomitant relations between families and day care centers, should be given considerable attention in subsequent research and experimental program development work.

Mediating Structures

The research on parent-staff interactions would suggest that a fruitful area for further study and experimental program work is the social milieu of the day care-family intersection. Joffe's findings of "underlife" in the

Berkeley child care program and Powell's discovery of friendship bonds among some parents and caregivers and among parents using the same center suggest that, at least in select cases, the friendship networks of families and child care staff encompass one another in a significant way. In the Powell study friendship relations among parents and caregivers were found to be a significant predictor of communication frequency and diversity. The finding that some parents and caregivers knew one another prior to the parent's use of the center suggests that parental social networks may have been used to find the child care center.

In cases where friendship networks exist among parents and between parents and caregivers, the parent-staff relationship may be best understood by examining the mediating structures between family and day care center. Perhaps a "lay referral system" which puts parents in contact with child care services through informal contacts is in operation for some parents. There is evidence of social networks having a major effect on relations between clients and formal human services. For example, informal referral systems consisting of lay consultants such as neighbors, co-workers, friends, and relatives have been found to have a definite influence on the utilization of health care services (Freidson, 1960; McKinlay, 1973). Further, there are descriptive data to suggest that friends, relatives and neighbors serve as informal referral agents for family day care (Sale & Torres, 1971), and evidence from an experimental intervention program that informal social networks can play an effective role in matching day care users and providers (Collins, Emlen & Watson, 1969). Further research is needed on the processes through which parents find child care, and how characteristics of this matchmaking process affect relations between parent and staff. It may be, for example, that neighbors, friends, and relatives play a mediating role in the day care-family relationship.

The importance of considering the social milieu of day care-family interaction may be extended to public policy issues. Berger & Neuhaus (1977), who suggest that mediating structures "stand between the individual in his private life and the larger institutions of public life," have proposed a new paradigm for pluralism in social policy that argues for public policy not to destroy or minimize mediating structures (neighborhood, ethnic, and racial subcultures) and, moreover, for policy to use these structures to advance legitimate social goals.

Organizational Context

There are many interconnections between professional socialization and organizational behavior and their influence on staff roles and relations with clients. For the purposes of this chapter I wish to maintain a fairly separate treatment of professionalism and organization behavior, recognizing fully the reciprocal relations among these variables.

There are two points to be made about the relation of parent-staff interaction to organizational behavior: first, structural dimensions of organizations influence parent-staff interaction and, second, perhaps nonschool-based child care centers have been and are patterned after public schools with respect to client relations. As will be discussed later, it seems appropriate to apply literature dealing with schools as formal organizations to the theoretical treatment of day care centers as small organizations. The parallels are many, and research data which view child care centers as organizations are not available. This is not to suggest that day care centers operate like schools, but it is to suggest that our understanding of parent-staff relations in day care can be enhanced through consideration of parent-teacher relations in public schools.

The distance and alienation of teachers from the communities in which they work has been a recognized issue in parent-teacher relations since Waller's (1932) classical study of the school as an organization. For the school the problem is one of maintaining parent interest in and commitment to the school program while preserving adequate parent-school distance to provide organizational and staff latitude. The tension is one generic to professionally staffed, client-serving organizations—to prevent client demands from defining client services (Bidwell, 1965). The differences between the family and school settings necessitate the development of a relationship that does not bring the two systems into such close contact that they impair the social structures that are required to sustain each (Litwak & Meyer, 1974).

In the case of schools (and day care centers) attempts at this delicate balance may be made through a maintenance of sufficient latitude vis-à-vis its constituency for the exercise of professional judgments regarding which kinds of specific program or educational outcomes best serve the client, and which procedures are best adapted to these ends (Blau & Scott, 1962). But again the major functional problem here is to sustain professional latitude without seriously diminishing constituency responsiveness. One approach to this problem is for the school to state its goals in ambiguous terms, thus allowing for flexibility in handling constituency expectations (Bidwell, 1965).

A recent exploratory analysis of selected organizational characteristics of 40 schools found several organizational variables related to the rate of face-to-face parent-teacher interaction and the frequency of parent-teacher disputes, as measured by teacher reports. The study found the rate of interaction declined with school formalization, centralization, solidarity of teacher organizations, and teacher's formal training, but interaction increased with staff seniority (Corwin & Wagenaar, 1976).

When the unit of analysis shifted from the organizational level to the individual teacher, there was evidence that teachers may use the organization as a protective mechanism against parental intrusion. The trend seems to be for teachers to form strong bonds among themselves and to seek institutional support to protect their interests from parental demands and criticisms (Lightfoot, 1975). Becker (1952) found relations among teachers and administrators in Chicago schools served largely as a form of mutual protection against parents. There seemed to be an implicit bargain between teachers and superiors whereby teachers would support the organization in return for institutional buffering from parents.

The numerous operational parallels between child care centers and public schools suggest the possibility that the activities and structure of day care centers have been patterned after those of public schools. Informal observations of the child care centers participating in the Powell study showed it common for caregivers to be referred to as "teachers" (although in many cases they lacked the traditional credentials); for the day care center to be informally or sometimes formally called a "school"; that centers defined their purpose in relation to schools (i.e., claiming that day care center experiences enhance formal schooling); and that some centers have an "educational component" as part of the day, the style of which was similar to formal learning activities typically pursued in grade school. Perhaps this institutional modeling has prompted parents and caregivers to relate to one another as teachers and parents traditionally relate in a public school setting.

If schools are inappropriate referent institutions for day care and if the existing patterns of day care-family interaction are in need of change, then alternative models need to be developed and disseminated. It is not within the scope of this chapter to debate the advantages and disadvantages of public schools serving as the major delivery systems for day care. But certainly an important contribution to this debate would be empirical evidence on how public school organizational properties influence interactions between parents and child care programs.

Staff Professionalism

The above discussion provides a context for appreciating the recent finding that teachers consider "good parents" to be those who abide by the teacher's rules and avoid intervention in classroom affairs (Lortie, 1975). Schoolteachers and child care staff do not have the power or status to implement a "hands-off" approach toward parents. On the one hand, parents are clients and are expected, at least theoretically, to adhere to the norms and wishes set forth by the professional staff. On the other hand, parents are constituents of public school systems and therefore have legitimate access to the policy-making mechanisms of schools or, in the case of nonschool-based day care centers, can withdraw their child from the program. The staff, then, does not enjoy complete autonomy and freedom, and here enters the influence of professional socialization on parent-staff interaction.

The child care and early education profession is an upwardly mobile one which seems to be achieving a more "professionalized" status. For example, the movement toward controlling entrance into the field (e.g., standards and credentialing) and efforts to develop a technical knowledge base (e.g., curriculum development) are indicative of attempts toward increased professionalism. It is a fledgling process, however, and several characteristics of the current professional status of child care workers appear to be related to the ways in which staff relate to parents. (See Joffe, 1977, for a cogent analysis of the current state of the child care professionalization process.)

One professional status issue which seems to prompt role confusion deals with the determination of services to be provided in child care programs. The problem is the degree to which services are limited to conventional educational approaches or broadened to include a range of services (e.g., psychological counseling to deal with family process problems) that heretofore have been the province of other professions and professionally staffed organizations. For caregiver roles, the problem is manifested in ambiguity surrounding the boundaries of legitimate services and the status of child care professionals in comparison with other human service professionals. The immersion of staff into the personal problems and lives of parents pulls caregivers away from their primary professional goal, the care and education of young children, and where information services are offered to parents, as in the child care program "underlife," the role ambiguity is heightened and movement toward increased professionalization is hampered (Joffe, 1977).

A perhaps more serious professionalization issue is the lack of a sophisticated technical knowledge base which affords caregivers authority and autonomy on the basis of specialized expertise. The care of normal preschool children is very familiar to parents and this familiarity makes it difficult for caregivers to boast of a vocabulary and skill that might move them several notches up the professional status ladder. However, it is well to emphasize the relationship between parental expectations and role status. Joffe (1977) has noted in analyzing her data that the desire of black parents to have a structured educational curriculum, while maybe disturbing to staff, actually serves to enhance the expert authority of the teacher. Caucasian parents, in their preference for a looser social-emotional program, dilute the need for staff with specialized knowledge and abilities.

The development of an expert knowledge base for caregivers may influence role status in yet another way. The more specialized the data base, the more specialized the program staff. Programs staffed by specialists contending with specific domains of children and the program tend to fragment and might cause problems for parent-staff relations. Experimental program planners might wish to examine program staffing with respect to the number of different caregivers responsible for a given child at different segments of the day and the degree to which this arrangement hinders or assists parents in forming a relationship with a caregiver who knows and deals with their child on an in-depth, daily basis.

SUMMARY AND CONCLUSIONS

The way parents and day care providers relate to one another is of increasing importance as multiple-system child rearing becomes a way of life for so many young children. The importance is heightened as more and more secondary child-rearing systems are nonfamilial and disconnected from family networks. The use of nonfamilial caregivers is not the problem. Rather, the critical issue is the social distance between family and secondary child-rearing system and the ways this distance affects children's experiences in crossing the boundaries of home and child care program. Adding further intensity to the issue are concerns that day care might supplant family child rearing, the newness of the coordinative child care role many parents now assume, and the assumption that incongruities between family and child care program result in negative experiences for children.

This chapter has suggested that parent-caregiver relations are embedded in a highly complex day care-family relationship and that the day care-family relationship as an interactional system is best understood within its socioecological context. This chapter has set forth as major components of a socio-ecological perspective of parent-caregiver relations the cultural values of family self-sufficiency, the mediating structures of informal social networks, structural dimensions of organizations, and staff professionalism.

The research and socioecological perspective of day care-family relations discussed in this chapter lead to several implications for improving the quality of child care program services. First, there is a need for new conceptions of the relationship between child care programs and parents, and for public and professional education efforts that project images of what the day care-family relationship might be like. The critical question in parent-staff relations is what is the best arrangement of family and secondary child-rearing systems for the care of young children. We need new designs of the scope and mode of services provided by child care programs, and new images and models of external relations of families that provide supportive services and networks. Perhaps we need new forms of the extended family, where mutual values and ideals for children rather than biological connections are the bases for family groupings. Galinsky and Hooks (1977) have carried out a descriptive study of new extended family arrangements for day care. Their work provides alternative conceptions of the day care-family relationship as well as model program designs. Further efforts of this sort are needed.

Second, program policies and practices should give increased attention to the interpersonal relationship between parents and staff. A good deal of the recent attention given to the relationship between parents and child care programs conceptualizes the parental role at a political level, having concern for parents in program decision-making capacities. While the significance of the program decision-making role for parents is not to be negated, it is incomplete and perhaps inadequate when considering the larger whole of the day care-family intersection. If the interpersonal relationship between parents and caregivers is to be valued and enhanced within programs, then one concomitant day care practice, for instance, might focus on the initial formative development of the relationship between parents and staff, making provisions for frequent periods of parent, caregiver and child interaction.

Third, the staffing of child care centers needs to be examined in relation to the amount and consistency of caregiver access to parents. Since the bulk of parent-caregiver communication occurs at the "transition point" when children enter and depart the day care center, attention needs to be given to (a) the number and types (role status) of caregivers available at these times, (b) the tasks and demands to which they must attend, and (c) the degree to which the physical environment is conducive to parent-caregiver discussion. A related fourth implication for service quality is that professional education programs need to be developed in the area of parent-staff relations. Relatively few child care training programs give attention to the interpersonal dynamics of relations between parents and child care workers.

Future research on parent-caregiver relationships needs to focus on the effects of the parent-caregiver and day care–family relationship on the development of children, and of the determinants of parent-caregiver interaction.

How should parents and child care programs relate to one another? Current practitioner literature and theoretical arguments suggest that the significant social distance of parents from child care programs is least desirable, and that fluid, close interdependent relationships between parents and child care programs are the most conducive to child functioning. Clearly an interdependent relationship would coincide with present notions of "parent-caregiver partnership" and "day care as a family support system." From a child development perspective, there are no empirical data to answer the question asked above. As was argued earlier in this chapter, research is needed to determine the effect of parent-caregiver relations on a child's experiences in dealing with possible incongruities between home and center.

An important question is what determines the nature of parent-caregiver relationships. This chapter has proposed a socioecological perspective of day care-family relations, suggesting several contextual variables that may have a major influence on interactions between family and child care program. Future research should give serious consideration to the possible influence of cultural values, mediating social structures, organizational structures, and staff professionalism.

Research must uncover how "matches" are made between parents and child care centers, the types of information that are exchanged in the process of developing a day care-family relationship, and precisely what transpires at the first face-to-face meeting of a parent and day care center staff member. With respect to the latter, are there significant formal/informal or verbal/nonverbal messages transmitted at this first meeting which shape subsequent development of the parent-caregiver relationship. For instance, can friendship relations be predicted from the type of interaction at the first meeting and, if so, what are the short- and long-term consequences for the child's integration into the day care center? Again considering the child's social world, it may be that life is much different for the child whose parents and caregivers maintain a friendship rather than a traditional client-professional relationship or no relationship at all.

American society is rapidly changing the ways in which its children are being raised. We know that families need help in rearing their children. But we do not know what constitutes the best arrangements of families and secondary child care systems when the needs of children and families are considered. While empirical answers to this question are needed, it also is essential that there be serious examination of the ways in which existing day care policies and practices influence parent-caregiver relationships. We must carefully analyze prevailing conceptions of the day care-family interface, explore the premises upon which current practices and policies affecting day care-family relations are based, and consider alternative ways to link families and child care program. A rethinking of the relationship between families and day care is necessary and, as this chapter has argued, an interpersonal approach to the problem may be the most productive way to proceed.

FOOTNOTE

1. Portions of this chapter are taken from the following summary report of this research: Powell, D. R., "The interface between families and child care programs." Detroit: The Merrill-Palmer Institute, 1977. This research was funded by Ford Foundation grant #750-0447.

REFERENCES

Becker, H. Social class variation in teacher-pupil relationships. *Journal of Educational Sociology,* 1972, *25,* 451–465.

Berger, P. L., & Neuhaus, R. J. *To empower people: The role of mediating structures in public policy.* Washington, D.C.: American Enterprise for Public Policy Research, 1977.

Bidwell, C. E. The school as a formal organization. In J. G. March (Ed.), *Handbook of organizations.* Chicago: Rand McNally, 1965.

Blau, P. M., & Scott, W. R. *Formal organizations.* San Francisco: Chandler, 1962.

Brim, O. G. Macro-structural influences on child development and the need for childhood social indicators. *American Journal of Orthopsychiatry,* 1975, *45,* 516–524.

Bronfenbrenner, U. The experimental ecology of education. *Educational Researcher,* 1976, *5,* 5–15.

Collins, A. H., Emlen, A., & Watson, E. The day-care neighbor service: An interventive experiment. *Community Mental Health Journal,* 1969, *5,* 219–224.

Congressional Record, 92nd Congress, 1st Session, December 8–11, 1971, *117* (Part 35).

Corwin, R. G., & Wagenaar, T. C. Boundary interaction between service organizations and their publics: A study of teacher-parent relationships. *Social Forces,* 1977, *55,* 471–492.

Deutsch, M. Facilitating development in the preschool child: Social and psychological perspectives. *Merrill-Palmer Quarterly,* 1964, *10,* 249–263.

Dreeben, R. *On what is learned in school.* Reading, Ma.: Addison-Wesley, 1968.

Freidson, E. Client control and medical practice. *American Journal of Sociology,* 1960, *65,* 374–382.

Galinsky, E., & Hooks, W. H. *The new extended family: Day care that works.* Boston: Houghton Mifflin, 1977.

Getzels, J. W. Education and socialization: A note on discontinuities. *Teachers College Record,* 1974, *76,* 218–225.

Joffe, C. E. *Friendly intruders: Childcare professionals and family life.* Berkeley, Ca.: University of California Press, 1977.

Keniston, K., & The Carnegie Council on Children. *All our children: The American family under pressure.* New York: Harcourt Brace Jovanovich, 1977.

Lightfoot, S. L. Families and schools: Creative conflict or negative dissonance. *Journal of Research and Development in Education,* 1975, *9,* 34–44.

Lippitt, R. Improving the socialization process. In J. A. Clausen (Ed.), *Socialization and society.* Boston, Ma.: Little, Brown, 1968.

Litwak, E., & Meyer, H. J. *School, family and neighborhood: The theory and practice of school-community relations.* New York: Columbia University Press, 1974.

Lortie, D. *Schoolteacher: A sociological study.* Chicago: University of Chicago Press, 1975.

Magnusson, D., Duner, A., & Zetterblom, G. *Adjustment: A longitudinal study.* New York: Wiley, 1974.

McKinlay, J. B. Social networks, lay consultation and help-seeking behavior. *Social Forces,* 1973, *51,* 275–292.

McPherson, G. *Small town teacher.* Cambridge, Ma.: Harvard University Press, 1972.

Minturn, L., & Lambert, W. W. *Mothers of six cultures: Antecedents of childrearing.* New York: Wiley, 1964.

Neubauer, P. B. (Ed.). *Children in collectives.* Springfield, Il.: Charles C. Thomas, 1965.

O'Neil, T. P. The vicious and dishonest campaign against the Child and Family Services Bill. *Congressional Record,* December 1, 1975, *121* (n. 175).

Prescott, E. *Children in group day care: The effect of a dual child-rearing environment.* Los Angeles: Research Department, Welfare Planning Council, Los Angeles Region, 1964. (mimeo)

Prescott, E., & David, T. *Effects of the physical environment on day care*. (Report prepared for the Office of the Assistant Secretary for Planning and Evaluation.) Washington, D.C.: Department of Health, Education, and Welfare, July, 1976.

Powell, D. R. *Day care and the family: A study of interactions and congruency*. (Final research report of the Parent-Caregiver Project) Detroit, Mi.: Merrill-Palmer Institute, 1977.

Powell, D. R. The interpersonal relationship between parents and caregivers in day care settings. *American Journal of Orthopsychiatry*, 1978, *48*, 680–689.

Powell, D. R. Correlates of parent-teacher communication frequency and diversity. *Journal of Educational Research*, 1978, *71*, 333–341.

Sale, J. S., & Torres, Y. L. *I'm not just a baby-sitter: A descriptive report of the Community Family Day Care Project*. Pasadena: Pacific Oaks College, 1971.

Smelser, N. J. The social challenge to parental authority. In S. M. Farber, P. Mustacchi, & R. H. Wilson (Eds.), *Man and civilization: The family's search for survival*. New York: McGraw-Hill, 1965.

Tizard, J., & Tizard, B. The institution as an environment for development. In M. P. M. Richards (Ed.), *The integration of a child into a social world*. London: Cambridge University Press, 1974.

Waller, W. *The sociology of teaching*. New York: Wiley, 1932.